COCKFOSTERS

ENFIELD WEST

SOUTHGATE

ARNOS GROVE

BOUNDS GREEN

WOOD GREEN

TURNPIKE LANE

MANOR HOUSE

WARE
BURNT OAK (WATLING)
COLINDALE
HENDON CENTRAL
BRENT
GOLDERS GREEN
RONDESBURY
HAMPSTEAD
AMPSTEAD BELSIZE PARK
CHLEY ROAD
CHALK FARM
SWISS COTTAGE
MARLBORO ROAD
ST. JOHNS WOOD
MARYLEBONE

HIGHGATE
TUFNELL PARK
KENTISH TOWN
CAMDEN TOWN
MORNINGTON CRESCENT
EUSTON

FINSBURY PARK
ARSENAL (HIGHBURY HILL)
DRAYTON PARK
HOLLOWAY ROAD
HIGHBURY & ISLINGTON
CALEDONIAN ROAD
KINGS CROSS ST. PANCRAS
CANONBURY & ESSEX ROAD

OLD STREET
ANGEL
MOORGATE

GWARE ROAD
BAKER STREET
GREAT PORTLAND ST. REGENTS PARK
EUSTON SQUARE
WARREN STREET
GOODGE STREET
FARRINGDON
ALDERSGATE
RUSSELL SQUARE
HOLBORN
CHANCERY LANE
POST OFFICE
LIVERPOOL STREET

PRAED STREET
BOND STREET
TOTTENHAM COURT ROAD
BRITISH MUSEUM
BANK
ALDGATE
SHOREDITCH

ARBLE RCH
OXFORD CIRCUS
ALDWYCH
COVENT GARDEN
MANSION HOUSE
MONUMENT
ST. MARYS
STE GR

PICCADILLY
DOVER STREET
RK CORNER
TSBRIDGE
OMPTON ROAD
LEICESTER SQUARE
STRAND
BLACKFRIARS
CANNON STREET
MARK LANE
ALDGATE EAST
WHITECHA
SHADWELL
WAPPING

TRAFALGAR SQUARE
TEMPLE
CHARING CROSS
LONDON BRIDGE
ROTHERHITHE
SURREY DOCKS

VICTORIA
WESTMINSTER
WATERLOO
LAMBETH NORTH
BOROUGH

SLOANE SQUARE
ST. JAMES PARK
ELEPHANT & CASTLE

KENNINGTON

NEW CROSS GATE

OVAL
STOCKWELL
CLAPHAM NORTH
CLAPHAM COMMON
CLAPHAM SOUTH
BALHAM
TRINITY ROAD (TOOTING BEC)
TOOTING BROADWAY
COLLIERS WOOD
SOUTH WIMBLEDON (MERTON)
MORDEN

UNDERGROUND

Underground
to Everywhere

Westminster Abbey looks on disapprovingly as its neighbourhood is ripped up to accommodate the new Metropolitan District Railway, about 1867. (Photograph Henry Flather. © Museum of London)

Underground
to Everywhere

LONDON'S UNDERGROUND RAILWAY
IN THE LIFE OF THE CAPITAL

STEPHEN HALLIDAY

SUTTON PUBLISHING

LONDON'S TRANSPORT MUSEUM

First published in the United Kingdom in 2001 by
Sutton Publishing Limited · Phoenix Mill
Thrupp · Stroud · Gloucestershire · GL5 2BU

in association with London's Transport Museum

British Library Cataloguing in Publication Data
A catalogue record for this book is available from the British Library.

ISBN 0-7509-2585-X

End-papers: front, the original version of Harry Beck's famous Underground map, for
which he was paid 5 guineas; back, a modern version of the Underground map.
(London's Transport Museum)

Typeset in 10/14.5pt Photina MT.
Typesetting and origination by
Sutton Publishing Limited.
Printed and bound in England by
J.H. Haynes & Co. Ltd, Sparkford.

CONTENTS

This gap in the elegant terrace of Leinster Gardens, Bayswater, was made to accommodate the Metropolitan Railway, now part of the Circle Line. It was filled with two dummy façades, 23–4 Leinster Gardens, with false doors and windows which were used to play practical jokes on novice postmen and messenger boys. (Photograph Henry Flather. © Museum of London)

FOREWORD

by Maxwell Hutchinson

I first travelled on the London Underground in 1953. I was five years old. My parents brought me down from Grantham in Lincolnshire by the *Flying Scotsman* to wave at the Queen the day after her coronation. It is a day that I will never forget.

I travelled on a mainline steam train for the first time in my life, but that experience paled into insignificance compared with my childhood discovery of the London Underground. My father, who was an architect, had endeavoured to explain to a child precisely what the Underground was. Firstly, he explained, there were moving staircases called escalators. I failed utterly to understand what he was talking about despite the eloquence of his description. At the bottom of these strange staircases that went deep under the earth's surface, there were trains travelling in tunnels – like the famous tunnels to the north and south of Grantham on the east coast mainline but (as I thought) hundreds of feet under the surface of London. To the young mind, the whole idea seemed utterly preposterous.

When we arrived at King's Cross, already soiled and a little weary from a hundred miles in the inadequate post-war carriages of the *Flying Scotsman*, we were carried along by the crowd still buoyed up by their enthusiasm for the coronation of our new young queen.

Descending the steps into the Underground, the first thing that struck me was the smell. It is still one of the system's mysterious trademarks that haunts me whenever I am away from London. There is nothing quite like the odour; it is unmistakable and lingers on the clothing with, for me, a mixture of abhorrence and affection. I am conscious that as a daily traveller on the Underground I must smell of the very place in what many consider to be an unpleasant way. On the other hand, I can wear this odour as a badge of honour. I don't own a motor car; I don't own a bicycle. For me, the Underground is my chauffeur-driven transport system. After the smell, I remember the intolerable crowds and the fact that everybody smoked. The escalator surpassed my wildest imaginings. It was with fear and trepidation that I stepped off the metal spikes at the top only to be transported down and down on a ride that was far better than anything I had experienced at a fairground. As for the trains themselves, frankly, I was terrified. The people, the dark, the snapping guillotine of the doors and the speed were like nothing I had ever experienced. Happily, that sense of wonderment, magic and respect has never vanished.

The London Underground system is one of the great wonders of the world. Londoners take it for granted. Infrequent British visitors boast of their command of the system and foreigners simply do not understand how it works. I have met many an American who has bought a ticket in Piccadilly Circus to travel to Leicester Square failing to understand their proximity and assuming, understandably, that the fact that both locations have stations means that they must be beyond walking distance.

At the beginning of the great endeavour beneath the streets of London, there was an ambition which seemed as impossible as supersonic flight, space travel, or the human genome project. Yes, it was proposed, trains could travel in tunnels to the very heart of the capital and carry willing commuters out to the sylvan glades of the suburbs. What heroism there was in the hearts and minds of the men who made this happen. When I explain to people at Baker Street or Great Portland Street that these stations were designed to accommodate steam trains, they cannot cope with the idea. Things are bad enough with electric power – how in the name of reason could trains have been pulled by steam? – but they were.

The economic, social and cultural history of the tube system seems to be cyclical. Success, failure, ambition, achievement, thrill, insolvency and personal ambition are woven into a 200-year history as rich and entertaining as any to be found.

Londoners never call it the Underground, quite simply, 'The Tube'. This is a term of affection, an endearing way of describing a system which has, at various times, facilitated travel, encouraged enterprise and protected the population from the dangers of war. I would like to believe, but this may not be borne out by fact, that at least until the 1970s, the London Underground was still considered by Londoners to be an efficient and beneficial contribution to their daily lives. It is sad indeed, at the beginning of the third millennium, that this awe-inspiring concoction of engineering achievements has become such a vile object of hatred. This reversal of public esteem has nothing whatsoever to do with the achievements, which are set out in this book. It is simply a product of neglect, under-investment and poor management.

In reading the gripping story so eloquently told in this book, I am struck by the role of certain individuals in the totality of the achievement. Will the American Bob Kiley, so ingeniously engaged by Mayor Ken Livingstone, match the achievements of his fellow American, Charles Tyson Yerkes? Will any of Leslie Green's neglected red tile tube stations ever be restored to their former glory? Harry Beck's map of the Underground is my favourite graphic device of the twentieth century. Frank Pick, in choosing Charles Holden as his principal architect, gave this country some of our most important icons of the modern movement. Nikolaus Pevsner told me that Arnos Grove station was as important as any of the buildings of the Bauhaus – I believed him, and when I saw it for myself, he was right (I actually prefer Southgate). Roland Paoletti's role in engaging the country's greatest architects to design the Jubilee Line stations continues this tradition of single-minded individuals who dedicated their time and energy to improving the transport conditions for Londoners.

It is sad that a younger generation of Londoners will not see the tube as I saw it for the first time. For them, it is unreliable, expensive, overcrowded, dirty and, with the rise in street crime, potentially dangerous. This book will, I am confident, re-kindle a sense of enthusiasm, respect and awe for the hidden glory of *London Town*.

© Maxwell Hutchinson, July 2001

ACKNOWLEDGEMENTS

In writing this book I have incurred many debts, not least among my family and colleagues, whose opinions on London's underground railways have often been canvassed by me at inconvenient times. My wife Jane, a midwife, my daughter Faye, a nurse in a Liverpool casualty department, and my son Simon, a soldier keeping the peace in one of the world's troublespots, all have more stressful jobs than I do but they have listened patiently to accounts of the more colourful characters and events that surrounded the building of the London Underground. These events included suicide, bankruptcy and the creation of what one commentator has called 'the largest art gallery in the world'. My colleagues, especially Jane Fletcher and Lucia Ingham, have helped me by doing parts of my job that I should have been doing myself. My employers, Buckinghamshire Business School, allowed me the time to do the research and the staff of the Guildhall Library, the Metropolitan Archives and the British Newspaper Library at Colindale demonstrated the tact which is such a necessary quality of librarians in helping me to find original materials when I didn't always know what I was looking for. Simon Murphy of the picture library at the flourishing London's Transport Museum in Covent Garden patiently found most of the pictures which the book contains. I was very fortunate in the latter stages of my research to make contact with Anthony Bull, whose clear and accurate memory of the underground, supported by comprehensive diaries, stretches back to before the Second World War; David McKenna, who worked with Frank Pick before the war and Sir John Elliot in the difficult period of the 1950s; Paul Garbutt, who witnessed and described the dramas of the 1980s; and Richard Hope, editor of the *Railway Gazette*, whose personal involvement with some of the people and events of the last twenty years gave me insights that documents alone would not have provided. Ian Arthurton began his career with the underground as an engineer, became chairman of the Railway Division of the Institution of Mechanical Engineers and moved on to become the London Underground's Director of Passenger Services. Fortunately for me he combines a keen interest in the early history of the London Underground with an ability to describe, clearly and succinctly, the mysteries of the Public Private Partnership that will play a crucial role in the future of the network.

As I began work on this book I learned of the sudden, untimely death of Roger Hoyle, whose friendship I enjoyed for almost forty years. Roger, an airline captain with British Airways, had a lifelong interest in railways and their history, which was eclipsed only by his devotion to his wife Jane and his three daughters, Susan, Sally and Anna. I regret that he will not be able to read this book, which I dedicate to his memory.

Stephen Halliday, May 2001

PROLOGUE

In the 1850s Victorian London was not a pleasant place, especially for the traveller. Gustav Doré has recorded the hideous congestion as pedestrians, horsemen and horse-drawn vehicles jostled for space in its overcrowded streets. The predominant smell was that of horse-droppings, thousands of tons of which awaited the arrival of flies to consume their daily feast. At the end of the nineteenth century the invention of the internal combustion engine was greeted as a solution to air pollution! In 1855 Sir Joseph Paxton, architect of the Crystal Palace and hero of the Great Exhibition of 1851, told a Parliamentary Select Committee that: 'It takes a longer time to go from the London & Brighton station at London Bridge to the Great Western station at Paddington than from London Bridge to Brighton.'

In 1815, in an attempt to improve the capital's traffic, more use began to be made of the Thames. A steamboat service began between Greenwich and the City, with departures every fifteen minutes, and in the following twelve years four new toll-bridges across the river were built at Vauxhall, Waterloo, Southwark and Hammersmith, each charging a halfpenny or more to cross. However, by the 1850s river transport offered no relief since the Thames was the receptacle for London's sewage, as well as a source of its drinking water. Pedestrians crossing its bridges during a hot summer did so at a steady jogging pace, handkerchiefs held to their noses. In July 1855 the great scientist Michael Faraday travelled by boat from London Bridge to Hungerford Bridge and recorded that 'The whole of the river was an opaque, pale brown fluid. . . . Near the bridges the feculence rolled up in clouds so dense that they were visible at the surface. The smell was very bad.' Three years later, in the hot summer of 1858, the stench was so appalling that Members of Parliament fled from the chamber, led by Benjamin Disraeli, who was heard complaining about 'that Stygian Pool' that the Thames had become. *The Times* called it 'The Great Stink'.

The solution to London's problems of congestion and filth required an unorthodox combination of heroic engineers, egotistical financiers and visionary managers. The engineers, working with new materials, new machinery and new techniques, built the world's first underground railways and the first tunnel beneath a river. They were first condemned by the press for their folly, then praised for their vision. Sir Edward Watkin,

Traffic on Ludgate Hill in 1872 as recorded by Gustave Doré; hence the need for underground trains. (London's Transport Museum)

the egotistical chairman of the Metropolitan Line, the world's first underground railway, attempted to make it part of a system running from Manchester to Paris via a Channel Tunnel, which he actually started to build until Parliament (of which he was a Member) stopped him. Whitaker Wright raised the money to start to build the Bakerloo Line but went bankrupt, was jailed for seven years for fraud and committed suicide in the hallowed precincts of the new Law Courts in the Strand. His successor was Charles Tyson Yerkes, an American financier who had been jailed for fraud in Philadelphia and confronted by an angry mob brandishing nooses and firearms in Chicago. He finally fled to London from a disorderly private life in the USA. Having raised the money to build three tube lines by a series of stratagems the legality of which was debatable, he died, leaving his organisation on the verge of bankruptcy. For most of its existence the network has struggled to gain the investment it needed.

In the twentieth century the London Underground served as a refuge from German bombs; as 'the biggest art gallery in the world'; as a symbol of London itself, through its famous route-map; as a political football; and even as a means of transport. In the years between the two world wars London's underground railway was the envy of other nations, setting standards of comfort, reliability and design to which other systems aspired. In the post-war period it has struggled to cope with London's ever-growing passenger traffic despite chronic under-investment, though its connection to Heathrow, the world's busiest airport, has more than fulfilled Sir Edward Watkin's dream of making it a link in an international transport system. A journey begun on the London Underground can literally lead to anywhere in the world: truly an Underground to Everywhere.

As the network enters the twenty-first century there are signs that the problems of investment are at least being confronted, although disagreement remains about how the money should be found. This is an account of the London Underground's eventful and often florid history, written in the hope that it will once again become the urban transport system that others envy and seek to copy.

CHRONOLOGY

1900   27 June: Central Line opens the 'Twopenny Tube'; 28 December: Whitaker Wright, instigator of the Bakerloo Line, flees from his creditors

1901   Charles Tyson Yerkes buys shares in the District Railway; buys the planned Charing Cross, Euston and Hampstead Railway (second component of the Northern Line); buys the Piccadilly Railway

1902   Yerkes buys the Bakerloo Railway; electrification of the Inner Circle begins

1904   January: Whitaker Wright commits suicide in the Law Courts; 14 February: Great Northern and City Tube opens

1905   December: Yerkes dies, leaving a chaotic legacy of debt

1906   10 March: Bakerloo Line opens; 15 December: Great Northern, Piccadilly and Brompton Railway (Piccadilly Line) opens

1907   Albert Stanley becomes general manager of the Underground Group; Watkin Tower blown up by its disappointed owners; 22 June: Charing Cross, Euston and Hampstead Railway opens, second component of the Northern Line

1908   30 June: Sir Edgar Speyer rescues Yerkes' railways from bankruptcy at the eleventh hour; the name The Underground is adopted by all the underground railways

1909   Frank Pick appointed traffic development officer for the Underground Group

1911   First escalator installed, at Earl's Court

1913   The Underground group, 'The Combine', owns all underground railways except the Metropolitan and the Waterloo and City Line

1914   Edward McKnight Kauffer meets Frank Pick and starts to produce posters for the Underground Group

1915   The name Metro-land coined by the Metropolitan Railway; Frank Pick founder member of the Design and Industries Association; women enter underground service as men join the military

1916   Albert Stanley enters Parliament and becomes President of the Board of Trade in Lloyd George's wartime coalition

1917   Londoners seek shelter from Zeppelin raids in Underground stations

1920   Albert Stanley becomes Lord Ashfield and leaves government to head the Underground Group

1921   Trade Facilities Act; first case of government support for underground railways

1924   Euston–Camden link creates the Northern Line

1926   *Golders Green Gazette* describes Edgware as a beautiful garden suburb

1927   Post Office Railway opens, Paddington to Whitechapel

1929   Development (Loan Guarantees and Grants) Act; second case of government support for underground railways; Chiltern Court opened; Piccadilly Circus station rebuilt beneath Eros, and later becomes a listed structure; 55 Broadway opens, with furore over Epstein sculptures

1930   Pick spends seventeen days visiting European countries seeking architectural models

1932   Piccadilly Line extended to Arnos Grove with some notable station architecture. Harry Beck's schematic map of the Underground adopted; Beck paid 5 guineas

1933   London Passenger Transport Board established, with Ashfield chairman, Pick vice-chairman

1935   £40 million plan to extend Central, Bakerloo and Northern Lines; third case of government support for underground railways

1938   Green Belt (London and Home Counties) Act sets limits to Metroland

1939   Pick's evacuation plan implemented; Pick enters government service; public forbidden to use Underground stations as shelters

1940   Pick rows with Winston Churchill at meeting of Political Warfare Executive; the Blitz; extensive use of Underground stations as air raid shelters; Down Street, North End and Brompton Road stations used for government and military purposes; deep shelters constructed

1941   Death of Frank Pick; military production commences at Aldenham depot and in tunnels of uncompleted Central Line; 11 January: serious bomb damage as eleven stations struck by bombs; London Aircraft Production Group set up under LT management, making military equipment in London Underground depots and tunnels

1942   London Transport Spitfire enters RAF service

1943   March: 173 people killed as they try to enter Bethnal Green station during an air raid; worst such incident of the war

1947   Central Line to Leytonstone opened

1948   British Transport Commission established, with London Transport as a subordinate executive; SS *Empire Windrush* brings first wave of Commonwealth immigrants; accommodated in Clapham Common deep shelter

1952   Route C proposed, later to become the Victoria Line; a long wait begins for authority to make the required investment

1955   Chambers Committee praises London Transport management but can do nothing to help overcome problems of under-investment; growth of car and television ownership leads to decline in off-peak travel on the Underground

1956   London Transport begins to recruit staff in Barbados

1962   Victoria Line investment authorised by HM Treasury, ten years after line first proposed; London Transport Board established, reporting to Minister of Transport

1967   Barbara Castle and Desmond Plummer agree transfer of London Transport to the Greater London Council

1969   March: Victoria Line officially opened; Automatic Train Operation

1971   Fleet Line (later renamed Jubilee Line) authorised

1975   Moorgate disaster

1977   December: Piccadilly Line extension to Heathrow opens; Horace Cutler leader of GLC

1979   Jubilee Line opens, Charing Cross to Baker Street, taking over Stanmore branch from Bakerloo Line

1981   Labour gains control of GLC; Ken Livingstone leader; Fares Fair policy begins and leads to litigation; zonal fares introduced; passenger numbers begin to increase

1983   Margaret Thatcher wins general election, promising to abolish GLC

1984   London Regional Transport takes over the Underground from GLC; long process begins of improving productivity; one-person-operation begins

1986   Poetry on the Underground launched

1987   July: Docklands Light Railway begins operation; November: King's Cross Fire, thirty-one deaths

1993   Private Finance Initiative enables capital assets to be financed by the private sector

2000   January: Maths on the Underground launched for World Mathematical Year; July: Transport for London, under the authority of the mayor, takes over responsibility for the Underground; October: Robert Kiley appointed as London's Commissioner for Transport; Public Private Partnership bids in preparation for management of the Underground's infrastructure

2001   Ken Livingstone threatens the government with court action over the future of the Underground

INTRODUCTION:
EARLY DAYS AND FALSE STARTS

A great trunk line capable of maintaining a frequent, rapid, punctual and cheap intercommunication between the City and the suburbs without courting dangerous collisions by commingling on the same lines, creeping goods wagons with flying expresses and mixing up erratic excursionists with the migratory population of the City.

(Charles Pearson, City Solicitor, describing his proposal for an *Arcade Railway* beneath the Farringdon Road)

The forthcoming end of the world would be hastened by the construction of underground railways burrowing into the infernal regions and thereby disturbing the devil.

(Dr Cuming's view of the likely effects of an underground railway)

TOO MANY PASSENGERS

In 1801, the year of the first census, the population of London was recorded as 959,000. By 1851 it had reached 2,362,000.[1] To this unprecedented growth in population must be added the daily flow of commuter traffic brought by the new railways. London Bridge, the capital's first terminus, opened in December 1836 and by 1854 that station alone was unloading 10,845,000 passengers each year on to the congested streets of the metropolis, while a further sixteen million were entering through other railway termini.[2] By 1860 the ring of main line stations that serves London today was almost complete. Beginning at the first, London Bridge, and moving clockwise, the circle was formed by:

London Bridge (opened 1836)
Waterloo (1848)
Victoria (1860)
Paddington (1838)

Euston (1837)

King's Cross (1852)

Shoreditch (1840) (replaced by Liverpool Street, 1874)

Fenchurch Street (1841 – the only terminus then within the City itself)

Others were to follow shortly, including Charing Cross (1864), Cannon Street (1866), and St Pancras (1868), and by 1860 a clear pattern had been established: the main line railways were very good at bringing passengers to the fringes of the cities of London and Westminster where, in thinly populated districts like those around St Pancras, land could be bought cheaply for terminal stations. This left the passengers to find their ways to their final destinations via bridges, streets and alleys which in some cases dated back to the Middle Ages. The resulting confusion is well captured in Gustav Doré's engraving of traffic on Ludgate Hill in 1872, shown on p. xii.

THE *OMNIBUS* COMES TO LONDON

Some commercial enterprises sprang up to meet the transport needs of London's growing population. George Shillibeer (1797–1866), a London coachbuilder, visited Paris in 1828 and admired the *Entreprise des Omnibus* introduced to that city by Stanislas Baudry the same year. Shillibeer began a similar service from Paddington Green to the Bank of

George Shillibeer's first omnibus which ran from Paddington to the Bank of England. Popular with passengers, it drove Shillibeer into bankruptcy. (London's Transport Museum)

HACKNEY COACHES

In the reign of Charles I Captain Baily, a retired sailor who had served under Sir Walter Raleigh, hired out from the Maypole Inn in the Strand (now the site of St Mary-le-Strand) four *coches hacquenees*: French for a coach pulled by an 'ambling horse' ('hack'), one of which the driver rode. Charles I attempted to suppress the coaches, which cluttered up London's narrow streets, in favour of the sedan chair but they survived and in 1654 Cromwell authorised the 'Fellowship of Master Hackney Coachmen', licences being issued to regulate the numbers. By 1662 three hundred such licences were being issued at £5 per annum though a black market soon developed in which they were traded at higher prices. They enjoyed a monopoly of wheeled public transport within the area bounded by Southwark to the south and the 'New Road' (Marylebone Road–Euston Road–Pentonville Road) to the north. In 1694 the Hackney Coach Office was established, with five commissioners to issue licences and agree fares. In the same year some masked ladies hired a Hackney Coach and took it to Hyde Park where they 'behaved disgracefully and deliberately insulted some very distinguished people driving in their private coaches', following which coaches (and hence taxis) for hire were banned from Hyde Park. The ban remained until 1924. In 1823 David Davies of Mount Street, Mayfair, introduced from France a new type of carriage: a one-horse two-seater *cabriolet*, quickly shortened to 'cab', painted yellow and black. In 1831 the limitation on the number of coaches was removed and stage coaches, from surrounding towns, were allowed to pick up within the area previously monopolised by the Hackneys, leading to disputes that foreshadowed the mini-cab wars of the 1960s. From 1850 control of the Hackneys passed to the Metropolitan Police who issued licences, laid down regulations on the construction of vehicles and, later, administered the dreaded 'knowledge' test. The first petrol-driven cab was licensed in 1903 and *taximeters* (a third French derivation, meaning 'tariff meter') were introduced in 1907. In the year 2000 there were about sixteen thousand licensed *taxi cabs*, technically known as *Hackney Carriages*, whose twenty thousand drivers would probably be surprised to learn of their dependence upon French terms to describe their vehicles. In July 2000 Transport for London, under the authority of the mayor, took over responsibility for regulating taxis.

England on 4 July 1829. He offered the service along the 'New Road' built in 1756 between Paddington and the Angel (now Marylebone Road, Euston Road and Pentonville Road) because this fell just outside the area within which Hackney Coaches enjoyed a monopoly of wheeled public transport, competing only with sedan chairs.

Shillibeer offered five services daily in each direction at a fare of one shilling and sixpence for 'inside passengers'; outside passengers paid one shilling. The novelty of such shared urban transport is reflected in his newspaper advertisements which emphasised that 'a person of great respectability attends his Vehicle as Conductor: and every possible attention will be paid to the accommodation of ladies and children'. Despite such reassurance the service was not a success either for George Shillibeer or for his Parisian mentor. Stanislas Baudry drowned himself in the Seine in 1830 while Shillibeer, less drastically, went bankrupt and fled to Boulogne in a vain attempt to escape his creditors. After a short spell in a debtors' gaol he achieved prosperity by patenting a new type of funeral carriage.

In 1831 the Hackney Coach monopoly (*see* panel) was effectively abolished and from this time omnibus operators were allowed to ply their trade within the central area. George Shillibeer had argued for the abolition of the Hackney monopoly on behalf of 'the middling class of tradespeople whose finances cannot admit of the accommodation of a hackney coach and therefore necessitated to lose that time in walking which might be beneficially devoted to business'. However, it may be doubted whether the congested streets of the central district would have enabled much time to be saved until the heroic street building programme of Sir Joseph Bazalgette began to take effect in the 1870s.

SIR JOSEPH BAZALGETTE, 1819–91

Between 1856 and 1888 Bazalgette, one of the greatest of Victorian engineers, built more of London than anyone else, before or since. He did this in his capacity as chief engineer to the Metropolitan Board of Works, London's first metropolitan government. Bazalgette built the system of sewers and pumping stations which intercept London's sewage and convey it to treatment works. Before his great works the sewage had flowed into the Thames and thence into the water supply, causing cholera epidemics which killed forty thousand Londoners. He built the Victoria Embankment between Westminster and Blackfriars bridges to house the largest of his sewers, to provide a route for the District & Circle Line and to provide a new road from Westminster to the City. He also built the Chelsea Embankment and the Albert Embankment on which St Thomas's Hospital stands. The embankments reclaimed 52 acres of land from the Thames, speeding the river's flow and helping to turn it into one of the cleanest metropolitan rivers in the world. He built three bridges across the Thames: Hammersmith, Putney and Battersea. He created many of London's finest streets, including Charing Cross Road, Shaftesbury Avenue, Queen Victoria Street and Northumberland Avenue, demolishing slum tenements and rehousing forty thousand people in the process. He also created some famous parks, including Battersea Park, Finsbury Park, Southwark Park and Victoria Park, Hackney. Virtually all of his works are still in daily use, unnoticed by most of those who depend on them to travel, relax or spend a penny. A full account of Sir Joseph Bazalgette's work is to be found in *The Great Stink of London*.

Sir Joseph Bazalgette, builder of Victorian London, whose Thames Embankment carries the District and Circle Line from Westminster to Blackfriars. (By courtesy of Rear-Admiral Derek Bazalgette CB)

MORE RADICAL SOLUTIONS

In other quarters it was coming to be recognised that a solution more radical than the omnibus was needed to the problems of moving millions of people in London's central area. In 1846 a body of commissioners was appointed to consider a number of railway projects which had been proposed to Parliament.[3] They heard evidence from one of the most celebrated railway engineers, Robert Stephenson, co-inventor, with his father George, of the *Rocket* and engineer of the London and Birmingham Railway. Stephenson explained that he had, in 1836, prepared plans to extend the London and Birmingham Railway all the way to the Savoy Wharf on the Thames, the site of the present Savoy Hotel. This was to be achieved by running in a tunnel beneath Gower Street and Covent Garden. This early plan for a railway beneath the streets of London had been abandoned in favour of a terminus at Euston. The commissioners were impressed by the many protests about the disruption to property, traffic and life that would be caused if main line railways were allowed to penetrate further into the densely populated cities of London and Westminster. For these reasons they concluded that 'on the North of the Thames no Railway now before Parliament or projected be permitted to come within the limit described' (south of the Marylebone Road–Euston Road–Pentonville Road line), thus excluding main line railways from the central area.[4]

CHARLES PEARSON'S ARCADE RAILWAY

However, during their deliberations the commissioners heard of another scheme with a similar vision of taking a railway into the heart of the City. This was the plan of Charles Pearson (1794–1862), solicitor to the City of London and MP for Lambeth from 1847 to 1850. A successful solicitor with a number of notable achievements already to his credit, Pearson had campaigned successfully against the practice of packing juries in political trials and secured the admission of Jews, previously barred, to the freedom of the City of London. He also persuaded the City authorities to remove from the inscription on the Monument the lines that attributed the Great Fire of 1666 to the machinations of Catholics. Pearson presented to the commissioners a blueprint for what was, eventually, to become part of London's first underground railway.[5] It was described as an 'Arcade Railway' which would run from Farringdon, in the City, north towards the projected Great Northern Railway terminus at King's Cross. The railway would run just below street level in an arcade, following the line of the River Fleet along what is now Farringdon Road. In the years that followed, Pearson developed and promoted his plan with single-minded determination in a series of pamphlets and public meetings. In 1852 he published a pamphlet calling citizens to attend a meeting at the London Tavern, Bishopsgate, a popular meeting-place for such events. He proposed to explain his 'City Central Terminus' at Farringdon which would link the City:

> by means of a great trunk line capable of maintaining a frequent, rapid, punctual and cheap intercommunication between the City and the suburbs without courting dangerous collisions by commingling on the same lines, creeping goods wagons with flying expresses and mixing up erratic excursionists with the migratory population of the City. Mr Pearson will explain and illustrate his project by models and maps of immense size.[6]

In his pamphlet Pearson argued, with remarkable foresight, that building more roads would simply generate more traffic and that sub-surface railway projects of the kind he was advocating were the only solution to London's overcrowded alleys and congested streets. Much of the area through which the railway was projected to run had recently been cleared by the City Corporation. In 1830 Farringdon Street, from Ludgate Circus to the present site of Holborn Viaduct, had been built by demolishing some slum dwellings. The Bartholomew Fair at nearby Smithfield had degenerated to a state of 'rowdiness and debauchery' for which it was shortly to be permanently suppressed. In 1852 the Corporation had acquired 75 acres in Copenhagen Fields, just north of King's Cross, to which it proposed to relocate the Smithfield cattle market; its continued presence in the City was alarming shopkeepers whose premises were regularly wrecked by livestock running wild, often with the encouragement of their drunken drovers.[7] A Clerkenwell

Charles Pearson's Arcade Railway from Farringdon to King's Cross was eventually incorporated in the plans of the Metropolitan, the world's first underground railway. (London's Transport Museum)

Improvement Commission, established in 1840, had set about extending Farringdon Street north of Holborn to create what is now Farringdon Road and, in the process, had demolished a lot of semi-derelict property but the area still accommodated some of London's worst slum tenements and sweatshops.

PARLIAMENTARY TRAINS

To rid the City of these embarrassments, Pearson's plan depended upon the use of 'parliamentary trains'. These had been created by Gladstone's Regulation of Railways Act of 1844 which required railway companies to provide a daily service of covered passenger carriages, travelling at an average speed of at least 12 miles per hour, and charging not more than one penny per mile. Pearson had calculated that fifty thousand slum dwellers could be rehoused in ten thousand 'artisan cottages' 7 miles to the north of Farringdon, each with 400 square yards of garden, and that parliamentary trains would enable them to travel each day to their places of work in the City. The area thus freed of slums could then be redeveloped for commercial purposes and this would more than compensate for the capital cost of the railway. Everyone would benefit. It was a visionary scheme that involved building six standard gauge and two broad gauge tracks (for Great Western trains) beneath a 100ft-wide road, which eventually became the site of the present

Farringdon Road. The eight tracks ran to a 20 acre terminus station at Farringdon with facilities for passengers and freight, the latter to serve the projected new Smithfield meat market which was eventually completed in 1868. Pearson's bold plan required a substantial initial investment for a radical but untried idea.

Pearson's scheme was not without its opponents. The fiery preacher Dr Cuming told an open air meeting at Smithfield that the forthcoming end of the world would be hastened by the construction of underground railways burrowing into the infernal regions and thereby disturbing the devil. Despite these apocalyptic prophecies Pearson's proposal attracted much admiration though not a penny of the money he needed. Nor did he have much luck. The Great Northern Railway had taken powers to subscribe £170,000 to the 'Arcade Railway', which would enable it to run trains from King's Cross to Farringdon. Unfortunately one of its officers, Leopold Redpath, had misappropriated the money and used it for 'the furnishings of magnificent houses and the purchase of articles of *vertu* by one who was undergoing the penalties of the law for his conduct'. Redpath was sentenced to transportation for life but that didn't help Pearson.[8] In 1859, in what can only be described as an early use of direct mailing techniques, Pearson mailed to fifteen thousand citizens a *Twenty Minutes Letter to the Citizens of London in Favour of the Metropolitan Railway and City Station*.[9] Each pamphlet, besides the customary arguments in favour of Pearson's scheme, contained a share application form and a penny black postage stamp to encourage a prompt reply. There is no record of the response to this enterprising piece of company promotion but neither this nor his 'models and maps of immense size' resulted in the project being started. Pearson's scheme had been overtaken by the events described below.

CRYSTAL WAYS

In the meantime Parliament had appointed a Select Committee on Metropolitan Communications which sat for three months in 1855 and considered a number of radical solutions.[10] Several of them involved trains which were to be propelled by atmospheric pressure, an idea that briefly attracted the interest of many eminent railway engineers – to their cost. The idea had been patented in 1838 by two engineers called Samuel Clegg and Jacob Samuda, and required a cast-iron tube to be laid between the running rails. Within the tube was a piston which was attached to the underside of a passenger train. At the end of the line a stationary steam engine pumped out the air in front of the piston, the resulting vacuum causing the piston, with the train attached, to be drawn forward into the vacuum by the air pressure behind it. The system was very attractive for railways being built in enclosed spaces since no smoke or steam was generated by the train itself. However, the idea depended for its effectiveness upon the creation of an airtight seal around the piston and this proved to be its fatal weakness. The inventors of the system, Clegg and Samuda, built a 2-mile demonstration railway at

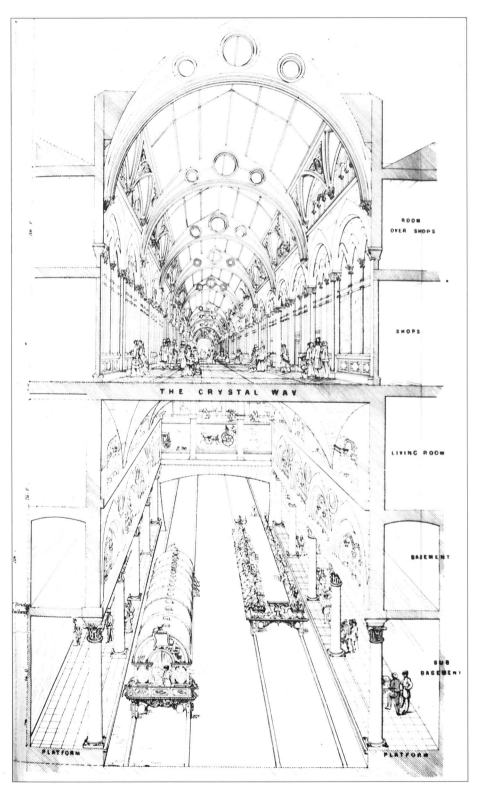

ROOM
OVER SHOPS

SHOPS

THE CRYSTAL WAY

LIVING ROOM

BASEMENT

SUB
BASEMENT

PLATFORM

PLATFORM

William
Mosley's
Crystal Way
would have
been the first
shopping mall;
visionary but
impractical.
(London's
Transport
Museum)

Dun Laoghaire in Ireland which worked intermittently and impressed several visitors, notably Isambard Kingdom Brunel who insisted to critics that 'mere mechanical difficulties can be overcome' and adopted the system for the South Devon Railway in the 1840s. Leather, beeswax and tallow were employed to create the critical airtight seal but the beeswax and tallow melted in hot weather and the leather became stiff and hard in cold or wet weather, so the system was reluctantly abandoned by Brunel. A similar fate befell the London–Croydon–Epsom Railway, where the 'airtight' pipe provided a comfortable home for rats.

Despite these setbacks the 'atmospheric' system of propulsion was proposed for two of the schemes that the Select Committee examined at length. On 10 May 1855 they examined a proposal from Mr William Moseley, an architect, called the *Crystal Way*. Moseley proposed to build a railway 12 feet below street level between St Paul's Cathedral and Oxford Circus, with a branch to Piccadilly Circus. It would be covered by a wrought-iron 'superway' across which pedestrians could pass for a toll of one penny, the trains being visible beneath them. The walkway itself would be enclosed within a glass arcade (hence the name *Crystal*), with arcades of shops, houses and the occasional hotel on either side. If it had been built it would have been a Victorian shopping mall with railway beneath. While recognising the visionary character of Moseley's scheme, costing an estimated £2 million, the committee members were more impressed by a similar scheme put forward by the 'apostle of glass' Sir Joseph Paxton MP.[11] Four years earlier Paxton had made spectacular use of glass in creating the pre-fabricated pavilion for the Great Exhibition of 1851. Contemptuously dismissed by *Punch* at the time as the

SIR JOSEPH PAXTON, 1801–65

Son of a farmer and apprenticed to a gardener, Paxton so impressed the Duke of Devonshire with his enthusiasm and ingenuity that the duke appointed Paxton head gardener at Chatsworth and took him on a tour of Europe to gather ideas. Paxton created the famous Chatsworth fountain, 267ft high, and a 300ft glass conservatory which he based on the structure of a lily brought home from South America by a botanist. The success of the conservatory inspired him to design, on similar principles, the 23 acre *Crystal Palace* (the name sneeringly coined by *Punch* in a critical article) for the Great Exhibition of 1851, after 233 other designs had been rejected by the organising committee. He completed the design, based on pre-fabricated interchangeable panels, in nine days. It held fourteen thousand exhibits, was visited by six million visitors and generated enough profit to start building the South Kensington museums. The structure was dismantled and re-erected at Sydenham, South London, by navvies whose work so impressed the authorities that they used them as a model for the 'Work Corps' employed in the Crimean War. They later developed into the Pioneer Corps. The Crystal Palace was destroyed by fire in 1936.

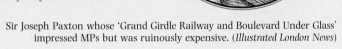

Sir Joseph Paxton whose 'Grand Girdle Railway and Boulevard Under Glass' impressed MPs but was ruinously expensive. (*Illustrated London News*)

'Crystal Palace', the pavilion had been a triumph so the committee paid careful attention to Paxton's proposal for a 'Grand Girdle Railway and Boulevard under Glass' which he had patriotically named the 'Great Victorian Way'. In his evidence to the committee Paxton claimed that it took longer to travel from London Bridge station to Paddington station than it did to travel from London Bridge to Brighton.

Paxton's solution was a railway, almost 12 miles long, built above ground but within a glass arcade, with shops and houses on either side. The line would link all of London's railway termini and would cross the Thames three times on enclosed bridges. As with Moseley's system, the trains would be powered by atmospheric pressure and the committee was assured that the great railway engineer Robert Stephenson MP had stated that the atmospheric principle would work in this case.[12] The railway would carry freight as well as passengers but the goods trains would only be allowed to run between nine in the evening and early the following morning: a suggestion that still appeals to many urban planners struggling with heavy goods vehicles in the twenty-first century. Paxton claimed further advantages for his system, insisting that, for those fortunate enough to occupy residences within his boulevard, it would 'almost be equal to going to

Sir Joseph Paxton's 'Great Victorian Way', linking all London's main line stations: it was visionary but impossibly expensive. (London's Transport Museum)

a foreign climate [and] would prevent many infirm persons being obliged to go into foreign countries in the winter'.[13] The cost was enormous: £34 million. In comparison, Brunel's Great Western Railway cost six million and Bazalgette's main drainage just over four million. Paxton acknowledged that the cost was too great for any company to bear and suggested that it be underwritten by public funds: a most unattractive proposition for Victorian politicians who were wedded to *laissez-faire* economics and still cherished the hope of abolishing income tax.

Nevertheless, perhaps out of respect for the hero of the Great Exhibition, Paxton's plan was one of nine selected by the committee for further consideration and it was particularly commended because it 'possesses many features of remarkable novelty'. However, they were even more impressed by the evidence presented by the ever-persistent Charles Pearson, campaigning for his Farringdon terminus. In his evidence Pearson gave some hint of the commercial pressures supporting his plan when he claimed it was:[14]

monstrous that commercial men should be tolerating a system where the poor are living upon ground which is worth £750 per acre per annum, when they might be transferred nightly in twenty minutes to land that is to be obtained for £200 an acre.

In their conclusions the committee recommended that 'the different metropolitan Railway Termini should be connected by railway with each other, with the docks, the river and the Post Office, so as to take all through traffic off the streets', adding that the work should be 'carried out by private enterprise'. They particularly commended 'Mr Charles Pearson's plan for a railway from Farringdon Street, communicating with the Great Northern station [King's Cross] and the Metropolitan Railway'.[15]

These few sentences formed the blueprint for London's first underground railways, into which Pearson's scheme would shortly be absorbed.

UNDERGROUND RAILWAYS IN OTHER CITIES

When the Metropolitan Railway opened in 1863, as described in Chapter One, it was the world's first underground railway. In February 1886 the Liverpool to Birkenhead railway opened (though it could be argued that this was little more than a tunnel beneath the Mersey). In the following month, March 1886, Glasgow, the second city of the Empire, inaugurated the Glasgow City and District Underground Railway, followed by the Glasgow District Cable Subway in 1897. The first foreign city to build such a railway was Budapest, whose 2-mile line opened ten years later, in 1896. The Paris *Metro*, its construction prompted by the advent of the 1900 Paris Exhibition, opened on 19 July, just in time for that event. Work on the New York Subway began in the same year and Berlin's followed in 1902. Madrid's Underground railway opened in 1919 and was a coveted prize during the Spanish Civil War. At one time in 1937 one end of the line was held by Franco's forces and the other by the Republican government. Moscow's system opened in the 1930s, much of it built by forced labour under the brutal direction of Nikita Khrushchev, whose reputation it thereby helped to make. In Italy Mussolini prepared plans for Rome's Underground railway but these were put aside during the Second World War and the system finally opened in 1955. Besides building the world's first underground railway London also built the first deep-level tube, now part of the Northern Line, as described in Chapter Two.

CHAPTER ONE
TERMINAL CONNECTIONS

Utopian and one which, even if it could be accomplished, would certainly never pay.
. . . The whole idea has been gradually associated with plans for flying machines,
warfare by balloons, tunnels under the channel and other bold but hazardous
propositions of the same kind . . . an insult to common sense.

(*The Times*, 1861, referring to the Metropolitan Railway)

The line may be regarded as the great engineering triumph of the day.

(*The Times*, 1863, referring to the Metropolitan Railway)

THE METROPOLITAN RAILWAY

Plans for a sub-surface railway to provide a link between the City of London and main
line stations to the north had been in existence for several years. The Great Western
Railway was particularly concerned that Brunel's terminus at Paddington, opened in
1838 on what was then the fringe of the built-up area, was too far from the City for its
passengers' convenience. In 1854 a Bill was presented to Parliament, the cumbersome
title of which reveals its purpose: 'The Metropolitan Railway, Paddington and the Great
Western Railway, the General Post Office, the London and North Western Railway and
the Great Northern Railway.' The plan, originally devised by a financier called William
Malins, was to link Paddington, Euston and King's Cross by a railway running beneath
the Marylebone–Euston–Pentonville road, picking up passengers from each station. The
inclusion of the General Post Office secured the support in Parliament of Rowland Hill
MP, who in 1844 had invented the penny post. A former chairman of the Brighton
Railway Company, Hill was an enthusiastic advocate of rail transport and was concerned
about the delays to the post caused by London's chronic traffic.

In 1854 a parliamentary committee considered the plan and, in particular, looked at
the problems posed by steam engines in long underground tunnels. John Fowler,
engineer to the projected line, had asked Robert Stephenson to design a locomotive that
could run the length of the proposed railway on heat and steam built up in the open air
before entering the tunnel. To reassure the committee Fowler produced as a witness

Isambard Kingdom Brunel himself, who insouciantly declared 'I thought the impression had been exploded long since that railway tunnels require much ventilation', and adding, enigmatically, 'If you are going a very short journey you need not take your dinner with you, or your corn for your horse.'[1]

Over the next four years the project underwent several changes of name, directors and route, the one constant factor being John Fowler, who remained the very well-paid consultant engineer to the company. By 1858 the Fowler railway project, its title mercifully shortened to the 'Metropolitan Railway', had in effect absorbed the plans for Pearson's 'Arcade Railway' referred to in the introduction. It combined the two schemes into a single line beginning at Bishop's Road, near Paddington, which would pick up passengers from stations at Edgware Road, Baker Street, Great Portland Street, Euston Square and King's Cross before turning south along Pearson's proposed route to Farringdon.[2] There would be connections to the Great Western tracks at Paddington and the Great Northern tracks at King's Cross so that the underground line could accommodate trains from these railways as well as offering its own shuttle service. The presence of Great Western trains meant that the tracks had to be laid to accommodate the company's broad gauge (7ft) rolling stock as well as the standard gauge (4ft 8½in) stock of the other services. There would also be a connection with the new Smithfield meat market for goods trains.

In 1858 *The Times* reported another meeting at the London Tavern, chaired by the Lord Mayor and addressed by Pearson and by Lord John Russell, MP for the City of London.[3] Their speeches prompted much cheering and some bold resolutions but this time they also produced some money. Earlier in the year William Malins had been replaced as chairman of the Metropolitan Railway by the stockbroker William Wilkinson, who enjoyed good City connections. The time was right. Much of the land through which the projected line would run was derelict and could be acquired at a reasonable price. In a few years' time it would be built upon and prohibitively expensive. Baron Lionel Rothschild reminded the meeting that land was changing hands in the City for as much as a million pounds an acre. Pearson had earlier urged the Metropolitan Railway directors to 'Tell the Corporation that if they do not come forward to help you, you will wind up the affair and that will be the end of it.'[4] Following the meeting the deal was done.[5] The Metropolitan Railway purchased the Fleet Valley land from the City for £179,157; in return the City Corporation subscribed £200,000 to the company's capital. The Great Western subscribed £175,000. The remainder of the capital, some £475,000, was raised from civil engineers like Morton Peto and Thomas Brassey,[6] who hoped to gain contracts, as well as from the Great Northern and Metropolitan Railway shareholders.

The new company moved into offices at 17 Duke Street, Westminster, the former home of I.K. Brunel. In February 1860 work at last began on the railway, watched with a mixture of curiosity and disdain by the press and the public. One observer recorded: 'A few

THE METROPOLITAN LINE

The Metropolitan Railway was the world's first underground railway, though it firmly believed that it was really a main line railway, part of which, by painful necessity, happened to be built just below street level. Its steam service opened on 9 January 1863 running from Bishop's Road station, near Paddington, to Farringdon Street in the City of London. Its tracks were dual gauge, accommodating both the standard gauge trains of the Metropolitan Railway itself and the broad gauge rolling stock of the Great Western running through from the main line at Paddington. In 1865 the line was extended to Moorgate Street and in 1868 further extensions were made, north to Swiss Cottage and south to Gloucester Road and South Kensington. From 1864 it also operated services via Westbourne Park and Shepherds Bush to Hammersmith, on what became the Hammersmith & City Line. After 1872 its new chairman, Sir Edward Watkin (*see* panel on p. 33), also chairman of the South Eastern Railway, embarked upon an ambitious programme of expansion and acquisition. In 1875 he extended the Metropolitan from Moorgate to Liverpool Street and in 1882 to Tower Hill. In 1878 he became chairman of the East London Railway (*see* panel on p. 31), from New Cross to Whitechapel, with an onward connection to Liverpool Street, to provide a link beneath the Thames to the South Eastern Railway. In the 1880s he extended the Metropolitan in a north-westerly direction to Harrow (1880), Pinner (1885) and Chesham (1889). Amersham and Aylesbury were reached in 1892, while in 1891 he had purchased the Aylesbury and Buckingham Railway, thus taking the 'Metropolitan' to the rural fastness of the Vale of Aylesbury. The original link to Paddington had become part of the Circle Line. Watkin's plan, a century before its time, was to connect with main line railways to the north and take passengers from Manchester, via London, Dover and a channel tunnel, to Paris. In 1899, after Watkin's retirement, a further acquisition took the Metropolitan's services to the village of Brill, 7 miles east of Aylesbury. Further extensions were built to Uxbridge (1904), Watford (1926) and Stanmore (1932), the last of these passing to the Bakerloo and then the Jubilee Line when it opened in 1979. In 1913 the Metropolitan had acquired the unloved Great Northern and City Tube (*see* p. 51) from Finsbury Park to Moorgate, which remained, however, unconnected to the rest of the company's network. The Metropolitan electrified its services from 1905, though the section beyond Amersham remained steam-operated until it was transferred to British Rail in September 1961 following electrification of the stretch from Rickmansworth to Amersham and Chesham. The Metropolitan maintained its independence of the rest of the network until it was finally absorbed, protesting, by the London Passenger Transport Board in 1933.

wooden houses on wheels first made their appearance; then came some wagons loaded with timber and accompanied by sundry gravel-coloured men with picks and shovels.'[7]

The Times was more astringent, describing the scheme as 'Utopian and one which, even if it could be accomplished, would certainly never pay'.[8] The writer added, with unconscious foresight, that 'the whole idea has been gradually associated with the plans for flying machines, warfare by balloons, tunnels under the Channel and other bold but hazardous propositions of the same kind'. The newspaper thought it 'an insult to common sense to suppose that people would ever prefer to be driven amid palpable darkness through the foul subsoil of London'.

The line was built by the 'cut and cover' method. A trench was dug, mostly along the line of the Marylebone–Euston–Pentonville roads, with appalling effects upon traffic. Once the line was built, the trench was covered over and the traffic resumed its normal, congested course. Benjamin Baker, who had joined John Fowler in designing the system, described some of the problems encountered in constructing the world's first underground railway at the Institution of Civil Engineers in 1885.[9] Baker and Fowler later collaborated on their most celebrated railway project, the Forth Bridge. The construction of the railway was closely followed, especially by the *Illustrated London News* which took many opportunities to publish engravings of the work in progress. On 15 February 1862 it published an illustration of the cutting as it passed 'the summer

The River Fleet bursts in on the Metropolitan Railway construction works, a scene 'well worthy of a visit' according to the *Illustrated London News*.

residence of Nell Gwynne'.[10] A more sombre note was sounded the following June when the Fleet sewer burst in upon the workings, and the newspaper marked the occasion with a scene of devastation on its front page and a vivid description of the event:

> A warning was given by the cracking and heaving mass and the workmen had time to escape before the embankment fell in . . . the massive brick wall, eight feet six

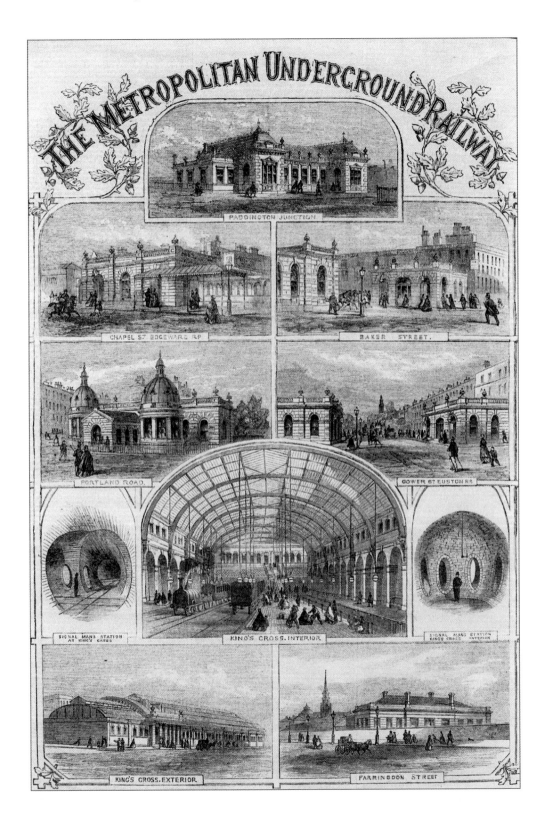

inches in thickness, thirty in height and a hundred yards long, rose bodily from its foundations as the water forced its way beneath. . . . The scene was, indeed, well worthy of a visit.[11]

Several inspection visits were carried out before the line officially opened, some of them arranged for publicity purposes. There exists a photograph of Gladstone on one of these occasions, looking distinctly out of place in an open goods wagon at Edgware Road in May 1862, shortly before the Fleet burst. On another such inspection visit, reported in the *Illustrated London News* on 6 September 1862,[12] the newspaper's correspondent described the curious sensation of agreeable disappointment – the open cuttings being more extensive, and the tunnels better lighted and ventilated, than was expected.

'THE GREAT ENGINEERING TRIUMPH OF THE DAY'

On 9 January 1863 the line was formally opened by the directors. Shortly before the opening they had referred to arbitration a late request for extra payments in connection with the opening by their engineer John Fowler, who was gaining a reputation for being distinctly acquisitive.[13] The previous week the *Illustrated London News* had announced the event and devoted a full page to illustrations of each of the seven stations served by the new route. A ceremonial tour of the new line was undertaken by the directors and about 700 guests. Sir Rowland Hill was among the guests but the Prime Minister, Lord Palmerston, was not. He had been invited but the 79-year old statesman had declined, saying that he hoped to remain above ground a little while longer. He died two years later. Another absentee was Charles Pearson. He had lived to see his idea taking shape but had died the previous September before it was completed. A banquet was held at the Farringdon Street terminus at which an atmosphere of mutual congratulation prevailed. The Metropolitan Police band played, speeches were made and toasts drunk to the manifold virtues of the City Corporation, the civil engineering profession in general and to John Fowler in particular. *The Times*, whose earlier scepticism was forgotten amid the enthusiasm of the occasion, declared:

The Metropolitan Railway has at length become 'a great fact' and, we may add, a great success . . . the line may be regarded as the great engineering triumph of the day . . . ingenious contrivances for obtaining light and ventilation were particularly commended.[14]

Opposite: Stations on the New Metropolitan Railway as shown in the *Illustrated London News* on the opening of the line.

The Metropolitan Railway at Baker Street with a Great Western broad gauge locomotive in steam. (London's Transport Museum)

The 'ingenious contrivances' consisted of lengths of cutting open to the sky (still a characteristic of much of the Metropolitan and Circle Line, for example at Farringdon) and coal gas lamps in huge globes hanging from the station roofs. Robert Lowe MP, Gladstone's future Chancellor of the Exchequer, made the principal speech, in which he expressed his confidence that the new line would form the basis of a 'Circle' of such railways within the metropolis. This would follow, but not until another twenty-one years had passed.

In his speech, John Fowler predicted that the 'ingenious' design of the locomotive would ensure that neither smoke nor steam would be emitted in the tunnels. In this he was radically wrong. In 1861 Robert Stephenson had delivered an experimental engine ordered by Fowler. It cost £4,518, about twice the price of a normal engine. It was tried out over a 7-mile stretch of the Great Western, but at the end of the run it was in such a poor condition, dangerously overheated and emitting steam from every orifice, that it had difficulty limping back to its depot. The Metropolitan Railway directors agreed to pay Stephenson for his engine and promptly attempted to sell it to the Great Western.[15] Instead, the line was worked by tank engines designed by Brunel's collaborator, Daniel Gooch MP, who neatly diverted the exhaust steam via a prominent pipe into a cold-

An early Metropolitan steam carriage, similar to those used on surface trains of the time. (London's Transport Museum)

water tank beneath the boiler. However, although this disposed of most of the steam it did nothing for the smoke which was released unimpeded into the tunnels.

Forty-five passenger coaches, made of teak and supplied by the Great Western, offered first, second and third class compartments, lit by coal gas carried in collapsible bags on the roofs of the carriages. The opening of the line had been delayed by the Chief Inspector of Railways, Colonel Yolland of the Royal Engineers, who was concerned about some of the finer points of the signalling equipment – though he appears to have overlooked the problems that could arise from the combination of bags of gas and locomotive sparks within a tunnel. Happily, no accidents occurred as a result of this hazardous arrangement and the line enjoyed an excellent safety record during its days of steam.

The *Illustrated London News* also gave generous coverage to the public opening of the line on 10 January 1863. It was estimated that thirty thousand people used the line on this first day, becoming the first paying passengers to use an underground railway service anywhere in the world. The crush of passengers was such that, for much of the day, the trains filled up at the terminus stations at each end of the line, Bishop's Road (Paddington) and Farringdon, and it became impossible to board the trains at intermediate stations.[16]

THE GREAT WESTERN WITHDRAWS

The enthusiasm of the crowds who attended the public opening was matched by the numbers who used the line in the months that followed. Fares were, according to class, threepence, fourpence and sixpence for full single journeys, fivepence, sixpence and ninepence return.[17] In the first six months almost thirty thousand passengers a day used the line and the service had to be increased to a frequency of ten-minute intervals at peak times and fifteen minutes at others. To supplement the service the Great Western brought in extra rolling stock and standard, non-condensing steam locomotives, causing two railwaymen to be removed, choking, to University College Hospital. Perhaps as a result of these extra services, problems quickly arose in the relationship between the Metropolitan Railway and its biggest shareholder, the Great Western, which had provided the locomotives and rolling stock for the trains. The locomotives were named after autocrats (*Czar, Kaiser, Mogul*) and unpleasant insects, (*Locust, Hornet, Mosquito*). The Great Western had backed the line because it wanted to gain access to the City for its main line passengers from Bristol and elsewhere. It had little interest in the Metropolitan's 'shuttle' service between intermediate stations and was consequently reluctant to devote more of its rolling stock, locomotives and staff to increasing the frequency of this service when the Metropolitan asked it to do so. The Great Western was also nervous about the Metropolitan's connections with other railway suitors so, when the Metropolitan Railway directors announced, in July 1863, that they were about to create a connection at King's Cross that would enable the Great Northern to run trains direct from Hatfield and Hitchin to Farringdon, the Great Western took what it assumed would be decisive pre-emptive action.[18] Its directors announced that they would withdraw all Great Western services in two months, leaving the line bereft of trains. They also refused to sell to the Metropolitan Railway the stock they had been using. In a series of hastily arranged meetings throughout July the Metropolitan Railway directors arranged to borrow some locomotives and rolling stock from the Great Northern and to purchase 18 tank locomotives and 34 passenger carriages. As a result of this swift action the Metropolitan was able to begin running its own services in August, well within the two months' notice served by the Great Western. By October peace had been restored. The Great Western sold its shares in the Metropolitan (at a profit) and resigned itself to the fact that it would now share the line not only with the Metropolitan's own services but also with the Great Northern, whose services began to run through to Farringdon from Hatfield and Hitchin via King's Cross in October 1863.

The directors of the Metropolitan showed some enterprise in securing revenue from sources other than fares. In March 1863, two months after the line opened, an advertising agent called James Willing[19] paid the company £1,150 for the right to sell books and place advertisements on the stations. The experiment must have been a success because in 1866 he paid over £34,000 for the right to continue the arrangement for another seven years. He renewed the contract at regular intervals until 1907, when it passed to W.H. Smith. In 1864 Felix Spiers and Christopher Pond, who had made a fortune selling refreshments to gold prospectors on the Melbourne to Ballarat Railway in Australia, signed an agreement to run refreshment rooms on Metropolitan stations, paying for this privilege 10 per cent of the takings, or at least £4,000 per annum.

WHATEVER BECAME OF THE EARTH?

A few weeks after the line opened the general manager of the Metropolitan Railway received a curious message from the manager of White's, that most exclusive of London's gentlemen's clubs, situated at the top of St James's Street: 'To save further heavy wagering within the precincts of the club, the manager would be grateful if you would inform him of what became of the earth removed from the tunnels.' The reply read 'Tell the manager to go to Chelsea and see for himself.' The excavated earth had been dumped on a greenfield site off the Fulham Road called Stamford Bridge. In 1905 it became the home of Chelsea Football Club, the embankments of earth being used to form terraces for spectators.[20]

Another curiosity of the line's construction was to be found in Bayswater at 23 Leinster Gardens, where a false house façade was created to conceal the trains running behind the neighbouring dwellings (*see* p. vi).

THE HEART OF THE CITY

It had long been the intention of the directors of the Metropolitan that the line should eventually run beyond Farringdon and soon after the line opened work began on an extension which took the line to Moorgate Street with an intermediate station at Aldersgate (now Barbican). The elliptical span of the station roof at the latter inspired John Betjeman's despairing poem 'Monody on the Death of Aldersgate Street Station', written in 1958 to lament the removal of the station roof, which had been severely damaged by bombs in the Second World War. Moorgate station was opened on 23 December 1865 and a year later a further connection was made with the Ludgate Hill station[21] of the London, Chatham and Dover Railway, thus creating the first connection between railways north and south of the river. The Metropolitan never took advantage of this link but the Great Northern used it to run freight trains across the river. In the meantime the construction of 'The City Widened Lines' (*see* panel) via a second tunnel through Clerkenwell made Moorgate Street and Farringdon accessible to the Great Western, Great Northern, Midland and London, Chatham and Dover Railways, which could also thereby gain access to the goods depot serving Smithfield meat market.

THE CITY WIDENED LINES

The so-called 'widened lines' were laid down in 1868 beside the existing Metropolitan Railway tracks (*see* panel on p. 14) between King's Cross and St Pancras to the north, and Farringdon and Moorgate in the City, an additional tunnel being created through Clerkenwell to accommodate them. They were built to make the City directly accessible to Great Northern trains from King's Cross and Midland Railway trains from St Pancras. There was also a connection with the London, Chatham and Dover Railway terminus at Ludgate Hill, thus linking railways north and south of the Thames. This through service for passenger trains ceased in the First World War but was reopened as Thameslink in 1988 following the electrification of suburban services from King's Cross and St Pancras. Trains now run from Bedford to Brighton and from Luton to Wimbledon via this route.

SMOKE, STEAM AND 'METROPOLITAN MIXTURE'

We do not need to imagine what the tunnels of the Metropolitan Railway were like as a growing number of steam locomotives poured through them from every direction since, once the initial enthusiasm for underground railway travel had waned, a number of contemporaries recorded their experiences of travelling through the dark, steaming, smoking tunnels. A letter to *The Times* described a journey in 1879:[22]

> The condition of the atmosphere was so poisonous that, although a mining engineer, I was almost suffocated and was obliged to be assisted from the train at an intermediate station. On reaching the open air I requested to be taken to a chemist close at hand. . . . Without a moment's hesitation he said 'Oh, I see, Metropolitan Railway', and at once poured out a wine glass full of what I conclude he designated Metropolitan Mixture. I was induced to ask him whether he often had such cases, to which he rejoined 'Why, bless you sir, we often have twenty cases a day.'

Even a supposedly flattering account of a journey in the 1890s in the *English Illustrated Magazine* conjures up a vision of a dentist from Hell, comparing the noise of the train with the 'shrieking of ten thousand demons above the thunder of the wheels. The sensation was altogether like the inhalation of gas preparatory to having a tooth drawn.' In October 1884 a leading article in *The Times*,[23] celebrating the completion of the Inner Circle Line, reminded its readers that early promises by the Metropolitan Railway to use locomotives which 'consume their own smoke and condense their own steam' had quickly been forgotten and added:

> A journey from King's Cross to Baker Street is a form of mild torture which no person would undergo if he could conveniently help it. Passengers have been consoled by the assurance that semi-asphyxiation by sulfurous fumes is not an injurious thing even for the asthmatic but this is a point on which coughing sufferers cannot be expected to agree with railway directors.

The reference to railway directors reflected the often-expressed conviction of these gentlemen that smoke-filled tunnels were not only harmless to humans but positively beneficial. In 1898 a Board of Trade Committee on Ventilation of Tunnels on the Metropolitan Railway was told that almost 550 passenger and goods trains were passing through the system each day, all, of course, drawn by steam locomotives. In his evidence to the committee the Metropolitan Railway's general manager, Colonel John Bell, assured his questioners that the company's employees were the healthiest railwaymen in the country, that the fumes were health-giving and that Great Portland Street station was 'actually used as a sanatorium for men who had been afflicted with asthma and bronchial complaints'.[24] Indeed, Bell attributed his own recovery from decades of tonsillitis to the 'acid gas' in the tunnels and claimed that another employee's bronchitis cure was due to the company's thoughtfulness in transferring him from a quiet, well-ventilated station at Bayswater to the fuming chasm of Euston Square. These strange assurances received some support from an independent quarter. In his book *The Soul of London*,[25] published in 1895, F.M. Hueffer (better known as Ford Madox Ford) wrote: 'I have known a man, dying a long way from London, sigh queerly for a sight of the gush of smoke that, on a platform of the Underground, one may see escaping in great woolly clots.'

However, the Board of Trade Committee heard some more unsettling evidence from a Metropolitan Railway train driver, Mr A. Langford. Having told the committee of his excellent health despite thirty-four years' subterranean service, he added, rather alarmingly, that 'very seldom' was the smoke so thick as to prevent him seeing the railway signals. The committee's reaction to this disconcerting news is not recorded but their deliberations achieved little since two years later the journalist R.D. Blumenfeld, a reliable chronicler of London at the turn of the century, recorded in his diary[26] his experience of a journey from Baker Street to Moorgate:

I had my first experience of Hades to-day, and if the real thing is to be like that I shall never again do anything wrong. I got into the Underground railway at Baker Street. I wanted to go to Moorgate Street. The compartment in which I sat was filled with passengers who were smoking pipes, as is the English habit . . . the smoke and the sulphur fill the tunnel, all the windows have to be closed. The atmosphere was a mixture of sulphur, coal dust and foul fumes from the gas lamps above; so that by the time we reached Moorgate Street I was near dead of asphyxiation and heat. I should think these Underground railways must soon be discontinued, for they are a menace to health.

Fortunately for Blumenfeld's son this gloomy prognosis was wrong since the son, Sir John Elliot, went on to become chairman of London Transport in the 1950s.

The problem of the fumes was eventually solved, after much hesitation and acrimony, in the early 1900s through the adoption of electric traction, though steam locomotives

---

R.D. BLUMENFELD, 1864–1948

Born in Wisconsin, the son of a German professor who had fled Germany after the 1848 revolution, Blumenfeld's persistent attempts to join the staff of the *New York Herald* as a journalist were repeatedly rebuffed by the proprietor, J. Gordon Bennett. His dramatic account of a fire he witnessed in New York led to his engagement by Albert Pulitzer to work on the *Morning Journal*, after which he was poached by Bennett and sent to London as the correspondent of the *Herald*. A chance encounter in a barber's shop in 1900 with Alfred Harmsworth (later Lord Northcliffe) led to his appointment as editor of the *Daily Mail*. Two years later he moved to the rival *Daily Express*, which he served as editor from 1904 to 1932. In 1907 he became a British subject. He was a pioneer in the use of dramatic stories and headlines on the front page to attract buyers and he was among the first editors to give extensive coverage to sports events. His diaries give a graphic account of life in the late nineteenth and early twentieth centuries, especially in London, where they include numerous references to travelling on the Underground. He was the father of Sir John Elliot (1898–1988), who anglicised his name in 1922; he was a prominent railway manager and chairman of London Transport from 1953 to 1959.

---

continued to be used for many years to haul engineers' trains for track maintenance. The last working steam train ran on 4 June 1967.

THE METROPOLITAN EXPANDS

In the meantime, despite the mounting anxiety of its customers about the atmosphere in which they were travelling, the Metropolitan embarked upon a rapid expansion of its business. In May 1864, within eighteen months of opening, it became the first railway to issue cheap 'workmen's tickets' for use on early trains. A threepenny return fare, almost half the normal rate, was offered on two trains which left Paddington at 5.30 and 5.40 a.m. The return journey could be made at any time after mid-day. The Metropolitan also began to expand its network, often by running its trains on surface lines (*see* panel on p. 14 for opening dates). First, it opened a joint venture with its former shareholder in the form of the Hammersmith and City Line, which ran partly over Great Western tracks to the east of Paddington.[27] By 1868 it was moving north-west of Baker Street towards what was eventually to become Metroland (*see* Chapter Five). It was also beginning to move south to Gloucester Road and South Kensington, creating the next stage in what was eventually to become the Circle Line.

NOT IN MY BACK YARD

The early success of the Metropolitan did not pass unnoticed among railway investors. In 1863, the year that the new line opened, promoters deposited bills before Parliament proposing almost 200 miles of additional railway tracks within the metropolis. Not everyone shared their enthusiasm. In 1861, while the Metropolitan was being built, the Revd William Denton, rector of St Bartholomew, Cripplegate, published a pamphlet with the cumbersome but informative title 'Observations on the Displacement of the Poor by Metropolitan Railways and by other Public Improvements',[28] in which he told his readers that a half-mile stretch of the Metropolitan had required the demolition of 899 dwellings housing 10,000 people. Thomas Hughes, MP for Lambeth (though better known as the author of *Tom Brown's Schooldays*), declared that the Metropolitan Railways were a 'social tyranny' inflicting suffering on 'the humbler classes, who have been turned out of their holdings . . . that a man might be able to get from one side of the town to the other in five minutes less time'. Residents of one neighbourhood were so alarmed at the onslaught that they formed an early 'fighting fund' to oppose the railway developments. One of its members told the select committee set up to examine the schemes that 'if London is to be cut up in such style, London will have to move elsewhere'.

A CIRCLE LINE?

Arguments of this kind no doubt helped the select committee to conclude that penetration by surface railways of the central metropolitan area was an issue to be handled with the greatest caution. Their recommendation was that there should be 'an inner circuit of railway which should abut upon, if it did not actually join, all the principal Railway Termini in the Metropolis'.[29] This was the blueprint for what, after much delay and some acrimony, would eventually emerge as the Circle Line. The committee also suggested that the whole circuit should be under one unified management, a visionary recommendation which was not to become fully effective until 1933, when the Metropolitan Railway reluctantly came under the management of the London Passenger Transport Board.

The obvious candidate to build the new line and complete the circle was the Metropolitan Railway, which in July 1864 gained the powers to extend its line from Paddington to South Kensington in the west and from Moorgate to Aldgate and Tower Hill in the east. As in the case of the original Metropolitan Railway, the main obstacle to the completion of the proposed Circle was finance, particularly since it would pass through the heart of the City and hence through or beneath the most expensive land in the world. However, there was an opportunity to construct a substantial part of the line through the proposed Victoria Embankment without having to pay extravagant compensation to property owners. Between 1863 and 1870 the embankment was built between Westminster Bridge and Blackfriars Bridge by the chief engineer of the Metropolitan Board of Works, Sir Joseph Bazalgette.[30] Originally designed to house the low level sewer which Bazalgette had designed to protect the Thames from sewage and the population from cholera and typhoid, this massive structure eventually reclaimed 37 acres of land from the Thames. In the process it provided land for the sewer, a major road, a service tunnel for water pipes and other utilities and a route for the District and Circle lines with stations at Westminster, Embankment, Temple and Blackfriars.

THE DISTRICT

Even with the availability of the relatively cheap land reclaimed by the Victoria Embankment it was estimated that the cost of the line would be almost £5 million and it was doubtful whether the Metropolitan, with its modest capital base and its existing commitments to extend its lines, would be able to raise this sum. In this respect it presaged the investment problems that were to beset socially desirable metropolitan railway projects throughout the following century. The ubiquitous John Fowler supported the idea of launching the railway as a separate company, raising money in its own right, linked to the Metropolitan at either end.[31] The new company would be called the 'Metropolitan District Railway', with four representatives of the Metropolitan Railway on its board. Fowler, of course, would be engineer to both of them. Bazalgette's stern and experienced eye evaluated forty-seven schemes for metropolitan railways and concluded that Fowler's proposal was the best one available.[32] The new line was incorporated as the Metropolitan District Railway Company in July 1864, with powers to complete the circle between South Kensington and Tower Hill. Four Metropolitan directors served on the board of the District. It was envisaged that, once the circle was completed, the two

---

THE DISTRICT LINE

The first section of the Metropolitan District Railway (later the District Line), between South Kensington and Westminster, was opened on 24 December 1868 on the day the Metropolitan also reached South Kensington from Gloucester Road. It was originally launched as a joint venture with the Metropolitan Railway (*see* panel on p. 14), the plan being to construct a circular line to link the main line terminus stations. The collaboration with the Metropolitan Railway did not long survive and

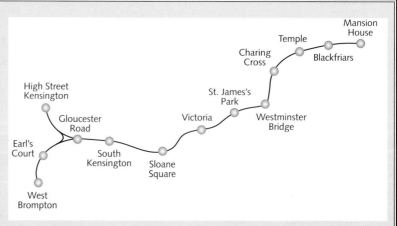

The Metropolitan District Railway, 1871.

the two became bitter rivals. In 1869 the District was extended west to West Brompton via Earl's Court and in 1870 it reached Blackfriars to the east. In 1871 it reached High Street Kensington and in the same year it reached Mansion House in the heart of the City. In 1874 the District began its long period of expansion to the west, reaching Hammersmith in that year, Richmond via London & South Western Railway lines in 1877 and Ealing in 1879. In 1880 the District built a 2-mile extension from West Brompton to Putney Bridge and in 1889 it began to run over London & South Western lines to Wimbledon. Meanwhile, in 1884 the District had finally completed the Circle Line by extending east from Mansion House to link with the Metropolitan Railway at Tower Hill. Electrification of the network began in 1902, the year the District was acquired by the Underground Group and began to run services over a new line from Whitechapel to Bow Road and thence via London, Tilbury and Southend Railway tracks to East Ham, Barking and Upminster. Services to New Cross via the East London Railway (1884, *see* panel on p. 31), South Harrow (1903), South Acton (1905), Uxbridge (1910) and Southend (1910) were later withdrawn or transferred to other lines.

companies would merge, though clashes of personality ensured that they never did. The differences between the two companies manifested themselves early, and in some curious ways. In May 1869 a Member of Parliament drew attention to the fact that the District permitted smoking and the Metropolitan did not. Thus a passenger travelling on a train using the lines of both companies would have to interrupt his smoking according to the whims of company policy. What was the Board of Trade going to do about it? John Bright, staunch advocate of free trade, answered that *laissez-faire* should prevail and that 'the question of cigars' should be left to the railway directors.[33]

Construction began in June 1865, and proceeded westwards. The contractors, Peto and Betts, had to confront a number of delicate engineering problems. At Sloane Square station the line passed directly through the course of the River Westbourne, which rises on Hampstead Heath, surfaces in Hyde Park as the Serpentine and enters the Thames at Chelsea. At Sloane Square it is a substantial river, crossing the platforms and tracks in a conspicuous 9ft-diameter iron casing, the purpose of which still baffles waiting passengers. Special precautions were taken as the line passed close to Westminster Abbey, a 7ft-thick layer of soft peat being placed outside the tunnel to absorb vibrations from passing trains.

Greater problems lay ahead. In May 1866 the London banking house Overend Gurney failed, precipitating a financial crisis that saw interest rates rise to the unheard-of level of 10 per cent. This was followed by the failure of thirteen other banks and the

An artist's impression of Sir Joseph Bazalgette's Victoria Embankment under construction at Charing Cross, complete with District Railway steam train. The planned 'atmospheric railway' (*see* p. 59) can be seen running from left to right beneath the river, but it was never built. (*Illustrated London News*)

The District Railway under construction at Westminster, with Big Ben, completed a few years earlier, in the background. (*Illustrated London News*)

consequent failure of many of their clients, among them Peto and Betts. New contractors were quickly found but the financial crisis made it even harder for the District to raise the capital it needed to meet its commitments. From 1864 onward Bazalgette's annual reports to his employers, the Metropolitan Board of Works, were loud with complaints about work on the Victoria Embankment being delayed while the District Railway sorted out its financial problems. In the event, Bazalgette proceeded relentlessly with the construction of the Embankment, some of which subsequently had to be re-excavated to enable the sub-surface train tunnels to be built. He also included some ventilation shafts in Victoria Embankment Gardens to enable smoke and steam to escape from the tunnels. They are still there, disguised by plinths, and people walking in the gardens can clearly hear the trains running beneath.

On 24 December 1868 the Metropolitan District Railway opened from South Kensington to Westminster. The *Illustrated London News* carried a short announcement of the opening,[34] in which it reminded its readers that the line 'forms a portion of the Metropolitan Inner Circle' and described the frantic pace of work which had characterised the last weeks of the construction in a desperate attempt to open the line in time to benefit from the Christmas traffic. Further capital was raised in July 1869 and the line opened to Blackfriars on 30 May 1870, shortly before the official opening of the Victoria Embankment itself. The first services on the new line were run by the Metropolitan Railway, which provided the locomotives and rolling stock in return for approximately half of the receipts. This arrangement echoed the Metropolitan's own relationship with the Great Western when its services began in 1863 but soon deteriorated into acrimony.

THE GREAT SCHISM BEGINS

On 3 January 1870 the District directors informed their Metropolitan colleagues that they were ending the agreement, giving eighteen months' notice. At the same time they appointed as chairman of the District James Staats Forbes, an experienced railwayman who was shortly to become chairman also of the London, Chatham and Dover Railway. This appointment was to have damaging consequences for the District's relationship with the Metropolitan, especially when the latter came under the chairmanship of Forbes's long-standing adversary, Sir Edward Watkin, of the rival South Eastern Railway.

In July 1871 the District extended its line from Blackfriars to Mansion House, within a mile of the Metropolitan's projected station at Tower Hill. The 'horseshoe' of the

JAMES STAATS FORBES, 1823–1904

James Staats Forbes was an early example of a 'company doctor' who spent much of his working life rescuing railways reduced to penury by incompetent predecessors. Born in Aberdeen, he worked for I.K. Brunel in the construction of the Great Western Railway. He refused the post of general manager at the enormous salary of £10,000, possibly because he was deterred by the prospect of working with the formidable and hot-tempered Brunel. He rescued a Dutch railway from insolvency and went on to perform the same service for the London, Chatham & Dover and for the District (*see* panel on p. 26), which he chaired from 1872 to 1901. Much of his energy was spent in protecting the last two from the designs of Sir Edward Watkin (*see* panel on p. 33), chairman of the Metropolitan Railway (*see* panel on p. 14) and of the South Eastern Railway, the latter being amalgamated with the London, Chatham & Dover in 1899. As emollient as Watkin was aggressive, Forbes persuaded shareholders by 'the delicacy of his touch, his light banter and personal charm', this being compared by the *Railway News* with Watkin's strategy of bullying his shareholders. In his last shareholders' meeting he reminded his audience 'much of my time has been spent in making apologies'. He was well rewarded for his labours, earning the colossal annual salary of £15,000 by 1884.

James Staats Forbes, bitter rival to Sir Edward Watkin. (London's Transport Museum)

combined Metropolitan/District lines was now almost the long-desired circle. It was no doubt for this reason that this modest 700-yard extension was celebrated with extravagant enthusiasm. Gladstone, at the banquet to mark the event, declared with characteristic portentousness that 'the Underground railway illustrated the present wants and destinies of London, the vast need that is felt for an increase in the means of locomotion and the novel and unheard-of resources that it is developing for the purposes of meeting the necessity'.[35] The air of celebration was only slightly marred by a letter sent to *The Times* the day after the public opening, complaining about the appalling unpunctuality of the trains.[36] The letter was signed, menacingly, 'MP' At the same time the District began to run its own services using its own locomotives and carriages, similar to those previously provided by the Metropolitan and lit by the same explosive compressed coal gas carried in bags on the carriage roofs.

MONEY PROBLEMS

The enthusiasm which greeted the opening of the new railway was not matched by its financial performance. By the time it opened it was burdened with heavy capital debts which became a permanent feature of underground railway facilities in the capital. Of its initial authorised share capital of £3.6 million it had only managed to raise £3 million, almost all of it spent to make its way through the expensive property between South Kensington and Westminster. Having survived the Overend Gurney crisis and the bankruptcy of its principal contractors, and having placated Bazalgette and the Metropolitan Board of Works who were anxious to press ahead with the Embankment, the District finally managed to raise £1.5 million in 5 per cent preference shares. This enabled it to complete the line through the Embankment and beneath Bazalgette's new Queen Victoria Street to reach Mansion House. The 5 per cent preference stock, with its first call on the District's profits, was to restrict dividend payments to ordinary shareholders for many years.

Largely for this reason, the District was very slow to construct the final link in the long-desired Circle Line. The expense and hazards of circumventing expensive property in the heart of the metropolis had not been lost on the District's directors. Having just managed to reach Mansion House they were daunted by the prospect of the further investment required to burrow beneath a thousand yards of the most expensive property in the Square Mile. In the years that followed, the company's revenues often struggled to meet the demands of its interest payments and preference shareholders, leaving ordinary shareholders at the end of a long queue.[37]

The District therefore sought to increase its revenues without heavy expenditure on new lines and over the following years it showed considerable ingenuity in doing this. Thus on 15 March 1871 Forbes was able to tell his shareholders at their half-yearly meeting that the District had made an agreement with the London and North Western

Railway whereby the latter would run its trains from its own lines, north of Euston, on to the District's system at South Kensington, reaching the latter via an under-used surface railway known as the West London Line. From Kensington it would use the District's tracks to run into Mansion House, thus giving it access to the City. In return the London and North Western would make a down payment of £100,000, thus reducing the District's burden of debt, and would pay tolls for the two trains an hour using the facility. The directors 'anticipated much advantage from this extension of the area from which traffic may be expected to arise' and invited other railway companies to enter into similar arrangements.[38]

At the same time Forbes sought cost-effective ways of extending the District's own services with minimal capital expenditure, using other companies' tracks where possible. (*See* panel on p. 26 for details of line openings.) Extensions were built to Hammersmith and Putney Bridge and beyond these stations the District secured an agreement with the London and South Western Railway to run over its tracks to Wimbledon and Richmond, and to gain access to Ealing via Turnham Green. By such measures the District was able to increase its suburban passenger revenue while making few demands on its over-stretched capital and without having to face too much competition from omnibus operators which, in the inner metropolitan area, was a continuing source of anxiety for the Metropolitan and the District at this time.[39]

THE CIRCLE BEGINS TO CLOSE

In the meantime, however, the City was beginning to fret over the continuing failure to complete the long-awaited Circle. In 1874 the prominent London solicitor George Newman secured parliamentary support for his 'Inner Circle Railway Bill'. This ambitious project proposed to close the circle by linking the District and Metropolitan

THE EAST LONDON RAILWAY

Authorised by an Act of Parliament in 1865, the purpose of this line was to link the main line railways north and south of the Thames, a noble aim never fully achieved owing to its inadequate connections to the main lines to the north. It passed through Marc Brunel's Thames Tunnel (*see* p. 40), opened in 1843 as a pedestrian tunnel but never a commercial success. The line opened throughout in 1876 between New Cross and Shoreditch, with a connection to the Great Eastern at Liverpool Street, but never ran its own trains. Its services were operated by main line companies (later comprising the Southern Railway) from the south, and by the Metropolitan and District Railways (*see* panels on pp. 14 & 26) from the north. In May 1878 Sir Edward Watkin (*see* panel on p. 33) was appointed as receiver to the line, which had run into difficulties through placing its financing in the hands of a colourful financier called Albert Grant – who later used some of his ill-gotten gains to restore Leicester Square. Watkin rescued the line from its immediate problems and became its chairman. A connection was made to the Metropolitan and Metropolitan District Railways in 1884. From 1913 its passenger services were operated by the Metropolitan; in 1925 it was transferred to the Southern Railway; in 1948 it passed to London Transport and has remained part of the Underground network ever since. Its continued use of Brunel's tunnel entitles this otherwise obscure line to lay claim to operating through the world's oldest railway tunnel beneath a river.

railways beneath the City, taking in a connection with the Great Eastern at Liverpool Street and with the East London Railway at Whitechapel. In addition, Fenchurch Street, beneath which the proposed link would run, would be widened, thereby easing one of the City's most notorious bottlenecks.

This was too good an opportunity to miss for the City Corporation and the Metropolitan Board of Works, which between them agreed to contribute £500,000 to the scheme.[40] Other investors, no doubt chastened by the experience of the impoverished District Railway, were more wary and Newman failed to gain support for his scheme, despite an alluring prospectus with confident predictions of capital gains of up to 46 per cent.[41] However, although Newman's company failed to raise the money it needed, it galvanised the District and Metropolitan Railways into a renewed effort to finish the job themselves.

THE WATKIN METROPOLITAN

In the meantime a change in management at the Metropolitan Railway had introduced an unpredictable factor into the equation: Sir Edward Watkin. In August 1872 Watkin was appointed chairman of the Metropolitan as a result of shareholder discontent with the line's level of profits and dividends. During the years that followed, Watkin's combative management style no doubt brought some benefits to shareholders and certainly enlivened their meetings but he also created enemies who would have been better kept as friends, notably among the directors of the Metropolitan District Railway. The situation was made worse by the fact that Watkin was chairman of the South Eastern Railway while James Staats Forbes, chairman of the District, was also chairman of the London, Chatham and Dover, the Kent competitors of the South Eastern.

Watkin began by addressing the problem of the Metropolitan's poor profits and ordered an immediate audit of the company's affairs. It revealed a sorry tale. In August 1882 two of Watkin's fellow-directors told of extravagant expenditure in the engineers' department (the chief engineer promptly left) and 'many false and fictitious entries' in the stores inventory.[42] Moreover the accounts were 'in an exceedingly unsatisfactory condition', to the point where it was not possible to say with any confidence what profits, if any, the company was making. Several items were missing altogether from the accounts, including an invoice from the omnipresent John Fowler for £11,765.[43] The board decided, somewhat belatedly, to appoint an accountant to see to these things. They also appointed Edwin Waterhouse,[44] founding partner of Price Waterhouse, to carry out a further investigation with the brief to 'ascertain what the defects in the past management have been which have brought the Company to such a low ebb'. Watkin was following the time-honoured tradition of heaping blame upon his predecessors and this he now proceeded to do with some justification and much success.

Waterhouse certainly provided Watkin with the evidence he sought. His report revealed that the previous chairman, Parson, admitted that he didn't understand

SIR EDWARD WATKIN, 1819–1901

Born in Manchester, Edward Watkin entered the railway industry in 1845 at the age of twenty-six and became associated with numerous railway companies and projects, his great and unrealised ambition being to link Paris and Manchester via a network of railways devised or dominated by him: the Great Central; the Metropolitan Railway; the East London (*see* panels on pp. 14 & 31); the South Eastern; and a channel tunnel of which he was an early and insistent advocate. Frustrated in this larger ambition he turned his considerable energies into needlessly antagonising other railway chairmen, notably James Staats Forbes, chairman of the District and of the London, Chatham and Dover Railway, thereby turning potential partners into bitter rivals. Watkin's expansion of the Metropolitan Railway north-west towards Harrow, Amersham and Chesham was responsible for the later creation of 'Metroland'. To stimulate suburban traffic further he promoted the 'Watkin Tower', 15ft higher than the Eiffel Tower, as a tourist attraction close to the railway. It was a commercial failure and was never completed. Its site is now occupied by Wembley stadium. He served three constituencies as an MP and was knighted in 1868 for his work in promoting Canadian federation through an effective rail network. He was an aggressive workaholic, but ill-health obliged him to resign the chairmanship of his three railway companies in 1894. When news of his resignation reached the Stock Exchange the shares of all three companies rose. He also paid for the building of the 'Watkin path' up Mount Snowdon so that he could reach his holiday cottage. The path is still used by tourists.

Sir Edward Watkin of the Metropolitan and James Staats Forbes of the District briefly suspended hostilities to complete the Circle Line. (London's Transport Museum)

accounts; that the stores inventory had been 'grossly mismanaged', the storekeeper absconding with his gains; and that extravagant payments had been made to civil engineering contractors, for whom John Fowler unwisely appeared as an apologist.[45] Shareholders' dividends had been paid from capital and the wretched Parson had concluded an agreement with the London, Chatham and Dover Railway, to give them access to the Moorgate station across Metropolitan tracks, on terms which were disadvantageous to the Metropolitan. Since the London, Chatham and Dover was one of Watkin's special *bêtes noires* he was particularly enraged by this news. The board was purged of most of its previous members, Watkin's salary was doubled and Watkin set about confronting the company's tribulations.

The first object of his wrath was John Fowler. As soon as he had read Waterhouse's report Watkin wrote to Fowler in terms which tell us much about the character of each man.[46] He started by making some reassuring noises about not wishing to quarrel and reminding Fowler that he had been paid £152,484 for his services by the Metropolitan and a further £330,000 by the District, huge sums by any standards. Watkin's analysis of the situation was unambiguous:

no engineer in the world ever was so highly paid . . . you have set an example of charge [sic] which seems to me to have largely aided in the de-moralisation of the Professional men of all sorts who have lived upon the suffering shareholders for the past ten years.

He added, disarmingly, 'I apologise in advance if I have given any offence.' There is no evidence that these strictures had the desired effect upon Fowler but later in the year Watkin returned to the theme in an intemperate speech to his shareholders when he berated 'Clodd, the great railway contractor, Plausible, the great railway engineer, and Vampire, the great railway Lawyer'. Having thus vented his spleen and appointed a competent accountant, Watkin turned his considerable energies to his longer-term interests, including creating a link between Manchester and Paris, entertaining his shareholders while abusing his fellow-railwaymen, especially James Staats Forbes, and planning a superior version of the Eiffel Tower.[47]

MANCHESTER TO PARIS

In 1878 Watkin became chairman of the East London Railway (*see* panel on p. 31). Although it remained a separate company from the Metropolitan it provided a potential link between the Metropolitan's tracks to the north of the Thames and those of Watkin's South Eastern Railway to the south. At the same time Watkin began to expand the Metropolitan to the north-west (*see* panel on p. 14). By 1891 he had reached Aylesbury. Watkin was not unopposed in his expansion to the north. One of his most persistent questioners was a clergyman who complained that the line to Aylesbury was fit 'only for ducks and drakes and donkeys' and pleaded that the directors concentrate their attention and resources on the original purpose of the railway – to carry passengers within the metropolis itself.[48] Watkin prevailed, reasoning to his shareholders that the Metropolitan could in this way be extended at little cost, passing over cheap rural land and picking up longer distance commuter traffic with little competition from other railways or from the omnibuses which were providing such severe competition in the Metropolis itself.

However, there is no doubt that his real aim was to link up with railways from the north, in particular the Manchester, Sheffield and Lincolnshire Railway, of which he was also chairman. Watkin made no secret of his enthusiasm for this network of routes which would enable trains from Manchester to reach central London using Metropolitan tracks. At many shareholders' meetings he took the opportunity to advise his audience of the advantages of such an arrangement. Thus in January 1891 he told them of the Manchester, Sheffield and Lincolnshire Railway's attempts to obtain parliamentary sanction for a connection with the Metropolitan's lines at Quainton Road, a small rural community near Aylesbury. He assured his shareholders: 'The benefits to your undertaking generally would be very considerable and your Directors have entered into

The East London Railway
emerges from Marc Brunel's
tunnel – the world's oldest
beneath a river. (*Illustrated
London News*)

an agreement with the Sheffield company for running powers for that company over
your system between Quainton Road and Baker Street.'[49] Over the next few years the
shareholders' meetings were updated with the progress of the Manchester, Sheffield and
Lincolnshire's progress south. Eventually, in 1899, the company ran along and beside
the Metropolitan tracks most of the way into its terminus at Marylebone, having
changed its name to the Great Central.

Watkin's ambitions were not confined to a Manchester–London–Dover link. His other
interests included a seat on the board of the 'Submarine Continental Railway Company'
which in 1881 had begun some experimental borings between Dover and Folkestone
with a view to building a channel tunnel, close to the site where the modern tunnel
itself now begins. The government intervened to prevent Watkin's subterranean
excavations on the grounds that he was infringing the Crown's rights to the foreshore.
Watkin tried to overcome this obstacle by trying, on three occasions, to introduce into
Parliament a Bill which would give his company the authority it required. *Herapath's
Railway Journal* in 1888 revealed that the reluctance of Parliament to authorise the
construction of the tunnel was based on grounds of national security, citing evidence of
'growing armaments on the continent' and dismissing Watkin's reassurance that 'the
tunnel could be flooded in three minutes and that a Minister in London, by pressing a
button, could blow it up in a few seconds'. The journal, writing of the cosmopolitan
nature of the company, suggested that 'many of the servants would probably be French'
and implied that they would sabotage any attempt to block the tunnel in the event of a
French invasion.[50] On one occasion, in a stunt designed to gain support for the tunnel,
Watkin brought to London the French engineer of the Suez Canal, Ferdinand de Lesseps,

and arranged for the distinguished visitor to be greeted at Charing Cross by working men who, after much rehearsal, were schooled to cry 'Vive la France! Vive le tunnel sous la Manche!' An account of the occasion assures us that 'Naturally Monsieur de Lesseps went back to France with a passionate belief in the intelligence of the British working man.' However, the incident did nothing to advance the cause of the tunnel.

The repeated failure of his Bill did not, however, deter Watkin from pressing on with the work. At the annual general meeting of the Channel Tunnel Company in December 1890 Watkin informed his shareholders that 2,200 yards of tunnel had already been bored. He rejected the alternative suggestion of a bridge, asserting with his customary optimism that 'the great advantage of making a tunnel was that they might afterwards make as many as they pleased'.[51] His venture eventually failed but it could not be said of Sir Edward Watkin that he lacked determination.

In 1890 he spoke again to his shareholders of the possibility of a link between Manchester and Dover using the Metropolitan tracks, and one report of the meeting wrote of his 'long-cherished dream' of an onward link to Paris.[52] He also proposed to build a luxurious 80-bedroom 'Metropolitan Grand Hotel' above the Metropolitan's headquarters at Moorgate to accommodate the clientele who, according to this plan, would be carried by his network from Manchester and Paris to London. On this occasion, however, the shareholders demurred. The hotel project lapsed.

DERIDING THE ENEMY

When he was not conceiving his grand Franco-British schemes Watkin amused himself, and his shareholders, by abusing the Metropolitan's foes. He was a fluent, witty speaker with a gift for the invective phrase, which he turned upon one Sir Randall Roberts at a shareholders' meeting in July 1889. Roberts, an obscure soldier otherwise unknown to history, had sued the Metropolitan for £5,000, claiming that he had been injured while on the company's premises. Watkin pursued him relentlessly and had him followed by private investigators whose testimony as to the gentleman's alleged injuries resulted in an award by a jury of £10 – a fraction of his costs; Watkin rejoiced in the result, reminding shareholders that this was 'an instance of the manner in which railway companies are involved in the expense of defending exorbitant claims'.[53]

He never lost an opportunity to pour scorn on competitors, especially the struggling District company and its chairman, James Staats Forbes. Having dismissed Randall Roberts, Watkin proceeded, at the same meeting, to reject the idea of a merger with the District on the grounds of the unprofitability of the latter. A year later, having told his shareholders of the riches that lay ahead on account of his visionary schemes, he reminded his laughing shareholders of the poor dividends that the District paid compared with those they received from the Metropolitan since he, Watkin, had been in charge. Modesty was never a problem for Sir Edward Watkin.[54]

His grasp of technical matters was less sure. Mounting criticism of the smoky tunnels had raised the question of electrification (covered in more detail in Chapter Two). Watkin was often questioned by shareholders about the Metropolitan's plans for adopting this novel form of traction. He was normally dismissive of such questions but on occasion he showed himself to be thoroughly confused by the competing claims of alternating and direct current, assuring one meeting that: 'The proposal was to have a carriage containing electric motors but the Board had come to the conclusion that they wanted a direct current which would do away with an engine altogether.'[55]

AN ARMISTICE

Despite the hostility between the Metropolitan and District Railways and the personal animosities of their respective chairmen, the advantages of completing the Circle were becoming clear to both boards. In December 1877 a contractor called Charles Lucas persuaded Forbes and Watkin to meet on the neutral ground of his office in the City, where they agreed what turned out to be a temporary armistice while they jointly approached the City and the Metropolitan Board of Works for their financial support. The City agreed to contribute £300,000 and the Board £275,000, later raised to £500,000.[56] These figures were achieved after some characteristically combative interventions by Watkin. Thus on 4 January 1881 he wrote to the secretary of the City Sewers Commission a letter that was both pained and threatening, in connection with a meeting he had attended concerning the comparatively minor question of the cost of the rail link disturbing the sewers beneath Trinity Square: 'Some days ago I read with great pain the notes of the discussion on 14th December. . . . Having noticed the insulting tone of the discussion . . . I am beginning to think that the whole scheme must be abandoned.'[57]

Despite Watkin's threats engineering began later that year, in September 1881. The Metropolitan reached Tower Hill on 25 September 1882, while the more financially constrained District proceeded at a slower pace, despite Watkin's urgings and occasional insults. The District finally arrived at Tower Hill on 17 September 1884. The work had been complicated by the attempts of the Metropolitan Board of Works to prevent the railway companies putting ventilation shafts ('blow holes') in the streets, which occasionally blasted out jets of air and steam. The Board even introduced a Bill to Parliament designed to close some shafts that already existed. The Bill was only partially successful but it helps to explain the appalling conditions which developed in the tunnels, referred to above.[58] Alan Jackson[59] was told by his father that these 'blow holes' provided a lunchtime diversion for young office clerks who kept them under close observation in the hope that a lady would walk over one while a train passed beneath, thereby raising her skirts to reveal her nether garments.

Trial working of trains around the system was undertaken during the first week of October, prior to the full official opening of the service on 6 October 1884.

Unfortunately no photograph exists of this occasion, as Watkin and Forbes sat awkwardly in the same train, no doubt studiously ignoring each other. The trials set a pattern whereby Metropolitan trains ran clockwise on the outer track, while District trains ran anti-clockwise on the inner track. This apparently harmonious arrangement brought neither peace between the two companies nor an orderly service for passengers.

CHAOS: HOSTILITIES RESUMED

The completion of the long-promised Circle was not greeted with enthusiasm in every quarter. The *Railway Times*,[60] which had long questioned the value of the project, printed a leading article headed 'The Inner Circle Delusion' a week after it opened. It questioned whether the estimated cost of the link, £1.2 million, could ever earn an adequate return and criticised it as an example of 'aerial castles, pleasing to the imaginative mind', built by Underground directors. Trains were running between one and three hours late and one group of passengers had staged a breakout from a stationary train marooned between stations: 'the deluded passengers who have paid their fare make a financial sacrifice and a stampede over the banks in search of some more reliable conveyance'.

The chaos prompted a renewal of hostilities. An early, comical incident involved a dispute over the right to occupy a siding at South Kensington station. The District left locomotives there. The Metropolitan indignantly removed them. The District chained its engine to the rails. The Metropolitan sent one, two and finally three locomotives to haul it away. On 30 August the *West London Advertiser* reported, 'A tug-of-war ensued in which the chained train came off the victor.' Forbes and Watkin blamed each other for the confusion, each claiming that the other was trying to run more than his fair share of trains, causing congestion at crossing points. On 23 October 1884, a fortnight after the Circle opened, a nervous arbitrator was appointed to hear the ripe exchange of insults which characterised the case put by each man. Watkin concluded by begging him to 'put us out of our misery'.[61] The arbitrator suggested that, as a temporary measure, each company should restrict itself to eight trains an hour with an 80-minute allowance for the round trip. The armistice was to last three months, after which the situation would be reviewed. But the verbal hostilities continued, Watkin telling his shareholders at the first opportunity that the perfidious District Railway had sneaked in an extra forty-six trains per day, this being the cause of 'the difficulty so shamefully and needlessly made'. The word 'shamefully' has been crossed out in the minutes by an official more squeamish than Watkin himself but it is clearly visible beneath.[62]

Forbes repaid the hostility in equal measure, though his financial case was weak. At this time, although the two companies shared stations on the Circle, they already had separate booking offices, each encouraging the passengers to use its own line and sometimes sending them the long way round the Circle in order to achieve that end. At a meeting shortly before the opening of the Circle, in August 1884,[63] Forbes told his impatient shareholders that no dividend was to be paid and that this was partly attributable to the fact that Metropolitan staff were under instruction to create difficulties for passengers wishing to use District trains.[64] Questioned on the possibility of a merger he was as dismissive as Watkin, telling his shareholders on the same occasion that, 'the time for celebrating the wedding would arrive when the chairman of the Metropolitan company entertained different views from those which he had recently expressed regarding the condition and prospects of the Metropolitan District company'.

Perhaps it is not surprising that the wedding never took place. In the meantime other lines were burrowing deeper below London.

CHAPTER TWO
DOWN THE TUBES

'Of my own knowledge I can speak of the interest excited in foreign nations for the welfare and success of this undertaking; they look upon it as the greatest work of art ever contemplated.'
>   (The Duke of Wellington, July 1828, speaking with pardonable exaggeration of
>   Marc Brunel's Thames Tunnel as it struggled to escape from bankruptcy)

'the very delectable, highly respectable, twopenny tube young man'.
>   (Gilbert & Sullivan's updated wording for the 1900 revival of *Patience*; a topical
>   reference to the Central Line, opened that year and quickly named the twopenny
>   tube)

NEW TUBES, NEW TRACTION

Further development of the underground railway system was inhibited by the expense and hazard of driving sub-surface lines through the web of sewers, gas and water pipes which lay beneath London's streets. At the very least, railway companies were faced with the cost of re-routing or reconstructing these subterranean obstacles, while property owners were quick to seize upon any suggestion that the railways had damaged their buildings, however rickety the previous condition of the structures. The solution to the problem required two innovations absent from the Metropolitan and District Railways: the development of deep tunnelling techniques that enabled 'tubes' to be driven through the blue clay which lay deep beneath existing pipes and sewers; and a form of traction, electricity,[1] which would keep these deep tubes free of steam and smoke.[2]

MARC BRUNEL'S THAMES TUNNEL[3]

As observed in Chapter One, the East London Line, an otherwise unremarkable railway connecting Whitechapel and New Cross, has the distinction of running through the world's oldest tunnel beneath a river, which was built by Marc Brunel and his son

SIR MARC BRUNEL, 1769–1849

The less well-known but equally ingenious father of Isambard Kingdom Brunel, Marc Brunel was taught by the French mathematician Gaspard Monge, who became secretary to the French navy under Napoleon. Marc entered the French navy but his royalist sympathies prompted him to flee to New York in 1793 where he became the city engineer. He submitted a design for the Capitol in Washington, though not the one adopted. He came to England in 1799 and invented a process for making ships' blocks, thousands of which were required to guide the ropes that hoisted the sails on a ship of the line. The process was adopted by the Admiralty as it expanded the Royal Navy to meet the threat from Napoleon and in this way Marc contributed to Nelson's destruction of the service for which his old tutor, Monge, was responsible. Marc also invented an early typewriter, a cotton winding machine, a knitting machine and a boot-making machine. He built the floating docks at Liverpool. He showed little commercial acumen in exploiting his inventions and in 1821 spent several months in a debtors' prison from which he was rescued by a £5,000 payment from a belatedly grateful Admiralty. His greatest achievement was the Thames Tunnel, the first tunnel ever constructed beneath a river. For this he invented the tunnelling shield, the design of which still underpins tunnelling methods. Work began in 1825 and, following many vicissitudes, was completed in 1843. It lost money but still carries the East London Line from Wapping to New Cross.

Marc Brunel, French father of Isambard and designer of the Thames Tunnel. (By courtesy of The National Portrait Gallery, London)

Isambard between 1825 and 1843. In 1818 Marc, a prolific inventor, had registered Patent no. 4204 which described two techniques for 'forming drifts and tunnels underground', better known as a tunnelling shield. The shield used to build the Thames Tunnel between Wapping and Rotherhithe was, in effect, a rectangular frame divided into three levels, or floors. On each level were twelve 'cells', each large enough to accommodate a man excavating the ground ahead of him with a pick and shovel, throwing the spoil to the rear whence it was removed from the tunnel. When each of the thirty-six men in the shield had excavated about six inches of ground, the shield was propelled forward by screw jacks and the men resumed excavating, protected from roof falls by the frame of the shield. Bricklayers followed, lining the tunnel with brickwork as it advanced. The novelty of Brunel's invention and the obvious advantages of linking the north and south banks of the Thames by a tunnel downstream from London Bridge were such that Brunel had little difficulty raising both enthusiasm and money for his proposed Thames Tunnel. Following a meeting in February 1824, at the familiar venue of the City Tavern, Bishopsgate (scene of later disappointments for Charles Pearson[4]), Brunel quickly raised almost £180,000 and set to work. In March 1825 a shaft was sunk at Rotherhithe and in November the shield was installed at the bottom. Tunnelling proceeded more slowly than had been expected, but when the pace quickened the shield collapsed and had to be replaced by a new one. The tunnel was flooded five times, killing many workmen, and on the second of these occasions, in 1828, Isambard Brunel narrowly escaped with his life. By this time Isambard had taken over much of the work from his father, who had suffered first a heart attack and then a stroke. The tunnel went bankrupt and was bricked up for seven years while more money was raised in the form of a loan from the Treasury, with the encouragement of no less a person than the Duke of Wellington, who stoutly declared: 'Of my own knowledge I can speak of the interest excited in foreign nations for the welfare and success of this undertaking; they look upon it as the greatest work of art ever contemplated.' The 1,200ft tunnel finally opened on 25 March 1843. A military band played 'See the conquering hero comes' as a long procession, led by a police constable appropriately wearing a Waterloo medal, marched through the tunnel to the sound of much cheering. The occasion was only slightly marred by a demonstration by Thames watermen, who flew black flags in protest at their prospective loss of trade.[5] One million people visited the tunnel in its first four months but its penny toll for pedestrians never yielded a profit and it was unable even to pay interest on the Treasury loan, which thus increased in size rather than diminished. By 1865 the loan had grown in value from £250,000 to £393,666 and in September of that year it was bought by the East London Railway for £200,000 – not enough even to discharge its debts.

THE TOWER SUBWAY

Although the Thames Tunnel was a triumph of civil engineering, it was not a happy financial precedent for anyone contemplating future tunnels beneath the metropolis. However, the concept of the tunnelling shield had been firmly established and Brunel's setbacks did not deter another civil engineer, Peter William Barlow (1809–85). In 1862, while sinking cast-iron cylinders into the London clay to form the piers of the old Lambeth suspension bridge[6] over the Thames, he conceived the idea of turning the cylinders on their sides to form a tunnel *beneath* the river. In 1864, building on the idea of Marc Brunel's shield, Barlow designed a cylindrical tunnelling shield which could be used to excavate a circular tunnel slightly larger than the prefabricated iron segments (not Brunel's brickwork) which would be bolted into place as the shield advanced. Liquid cement would then be forced through holes in the segments so that they were firmly secured to the outer ring of London clay.

Barlow used this system to create the 'Tower Subway', which ran 400 yards beneath the Thames from Tower Hill to Pickleherring Street (the latter no longer exists but was close to the present site of HMS *Belfast*). The subway was opened on 7 August 1870. Passengers paid twopence first class and a penny second class to be drawn in 2ft 6in gauge cable carriages across the river. A cable was attached to the carriages at one end

The Greathead Shield and Price's Rotary Excavator (seen here) between them transformed the construction of tube tunnels. (London's Transport Museum)

while a stationary steam engine at the other end provided the traction. This was the first 'tube' railway but it attracted few passengers since they could use the nearby London Bridge, toll free and without having to wait for a cable carriage. In 1870 a receiver was appointed, the railway was removed and the subway became a foot tunnel, which accommodated one million pedestrians a year.[7] Peter Barlow devoted his energies thereafter to campaigning against other means of crossing the Thames by writing pamphlets with such revealing titles as *The Tower Bridge: observations to prove that a new bridge east of London Bridge is unnecessary*.[8] Happily for London, Barlow's attempts to vilify Sir Joseph Bazalgette's proposals for a new 'Tower Bridge' were unsuccessful and after the latter opened in 1894 the Tower Subway was closed to pedestrians. It still exists, however, serving as a means to conduct water and power lines beneath the river.

THE CITY AND SOUTH LONDON RAILWAY: THE BEGINNINGS OF THE NORTHERN LINE

Undeterred by the financial failure of his Tower Subway, Peter Barlow began to campaign for a much more ambitious scheme: a City and Southwark Subway, over a mile long, between the City and the Elephant and Castle. Barlow was greatly assisted in his advocacy of the scheme by James Henry Greathead (1844–96), a South African engineer who had come to England in 1859. Greathead had worked with Barlow in the construction of the Tower Subway and had also designed a new type of cylindrical tunnelling shield with sharp steel blades that were forced forward into the clay by hydraulic rams operating at a pressure of a ton per square inch. Workmen, described as 'miners', then excavated the loosened clay which was hauled away in wagons pulled by ponies. This speeded up the tunnelling process and was the basis of future shield technology. The shield could also be 'steered' to left or right, up or down, as the route of the line required, by applying varying degrees of pressure to the rams around the circumference of the shield. As with the Metropolitan Railway, it was not easy to raise the capital. The public issue of shares, at £10 each, was under-subscribed and the contractor, Edmund Gabbutt, had to take some of his payment in unsold stock. Altogether £600,000 was raised from the issue of shares before the line was completed and Parliament granted additional borrowing powers of £175,000.[9]

Tunnelling began in May 1886, from a shaft sunk into the Thames just west of London Bridge.[10] From this point, two tunnels 10ft 2in in diameter were excavated, north to a terminus in King William Street and south towards the Elephant and Castle. Soon after construction began, powers were granted to extend the line further south, to Stockwell, and the company changed its name to the City and South London Railway. The tunnels were 40ft or more below the surface, well beneath sewers and foundations, and followed the line of the streets above to forestall any damage claims from property owners. For the same reason, where streets were narrow one tunnel ran above the other

THE CITY AND SOUTH LONDON RAILWAY

The **City and South London Railway** was the world's first deep-level tube railway, constructed by tunnelling rather than by the 'cut-and-cover' methods used on the earlier sub-surface lines. It was also the first to use electric traction. It was formally opened on 4 November 1890, extending from a station at King William Street, in the City, to Stockwell, 3½ miles to the south. Its tunnels, with a diameter of only 10ft 2in, were 18in narrower than those of later tubes. In 1900 the railway opened a northern extension to Bank, adding an intermediate station at London Bridge, at the same time closing the King William Street station. In 1900 it also extended south from Stockwell to Clapham Common and, in the years that followed, it reached north, to Angel (1901) and to King's Cross and Euston (1907). In 1913 the City and South London was bought by the Underground Group, which decided to enlarge its tunnels to the standard 11ft 8in gauge and link it with the Charing Cross, Euston and Hampstead Railway by building a tunnel from Euston to Camden Town which united the two railways. The completion of this link in 1924 created the Northern Line, though this name was not adopted until 1937. In 1926 the southern branch was extended from Clapham Common to Morden and a further link to the rest of the Northern Line was established by building a line from Kennington to the present Embankment station.

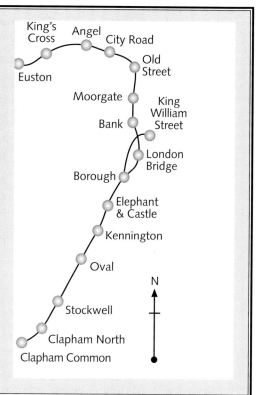

The City and South London Railway, 1907.

rather than by its side. Greathead also took the precaution of photographing buildings along the route of the tunnels to counter any claims of damage from opportunistic owners; thus when claims were lodged, in the words of *The Engineer*, Greathead's 'awkward pictorial evidence of old cracks provided very rapid means of settling disputes on the subject'.[11]

ELECTRIC RAILWAYS

The company initially intended to operate cable cars, using a method developed by a Londoner called Andrew Hallidie and applied by him in 1871 to the cable cars of San Francisco. Trains would clamp themselves to a continuously moving, endless cable, detaching themselves when they wanted to stop at a station. In 1883 the Patent Cable Tramways Corporation had been established to market Hallidie's system in Britain and operated a pioneer tramway up Highgate Hill. Directors of this company were used by Greathead to persuade Members of Parliament that the City and South London Railway should be authorised to proceed and a group of MPs were taken to Highgate and given a ride on the novel form of traction. However, as the railway extended from the Elephant and Castle to Stockwell, the directors of the company began to doubt the wisdom of using the endless cable system over a distance of 3½ miles along a route with numerous curves. Their doubts were sharpened when, in January 1888, the Patent Cable Tramways Corporation went bankrupt.

The board then took the imaginative step of deciding to consider the still novel, and far from proven, system of electric traction. This was not the first time that electricity had come to the capital. In 1878 Sir Joseph Bazalgette had introduced electric lighting to the Victoria Embankment, discontinuing the experiment when the French company that supplied the generator went bankrupt.[12] The following year Werner von Siemens had demonstrated a small electric traction engine at the Berlin Trade fair and in 1883 his compatriot Magnus Volk had installed an electric railway on the seafront at Brighton, the infrastructure of which is still in use today. After consulting many authorities about these small-scale experiments, including John Fowler who charged the typically enormous fee of £2,500, the directors decided in 1888 to ask the Manchester engineering firm of Mather and Platt to electrify the line. It was an excellent choice. In 1883 the chairman of the firm, Sir William Mather, had visited America and secured the British rights to manufacture Thomas Edison's dynamo. He then employed two outstanding scientists from Cambridge, the brothers John and Edward Hopkinson, to make some dramatic improvements to Edison's design.[13]

Mather and Platt built a power station at Stockwell, supplied with Edison-Hopkinson dynamos, and designed an electric locomotive which ran at 25 miles per hour on 450 volts of current. Fourteen were supplied. Each train consisted of three wooden carriages, each accommodating thirty-two seated passengers and lit by electricity. The only windows were narrow horizontal slits just beneath the roof, presumably because the passengers would have nothing more to look at than the tunnel walls. These claustrophobic vehicles quickly became known as 'padded cells' but passengers were not deterred by this unflattering description or by *Punch*'s sobriquet 'the sardine box'. In fact the latter term derived from the early popularity of the line which caused overcrowding. In its first full year of operation the line carried 5,161,398 passengers at a uniform fare of twopence, though penny fares for early and late trains were introduced shortly after the line opened. No tickets were issued, a turnstile being employed to control access to the platforms.

A Royal Occasion

The formal opening of the world's first underground electric railway was a grand occasion, carried out by the Prince of Wales on 4 November 1890, though the service was not opened to the public until 18 December. The prince was cheered, Greathead was cheered, Mather and Platt were particularly loudly cheered and the prince was presented with a gold key with which he switched on the current.[14] Much of the

An early City and South London Railway electric locomotive, which struggled, lights flickering, up the incline to the King William Street terminus. (London's Transport Museum)

One of the City and South London's 'Padded Cells', so-called because of their lavish upholstery and slit windows. (London's Transport Museum)

A great occasion: the Prince of Wales opens the world's first tube railway at Stockwell on 4 November 1890. (London's Transport Museum)

extensive coverage of the opening of the line concentrated on the novel form of traction. Thus the *Illustrated London News* explained, with pictures and diagrams, how electricity was generated and how it was applied to turn the wheels of the locomotives.[15] Much space was also devoted to commenting on the fact that, for the first time, there was no distinction between first and second class passengers. The *Railway Times* thought this was a dreadful state of affairs, commenting that 'we have scarcely yet been educated up to that condition of social equality when lords and ladies will be content to ride side by side with Billingsgate "fish fags" and Smithfield butchers'.[16] Nevertheless this one-class pattern was quickly accepted and became the norm for underground travel. However, one form of discrimination was preserved. Each train carried a smoking carriage from which ladies were excluded. A bizarre notice threatened a £2 fine for anyone travelling on the roof of the trains,[17] though since the culprits would presumably have been decapitated it is hard to see how the penalty could have been imposed.

The trains served six stations, at Stockwell, Oval, Kennington, Elephant and Castle, Borough and King William Street. There was an upward slope into the King William Street terminus and at this point, furthest from the power station, voltage was lowest. For this reason trains often struggled to reach the terminus, their electric lights dimmed by the effort. Sometimes the trains failed to reach the summit, having to slip back to take a run at the slope. The stations were of brick construction, surmounted by prominent domes to house the lift mechanisms which took passengers to and from the platforms. An illustration survives of one of the lifts, looking rather like a forbidding cupboard.[18]

Within three years of the line opening, plans were made to extend it. The King William Street station was abandoned and the line diverted so that from 1900 it served London Bridge (with its substantial volume of commuters), Bank and Moorgate, the last already served by the Metropolitan. To avoid the need to purchase ruinously expensive City property for its station at the Bank the directors arranged to build a booking hall in the crypt of St Mary Woolnoth, but this proved to be a false economy. Anxieties over damage to this fine Hawksmoor church occupied many of the company's board meetings at this time and at one point a claim of £300,000 was entered against the company, leading the desperate directors to pursue a false rumour that the church was for sale. Eventually, after a civil action which went all the way to the House of Lords, the railway had to pay £170,000 to the church as compensation for damage caused to its structure.[19] The line also extended south to Clapham Common. Further extensions are described in the *City and South London Railway* panel on p. 45.

The City and South London was the world's first deep-level electric railway and it was a triumph of engineering enterprise. However, like the other London Underground railways, before and since, it could not achieve adequate financial rewards for its investors. It paid no dividend for the first year and was paying only 2 per cent after seven years – no more than bank rate. Once again the revenue generated from fares was inadequate to support the heavy capital cost – £775,000 – of constructing a railway

---

LOST STATIONS: KING WILLIAM STREET

King William Street was the original terminus of the City and South London Railway, built on a cramped site on the corner of King William Street and what is now Monument Street. It opened in December 1890. The approach to the station was made awkward by the fact that the line had to run below the narrow streets, which required the northbound tunnel to run above the southbound tunnel. Awkward curves required the tunnels to cross each other so that the normal 'keep left' rule which applies on railways was altered to 'keep right' for a short distance beneath the river and beyond. This feature remains between Moorgate and London Bridge. In 1900 the line was re-routed via London Bridge station and by-passed King William Street which closed in February 1900. A proposal to grow mushrooms in the tunnels came to nothing and at the outbreak of war in 1914 a search by the police for a suggested *cache* of enemy agents and explosives revealed nothing but led to the boarding-up of the tunnels. In January 1940 the station and disused tunnels were converted into an air raid shelter. It was later used as a document store by the tenants of the offices above, Regis House.

St Mary Woolnoth church, the crypt of which provided a temporary home for the Bank station booking office, with almost disastrous results for the structure of Hawksmoor's masterpiece. (By courtesy of the Guildhall Library, Corporation of London)

beneath the streets of the capital. For this reason, ten years elapsed before another burst of investor optimism led to the opening of the next major tube line, the Central London Railway or 'Twopenny Tube'. In the meantime the only new underground railways were the Waterloo and City Line and the Great Northern and City Railway. Both were built as extensions to main line railways although they enjoyed very different fortunes.

THE WATERLOO AND CITY LINE: 'THE DRAIN'

The Waterloo and City Line was a protégé of the London and South Western, which was anxious to transfer its commuters from its terminus at Waterloo to the City. It connected Waterloo to the Bank, with no intermediate stations, its 12ft-diameter tunnels running for most of its 1½ miles beneath the Thames, so there were no problems with wayleaves or litigious landlords. The London and South Western underwrote a dividend of 3 per cent and capital of £540,000 was easily raised, early shareholders being able to sell quickly at a profit.[20] Tunnelling began in November 1894 and the line was officially opened on 11 July 1898. Public services began on 8 August.[21]

The line, soon known affectionately as 'the Drain', had no connection with any other railway at either end so rolling stock had to be lowered on to the tracks at the Waterloo end by hoist. Each train consisted of two electric motor coaches and two trailers, with seating altogether for 222 passengers. The rolling stock was much lighter and cheaper to operate than the locomotive-hauled stock later adopted by the Central London Railway. The service was operated by the London and South Western, with peak hour trains departing every five minutes. The service was popular from the first day and peak hour frequency was soon increased to departures every four minutes. By 1900 this little railway, unlike most of its larger brethren, was paying dividends of a respectable 3 per cent or more. In 1907 it was absorbed by its faithful parent, the London and South Western, and it remained in the control of the railway's successors, the Southern Railway and British Rail, until it was transferred to the London Underground in 1994.[22]

THE GREAT NORTHERN AND CITY: THE ORPHAN LINE

By the 1890s commuter traffic on Great Northern suburban services to Finsbury Park and beyond had grown to the point where the railway could no longer accommodate it. Stories abounded of commuters travelling in conditions of intolerable discomfort and of passengers already in compartments resolutely grasping the door handles to prevent others from entering.[23] The Great Northern therefore initially supported a proposal to build a 3 mile line from Finsbury Park, where congestion was worst, to Moorgate, an area already served by the Metropolitan and by the City and South London Railways. The Great Northern insisted that the tunnels should be a full 16ft in diameter so that its suburban trains could, if required, themselves run directly to the new station. No sooner had Parliament, in 1892, given its assent to the new railway with its huge, expensive tunnels than the Great Northern lost interest in it. Pressed by competition from a new railway which finally took form as the Great Central, and presented with a more attractive alternative proposal which eventually became part of the Piccadilly Line, the Great Northern distanced itself from its former protégé which consequently had great difficulty raising capital. Eventually the building contractor Sir Weetman Pearson (the future Lord Cowdray) agreed to build the line, buy many of its shares and underwrite a 3 per cent dividend. Construction then began, whereupon the Great Northern, alarmed at the growth of its orphaned child, refused access to its Finsbury Park station. The new railway therefore had to create its own Underground station at Finsbury Park, separate from the Great Northern station and connected to it by an awkward vertical interchange.

The new line, its original purpose vitiated by Great Northern hostility, opened on 14 February 1904, an event virtually unnoticed by the press. Its very cheap twopenny fare for the 3½ mile journey was dictated by competition from horse trams. The Great Northern ignored the existence of its unloved offspring, an article in the *Railway Times* observing that, 'One can travel from end to end of the Great Northern's suburban district without seeing a single notice that a new underground route has been opened from Finsbury Park to the City.'[24] Pearson's, which operated the line for the first three years, took about £90,000 in fares in the first year against the £143,000 expected and the line never made a profit. In 1913 it was bought by the Metropolitan Railway, which had no coherent plans for it, and it was never integrated with the Metropolitan's other operations. In 1968 a short section was transferred to the new Victoria Line and in 1975 its original purpose was finally achieved when it was transferred to British Rail for inclusion in its Great Northern suburban electrification scheme.

'THE TWOPENNY TUBE'

Despite the disappointing financial returns of the City and South London Railway some investors remained convinced that profits could be made from tube railways deep beneath London's streets. Most of them, it must be said, were foreign investors, a pattern that was to remain true for much of the early history of the London tube system. The most prominent member of the syndicate which promoted the Central London Railway was Sir Ernest Cassel (1852–1921), a banker who came originally from Frankfurt and whose philanthropic work earned him the friendship of King Edward VII and a knighthood. He was joined by Henry Oppenheim (1835–1912), another banker from Frankfurt and Darius Ogden Mills (1825–1910), a New York banker and director of eighteen American companies. On 5 August 1891, at the third attempt, the promoters succeeded in gaining parliamentary authority for a railway from Shepherd's Bush to the Bank, extended the following year to Liverpool Street. The Act of Parliament had to

THE CENTRAL LINE

The Central London Railway was officially opened on 27 June 1900, running from Bank (originally called Cornhill) to Shepherd's Bush. It was the first local line to run all day on Sundays, other lines stopping for a 'church interval'. It was an electric railway from the start, most of the equipment coming from the USA. In 1908 a short western extension was built to serve the Franco-British exhibition at Wood Lane, later renamed White City, and in 1912 the line was extended east to Liverpool Street. In the following year, 1913, it was acquired by the Underground Group (*see* p. 83). In 1920 the Central secured powers to run over Great Western tracks from near White City to Ealing Broadway. There was no further growth until the late 1930s when the management of the London Passenger Transport Board was encouraged by the government's New Works Programme to begin a major suburban expansion to the north-west and north-east. At this time, 1937, the name 'Central Line' was officially adopted. To the north-west new tracks were built beside the Great Western lines to West Ruislip, and to the north-east an extension was built to Stratford and Leyton from where the Central ran over LNER tracks to Ongar and Hainault. These lines were begun before the war but hostilities delayed their completion, Ruislip being reached in 1948 and Epping in 1949. A shuttle service from Epping to Ongar ran from 1957 to 1994 when it was closed.

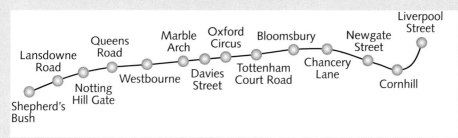

The Central London Railway in 1912, showing original station names.

overcome the opposition of both the Metropolitan and District Railways, Watkin in particular objecting to the use of electric traction on the grounds that steam was 'the only efficient form of locomotive power'.

The strenuous efforts of Ernest Cassel and his numerous contacts in banking circles ensured that three-quarters of the £10 shares were eventually sold to a group of financiers in which foreign interests predominated, with financiers from Germany, Austria, France and the USA particularly prominent.[25] Nevertheless an examination of the register of shareholders reveals some more homely investors, including a pig-keeper from Berkhamsted, Hertfordshire, a piano-tuner from Regent's Park, London, and numerous clergymen. The unsold shares were taken up by the Electric Traction Company which was contracted to build the line, a financing method noted previously in the construction of earlier lines. In this case, however, the contractor was also owned by Cassel and his associates.

Tunnelling began in April 1896, the contractors working under the technical direction of Sir John Fowler, Sir Benjamin Baker and James Greathead, a trio by now uniquely qualified to advise on such matters and rewarded accordingly with a payment of £93,000. Greathead shields were used to cut the 11ft 6in diameter tunnels, lined by cast-iron segments as on the City and South London Railway. Fourteen stations were served by the line. Particular care had to be taken at the City end, where the tunnels ran perilously close to the vaults of the Bank of England. In 1892 a Parliamentary Committee had recommended that where tubes ran beneath streets free wayleaves should be granted to the companies, thus relieving them of the need to enter into protracted negotiations with litigious property owners; so, as with later tube railways, the line followed the course of the streets above.[26] For this reason, where the street was narrow the two train tunnels, eastbound and westbound, were built one above the other rather than side by side, a feature particularly evident at St Paul's station. For the first time, stations were designed as shallow 'humps' which helped trains to slow down as they entered stations and to accelerate as they left. This is still evident to the careful observer, especially on the eastbound line at Tottenham Court Road. The station at Bank, by agreement with the City Corporation, was constructed beneath the seven streets which meet outside the Bank of England, on the understanding that the station concourse could also be used as a subway for pedestrians wishing to cross this hazardous junction. It continues to serve this valuable purpose though the cost of constructing this station greatly exceeded the estimates and helped to account for the fact that the capital cost of building the line was not far short of £4 million.

Much of the line's equipment was purchased from the USA. General Electric, of which Darius Ogden Mills was a director, supplied the power stations and locomotives, the latter being taken by barge from London Docks to Chelsea harbour, whence they were taken by horse-drawn wagons to the company's depot at Wood Lane, Shepherd's Bush, for final assembly. Granville Cuningham, a Scotsman with experience of running tramways in Montreal, was appointed general manager of the line and recommended one class travel and a flat fare of twopence, with penny fares on early morning trains to conform with the 'cheap trains' provisions of the Act which had created the company.[27]

The line was officially opened on 27 June 1900, though it didn't open to the public for another month. The ceremony was once again performed by the Prince of Wales, who was by now quite accustomed to opening underground railways. Much of the newspaper comment was directed towards the presence in the official party of Samuel Clemens, better known as Mark Twain, who was then living in London and giving public lectures in an attempt to recover a fortune lost in unwise speculation in his native America. The party travelled from Bank to the Shepherd's Bush terminus where they enjoyed a banquet in a marquee. Railway staff were later allowed to finish the remnants of the banquet but when they took up this offer they found some food but no drink – and a lot of inebriated waiters.[28]

Press coverage of the new line was generous despite the fact that, at the time, the illustrated papers were distracted by the more visually dramatic events of the Boer War. The *Daily Mail*, in its report, wrote of the 'palatial, luxuriously upholstered passenger cars'[29] and 'the long, brilliantly lighted train' with its glass-shaded electric lights, while *The Times* commented on carriages 'open from end to end, after the American fashion',[30] a great improvement on the 'padded cells' of the City and South London Railway. The 'cars', as the *Daily Mail* called them in this early use of the American term, had in fact been built in Manchester though American influence was apparent in their design, with generous use of brass and leather. The carriages were painted crimson with the name of the Central London Railway picked out in prominent gold lettering. Passengers entered and left the carriages by end-doors which were opened and closed at stations by 'gatemen'. Forty-eight lifts supplied by the American Frank Sprague were installed at the stations.

When the line opened to the public on 30 July 1900, the *Daily Mail* became effusive, writing of 'voracious curiosity, astonished satisfaction and solid merit . . . if this kind of thing goes on London will come to be quite a nice place to travel in'. The coyness of the staff was particularly applauded: the 'conductor was all of a quiver of joy and pride. But there was no indecorous exhibition of emotion: every man was resolutely British.'[31] Some more surprising claims were made by that normally sober journal, the *Railway Times*. On 25 August it claimed that motorists and cyclists were so much calmer as a result of the new railway that the number of traffic summonses had fallen dramatically. The following week, in an article headed 'The Temperature of Tunnels', it wrote: 'It has been stated that a person who suffered from anorexia for eighteen months suddenly developed a ravenous appetite after a single journey by the new underground electric railway vulgarly known as the "Twopenny tube".'[32] This remarkable outcome was attributed to the cool temperature in the tunnels.

The trains were expensive to operate because of the number of crewmen required. Each locomotive was driven by a two-man crew from a cab located in the centre so that

Hump-back electric engine of the Central London Railway, whose great weight and inadequate suspension prevented Cheapside draughtsmen from drawing straight lines. (London's Transport Museum)

the driver and his assistant could look out in both directions. In addition to the locomotive crew, two guards and four gatemen travelled on each seven-car train and at every stop a complicated ceremony of hand signals was enacted between train crew, guards and gatemen before the train could proceed on its journey.[33] Crews worked punishing ten-hour shifts without meal breaks and a routine became established whereby signalmen would brew tea and prepare snacks for crewmen who collected them as they passed.

The enthusiasm of the press was matched by that of the travelling public. In the remaining five months of 1900 almost fifteen million passengers were carried at the flat fare of twopence, which soon earned the line the popular sobriquet the 'Twopenny Tube'. The following year forty-one million passengers used the line, eight times as many as had used the City and South London in its first year, and the railway was able, within months of opening, to pay a dividend of 2½ per cent on its ordinary shares in contrast with its impecunious south London cousin. The line benefited not only from commuter traffic but also, outside the peak period, from passengers travelling to and from the West End theatres and shops. Some of these were already open when the line began to operate and others followed soon afterwards, many of them situated in or near Oxford Street, beneath which much of the line ran. The shops included Liberty's (1875), D.H. Evans (1879), Peter Robinson (1900) and Selfridges, whose owner, Gordon Selfridge, tried without success to persuade the railway to rename its Bond Street station 'Selfridges' when his store opened in 1909. Prominent places of entertainment which attracted further passenger traffic included the Princess's Theatre, on Oxford Street itself, which opened in the 1840s and the Queen's Hall, Langham Place (1893). Recognising the opportunities offered by these premises, in 1912 the Central introduced cheap 'shopping tickets' for use in off-peak periods to visit the sales.

Unfortunately much of the success of the Central Line in attracting passengers was achieved at the expense of other lines, particularly the Metropolitan, which was prompted to implement three reductions in its fares in the early years of the new century.[34] It was at this time that the underground railway began to make an impact on the world of literature, and one writer used the Metropolitan's deserted carriages as the basis for a detective story. John Galsworthy sent Soames Forsyte on many underground journeys in *A Man of Property* (1906) but it was Baroness Orczy who made the Metropolitan Line a central feature of her detective story *The Mysterious Death on the Underground Railway*, in which she explained that 'the good old Metropolitan Railway carriages cannot at any time be said to be overcrowded'.[35] A young woman is found dead in a carriage at Aldgate station and the absence of other passengers in the carriage helps to ensure that the culprit escapes justice. The Baroness (more prosaically, Mrs Montague Barstow) had more than a passing interest in the underground since she claimed to have conceived the idea of her most famous work, *The Scarlet Pimpernel*, while buying a ticket at Tower Hill station. Presumably there was a long queue.

MURDER ON THE UNDERGROUND[36]

Baroness Orczy created a fictional murder on the Underground but sadly there have been several of the grimmer kind. On the evening of 25 May 1957 Countess Teresa Lubienska, descendant of a Polish landowning family, was stabbed to death at Gloucester Road station. A survivor of the Nazi Ravensbruck concentration camp, she lived in Kensington and was a prominent member of the Polish community. The person responsible for this apparently motiveless murder was never found. Two years later, on 13 July 1959, two policemen arrested a petty criminal called Gunther Podola while he was trying to blackmail a housewife from a telephone booth at South Kensington station. Podola shot dead Detective Sergeant Raymond Purdy, who was married with three children. Podola was later re-arrested, tried, found guilty and hanged on 5 November 1959: the last person to be hanged for murdering a policeman. On 15 March 1976 an Irish terrorist called Vincent Kelly was carrying a bomb on a District Line train at West Ham when the bomb began to give off smoke. Panicking, Kelly threw the bomb down the carriage, where it exploded, injuring nine passengers including himself. He fled from the train and was pursued, heroically, by the driver, Stephen Julius, a married man originally from the West Indies. Kelly shot Stephen Julius dead, injured a post office engineer with another shot and, when cornered, tried to shoot himself. The most recent murder was at Holborn station on 9 December 1988 when a tourist was stabbed to death by a mugger. The culprit was subsequently arrested and convicted.

SHAKES AND SMELLS

After its promising start the new railway soon ran into difficulties. The first concerned the fearful vibrations caused by the weight of the trains and particularly of the locomotives with their primitive suspension. In March 1901 a Member of Parliament called Rickett[37] asked Gerald Balfour, President of the Board of Trade and brother of the future Prime Minister A.J. Balfour, what was to be done about the disturbance to buildings on the surface caused by the trains. After some prevarication the Central's Board of Directors considered the matter, having been told by Balfour that 'the public would not be satisfied with an investigation by the company alone'.[38] Accordingly the Board of Trade set up a committee of three scientific experts who heard evidence from people living in the vicinity of Hyde Park and from others whose dwellings or offices were along the route. One of the experts was Sir John Wolfe-Barry, designer of Tower Bridge, and he and his two fellows quickly became known as the 'vibration committee'. Nine witnesses attested to the fact that buildings shook when the trains passed beneath them and it was claimed that draughtsmen in offices in Cheapside were thereby prevented from drawing straight lines. The blame was laid on the heavy, 43-ton locomotives, some of which were therefore adapted, with improved suspension and geared operation. This reduced the vibrations but the problem was not fully solved until the locomotives were replaced with luxurious multiple units. These were also the first to be equipped with a 'dead man's handle' – a safety device for the driver imported from the United States, which stopped the train if the driver became incapacitated. The changeover was completed by March 1903.

Having dealt with the shakes the company turned to its other pressing problem: smells. The Board discussed the question of unpleasant odours on its platforms within six months of the line opening but the problem did not seriously engage their attention until

November 1901, when a lengthy discussion was devoted to the subject.[39] Having heard reassurances from Granville Cuningham, the line's general manager, about the vibrant health of its employees despite the smells, the directors considered a letter from the Reverend Professor George Henson, Professor of Botany at the Royal Horticultural Society. He suggested that the smell was caused by excessive carbonic acid and that this should 'be removed in a natural manner by placing evergreen shrubs with plenty of leaf surface such as hollies, rhododendrons etc. on the station platforms'. Granville Cuningham was enthusiastic and sought permission to proceed with the experiment, suggesting that 'the presence of healthy shrubs on our platforms would have a reassuring effect on the public mind'. Since the Board immediately proceeded to discuss other matters we may conclude that they were not convinced so the Reverend Professor never discovered what would have been the effect upon his plants of immersion in the sunless depths of the Central London Railway. The arguments about the smells rumbled on and were considered by the Royal Commission on London Traffic which sat in 1904.[40] Cuningham acknowledged the existence of 'that peculiar smell in the tunnel which is very difficult to account for' and did not dispute the assertion by one Member of Parliament that the smell 'really is the main objection of very many people – delicate people, ladies and others – to travelling on your line'. The humidity of the air in the tunnels was found to be little more than half that on the surface and one visitor from Africa observed that the smell in the tunnels reminded him of a crocodile's breath – though he omitted to explain how he had smelt a crocodile's breath and survived to make the comparison. The installation of a huge fan at the company's Wood Lane depot, designed to replenish the tunnels with fresh air overnight, failed to solve the problem and the smells remained until a system for pumping cleaned, ozonised air into the tunnels was installed from 1911.

EXTENSIONS TO EAST AND WEST

On 14 May 1908 the Central opened a loop west of its depot at Wood Lane in order to benefit from passenger traffic to the Franco-British Exhibition which opened its doors on the same day. The exhibition buildings were concrete structures painted white, which earned the rather ugly complex the nickname 'White City'. The same name was attached to the athletics stadium which opened the same year to host the Olympic Games and this facility also brought further traffic to the line. Four years later, in July 1912, the line extended east from Bank to Liverpool Street, where the line could pick up Great Eastern passengers from there and from nearby Broad Street. The Act permitting this extension included the curious provision that no foul air should escape into the stations above – a legacy of the 'peculiar smell' that had so worried the Royal Commission. In 1911 a 'Lightning Parcels Express' was opened, conveying light packages on tricycles between Central Line stations and nearby premises. The service was ended in 1917 owing to wartime labour shortages and was never resumed.

The Central had demonstrated that it *was* possible, albeit with some difficulty, to raise enough money to build a deep-level tube through the heart of the metropolis and to operate it at a modest profit with innovative engineering. More ambitious schemes would have to await ingenious methods of financial engineering imported, like much of the Central's equipment, from across the Atlantic. These steps would be taken by the directors of the Underground Group who, in 1913, took over the Central London Railway.

THE FORGOTTEN TUBE

The idea of dispatching goods traffic along a tube beneath the streets of London can be traced back to 1855 when Rowland Hill, inventor of the penny post, proposed the construction of a tube between the headquarters of the Post Office, at St Martin's le Grand near St Paul's Cathedral, and a post office in Holborn which was particularly difficult to reach because of London's appalling traffic. Hill's proposal led to the formation, in 1859, of the Pneumatic Despatch Company, with a board of directors that included the chairman of the London and North Western Railway and W.H. Smith, who was interested in any proposal which would enable him to distribute newspapers and magazines to his shops. The company constructed an experimental line in Battersea, on the site of the present power station. An oval tube, 452 yards long, with a circumference of about 9ft, was constructed. A centrifuge at one end blew air into the tube while a similar device at the other sucked the air out, creating a partial vacuum. The wagons were surrounded by a rubber flange which formed a more or less airtight seal and caused them to be drawn into the vacuum at speeds of up to 30mph.[41] The success of this experiment led the company to construct a 2ft gauge tube between Euston, the London terminus of the London and North Western Railway, and a district post office 400 yards away in Eversholt Street, along which thirty trains a day ran from 20 February 1863. The new tube, opened a month after the Metropolitan Railway's services began amid so much acclaim, was received with great enthusiasm, *The Times* confidently predicting that, 'the days ought to be fast approaching when the ponderous goods vans which now ply between station and station shall disappear for ever from the streets of London'.[42]

Visitors to London were taken to see the novel device and some of them, despite warnings from their anxious hosts, insisted on taking a ride. Once of the intrepid travellers was Prince Jerome Napoleon, nephew of the late emperor. In the years that followed the tube was extended first to Holborn and finally to the Post Office headquarters at St Martin's le Grand, which it reached in May 1869. Plans were made to extend the system beneath the Thames to Waterloo via Charing Cross, as shown in the illustration on p. 27, but this extension was never built. Legends quickly attached themselves to this novel facility, a writer in the *London Journal* claiming that:

a lady whose courage or rashness – we know not which to call it – astonished all spectators, was actually shot the whole length of the tube, crinoline and all, without injury to person or petticoat.[43]

In 1870 the Victoria Embankment opened, built by Sir Joseph Bazalgette[44] to provide both an additional route between Westminster and the City and a tunnel for the underground railway. This had such a beneficial effect on road traffic that the Post Office had fewer problems connecting its offices by road, thus diminishing the attractions of the tube. At the same time the railway ran into the difficulties which had beset Brunel's experiments with pneumatic power: how to maintain an airtight seal.[45] The volume of traffic failed to reach the required levels and in 1882 the operation ceased. Further attempts to revive it failed and it was eventually taken over by its faithless customer, the Post Office, not for carrying mail but as a route for telephone lines.

The Post Office Railway, opened in 1927, still carries mail from Paddington to Whitechapel. (Reproduced by permission of Consignia. The ownership of the postal imagery is vested in Consignia and the trade marks are the trade marks of Consignia.)

However, this did not mark the end of plans for the subterranean carriage of postal traffic. In 1913, following a study of systems used in New York and Chicago, the Post Office obtained powers to build a 2ft gauge railway running 6 miles from Paddington to Whitechapel via Mount Pleasant and Liverpool Street, serving eight postal stations altogether. The capital cost was estimated as £871,930 and even at that price it was acknowledged that the enterprise would be more expensive than carriage by road. Asquith's cabinet authorised it on the grounds that benefits would arise from the swifter carriage of the Royal Mail: the first example of a crude form of cost-benefit analysis being applied to an underground railway. It eventually cost £1,700,000, twice the original estimate. Construction began in 1914 but was held up by the First World War and its aftermath. During the war the partly completed tunnels were used to store objects from the Tate Gallery, the National Portrait Gallery and the Public Record Office. The line finally entered service in December 1927. The electric trains are driverless, operated by remote control from the stations. Most people are unaware of its existence, though it achieved a brief moment of fame in 1954 when Brian Johnston, better known for his cricket commentaries, took a trip along it when accompanying a parcel from the BBC headquarters in London to the BBC offices in Bristol.

CHAPTER THREE
THE AMERICAN CONNECTION

You go to penal servitude for seven years.

(Mr Justice Bingham, sentencing Whitaker Wright,
the financier of the Bakerloo Line)

Buy up old junk, fix it up a little and unload it upon other fellows.

(Charles Tyson Yerkes, founder of *Underground Electric Railways of London*,
describing his business methods)

NEW LINES, NEW PEOPLE

As the twentieth century dawned two pieces of unfinished business remained for the management of London's underground railway system. The first task involved converting the Metropolitan and District 'Circle' from steam to electric traction, thereby sparing the passengers the horrors of the sulphurous tunnels described in Chapter One.[1] The second concerned a number of proposed new lines whose promoters had gained the sanction of Parliament for their construction but had failed to attract the interest of investors. Both of these challenges were taken up by American entrepreneurs headed by the flamboyant figure of Charles Tyson Yerkes (rhymes with 'turkeys'), a dynamic if unlikely benefactor of London's underground railways.

As early as 1893 Parliamentary authority had been gained for the Charing Cross, Euston and Hampstead Railway – later to become the northern section of the Northern Line; and for the Baker Street and Waterloo Railway – later to be known as the Bakerloo Line. The latter scheme incurred the wrath of the combative Sir Edward Watkin as he approached the end of his chairmanship of the Metropolitan Railway. Watkin's spokesman, the engineer Sir Benjamin Baker, told the Parliamentary Committee examining the Baker Street–Waterloo proposal that it would, in some unspecified way, interfere with Watkin's grand design for a railway from Manchester to Paris and that, in Baker's disparaging phrase, 'a little electric omnibus line like this is to block big companies with millions and millions of money'.[2] Nevertheless this line was also authorised and the promoters of both new railways then set about trying to raise capital from investors. In this they were notably unsuccessful.

THE BAKERLOO LINE

Plans for a link between Waterloo and Charing Cross went back almost thirty years. In 1863 a proposal had been made for a goods railway between Waterloo and Charing Cross driven by pneumatic power. It may be seen in the artist's impression of the Victoria Embankment which is reproduced on p. 27. The scheme made little progress despite this engraving appearing in the *Illustrated London News* in June 1863. A further scheme, known as the Charing Cross and Waterloo Electric Railway, was authorised by an Act of 1882. It was to cross the Thames in iron caissons laid in a trench in the river bed and would have linked Waterloo to Westminster just as the later Waterloo and City Line linked it to the City. Dr Siemens was the company's electrical engineer but the promoters failed to arouse the interest of investors and Siemens' death in 1883 sealed the fate of the scheme.

At first, the Baker Street and Waterloo Railway was no more successful in raising money so in 1897 the directors of the fledgling line were relieved when they were approached by Whitaker Wright on behalf of the London and Globe Finance Corporation. Wright was the first of a line of colourful characters who were to play a critical role in financing the construction of the Underground. Whitaker Wright (1845–1904), an Englishman, had made a fortune from mining in the USA and was a millionaire by the time he was thirty-one. In 1897, having returned to England,

Cyanide tablets and revolvers are not normally encouraged in the Law Courts, where Wright, originator of the Bakerloo Line, was sentenced to seven years' hard labour – shortly before he committed suicide. (By courtesy of the National Portrait Gallery, London)

he became managing director of the London and Globe Finance Corporation, in which he owned almost one-third of the shares. Operating from a small office in the City he proceeded to acquire interests in mining and other activities, one of these being the Baker Street Railway – which thereby acquired £700,000 of badly needed finance with which to begin building. Wright was adept at placing on company boards well-known public figures whose presence would reassure investors. Thus Quintin Hogg[3] (1845–1903), a prominent Christian philanthropist and founder of the polytechnic movement, became a director of the Baker Street and Waterloo Railway. He later helped to rescue it from the consequences of Wright's financial machinations.

DEATH IN THE LAW COURTS

Construction of the new railway began in August 1898, from a temporary platform in the Thames just upstream from Hungerford Bridge. Greathead shields were used to drive tunnels north to Baker Street and south to a terminus beneath Waterloo. Work proceeded for eighteen months at a cost of about £650,000 but then the London and Globe ran into difficulties, largely as a result of the collapse in the share price of one of its other investments. An attempt by Wright to 'rig' the market by buying up London and Globe shares resulted in further disastrous losses, whereupon he tried to unload on to the market shares in the still-embryonic railway. This, predictably, failed as did a wildly optimistic speech to shareholders as the company plunged further into chaos. On 28 December 1900 the London and Globe was declared bankrupt and railway construction work ceased as contractors waited to be paid. Wright prudently fled to France. George Lambert, MP for a Devon constituency, proposed a motion regretting that Wright had not been prosecuted[4] and pressed in Parliament for Wright's prosecution; however, the Solicitor-General, Sir Edward Carson,[5] argued that the matter was civil rather than criminal. Nevertheless, a determined creditor succeeded in obtaining an arrest warrant from a judge in March 1903 but Wright, anticipating this event, had fled from France to New York four days earlier. He was arrested in New York and returned to England where he was arraigned for larceny, the prosecutor being the celebrated QC Sir Rufus Isaacs.[6] On 26 January 1904 Wright was convicted of defrauding investors to the value of £5 million and, in the words of Mr Justice Bingham, sentenced to 'the severest punishment which the Act permits, that you go to penal servitude for seven years'.[7] Wright left the courtroom proclaiming his innocence and his intention to appeal. A few minutes later he collapsed in the Law Courts, dead from a cyanide capsule he had been carrying. More alarmingly, when the police searched his body they found a loaded revolver which he had presumably had with him throughout the trial.[8] He was buried in the grounds of his palatial mansion at Lea Park, Witley, Surrey, amid his landscaped gardens, private theatre, observatory, lakes and an underwater billiard hall encased in glass. His obituary in the *Illustrated London News*

THE BAKERLOO LINE

The Baker Street and Waterloo Railway, as it was originally called in the 1893 Act that authorised its construction, was rescued from the bankruptcy, conviction and subsequent suicide of its original promoter by an equally flamboyant American financier, Charles Tyson Yerkes. It opened on 10 March 1906 between Baker Street and Lambeth North, extending to Elephant and Castle later the same year. The press, and soon afterwards the company, quickly adopted the name 'Bakerloo Line'. In 1907 the line reached Edgware Road and, in 1913, Paddington. It then expanded in a north-westerly direction over the tracks of other railways. Thus it used the lines of the London and North Western Railway to reach Willesden Junction in 1915 and Watford Junction in 1917. In 1939 it reached Stanmore via the tracks of the Metropolitan Railway (*see* panel on p. 14), though this last branch was transferred to the Jubilee Line in 1979. Since 1984 the former service to Watford Junction has terminated at Harrow and Wealdstone.

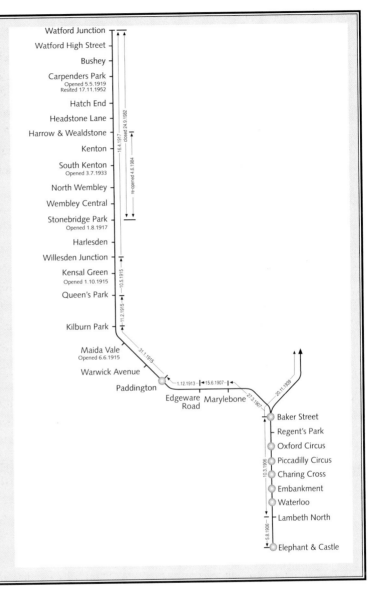

The Bakerloo Line, opened in 1906 and later extended, temporarily, as far as Watford.

remarked that 'At Lea Park in Surrey he played a part not unlike that of Rudolph, the mad king of Bavaria',[9] while his entry in the *Dictionary of National Biography*[10] observes that 'his abilities as a public speaker were turned to good account at shareholders' meetings and inspired confidence in his most disastrous undertakings'. Upon such men was the London Underground dependent in the early days of the twentieth century. His place was soon to be taken by another. The Baker Street to Waterloo Railway was rescued from the wreckage of the London and Globe bankruptcy by the even more flamboyant figure of Charles Yerkes.

CHARLES TYSON YERKES (1837–1905)

Charles Tyson Yerkes was born in Philadelphia to a Quaker family, though his life showed little evidence of his Quaker upbringing. He set himself up as a banker and stockbroker but the methods he used to sell municipal bonds for his native city led to an early brush with the law and a two-year prison sentence, of which he served seven months, for 'technical embezzlement'. He then moved to Chicago and applied his talents to the financing and construction of that city's famous 'Loop' railway but the Illinois state government was so alarmed at the financial webs he employed to create his 'Chicago Traction Tangle' that they took it under their own management. One meeting, protesting at Yerkes' attempts to bribe the legislators to reverse this decision, was attended by angry citizens brandishing nooses and firearms. Stock which he sold to investors in 1899 for $100 million was valued four years later at $15 million. He later described his methods of business as to 'buy up old junk, fix it up a little and unload it upon other fellows' so it is sobering to reflect that his purchase of the District Line and his critical role in the construction of early tube lines give him a strong claim to be one of the most influential figures in the early history of the London Underground. His colourful life was the thinly disguised subject of a trilogy of novels by the American writer Theodore Dreiser.[11]

It seems likely that Yerkes' interest in London's underground railways originated in his improbable friendship with (later Sir) Robert Perks (1849–1934).[12] Perks, a devout Methodist, was a most unlikely collaborator with Yerkes, the licentious lapsed Quaker but together they formed a formidable partnership in the creation of London's tube network. It is possible that Yerkes was attracted to London to escape a chaotic private life in New York involving a wife, an ex-wife and numerous mistresses. Perks was a solicitor who specialised in promoting railway bills in Parliament and in 1892 he acquired a substantial shareholding in the under-performing District Railway. When not engaged on railway matters Perks devoted his considerable energies to advancing the cause of Methodism. In Parliament, as MP for Louth between 1892 and 1910, he created a strong nonconformist lobby within the Liberal Party and at the turn of the century he led a campaign which raised 'one million guineas from one million Methodists' to build the Methodist Central Hall in Westminster. He may have met Yerkes during a trip to New York in the 1890s and he certainly persuaded the American to bring his financial acumen to bear in raising money to electrify the District Line. It was hoped that a change in traction would lead to a corresponding improvement in the financial performance of the line.[13] In April 1901 *Tramway and Railway World* became impatient with the management of the District which was dithering over whether to electrify its lines, running an experimental electric service between Earl's Court and Kensington at what the magazine called 'the phenomenal price of one shilling'. The article referred to rumours that Yerkes was buying up the stock of the District and commented:

'Buy up old junk, fix it up a little and unload it upon other fellows' was the motto of the American entrepreneur Charles Tyson Yerkes, who built much of London's tube network. (London's Transport Museum)

It is to be hoped that the rumours which recently have been circulated with regard to Mr Charles T. Yerkes' plans for a controlling interest in the Metropolitan District Railway may prove to be well founded. . . . Half measures have never characterised Mr Yerkes' undertakings and he is not accustomed to hesitating at trifles.[14]

On 6 June 1901 James Staats Forbes, still chairing the ailing District, told his shareholders that 'gentlemen of reputation, acknowledged ability and financial means had been found who had come forward to assist the company'.[15] This assistance had taken the form of share purchases, by Yerkes and his associates, at one-third of the shares' face value, which gave them control of the company. The 'financial means' referred to would enable the company to electrify its trains and, it was hoped, its finances, since electrification was predicted to bring about a major reduction in operating costs. Perks, the second largest shareholder and a friend of Yerkes, spoke in favour of the new investors so the long-suffering shareholders, recognising a *fait accompli*, voted unanimously to back them.

CREATIVE FINANCE

In the previous two months, April and May 1901, Yerkes had been in the USA raising money for a more ambitious scheme which, after several changes of name, size and ownership, became the Underground Group, the dominant force in London's transport system for much of the twentieth century. It began life as the Metropolitan District Electric Traction Company with a capital of £1 million of which 95 per cent was held by American investors, mostly from Yerkes' old haunts of Chicago, Philadelphia and New York. This company bought Yerkes' shares in the District and thus assumed control of the line but this was not the limit of his ambition. After long and tortuous negotiations with the Great Northern Railway and other parties the company bought up the right to construct what would eventually become the Piccadilly Line, running from Hammersmith to Finsbury Park via Piccadilly Circus. In the process Yerkes had to outwit J. Pierpont Morgan, a fellow-American of equal ruthlessness and determination, who was promoting a rival scheme. Yerkes exploited a temporary disagreement between Morgan and one of his partners by a manoeuvre which led one speaker in a parliamentary debate to doubt 'whether for a long time, if ever, such a very dirty transaction was ever done by parties coming before Parliament'.[16] Morgan's own verdict was that it was 'the greatest rascality and conspiracy I ever heard of',[17] an unintended compliment from one not noted for excessive scruple. This transaction was completed in November 1901. In a further burst of activity in the same month the company also acquired the unbuilt Charing Cross, Euston and Hampstead Railway. Four months later, in March 1902, the bankrupt Bakerloo fell into the embrace of Yerkes and his syndicate which now owned one ailing railway, the District; one half-completed, the Bakerloo; and two new ones yet to be built: the Piccadilly and the Charing Cross, Euston and Hampstead Railways.

The million pounds of share capital of the Metropolitan District Electric Traction Company (MDET) was clearly inadequate for the tasks it now faced. Yerkes therefore approached the German-born banker (later Sir) Edgar Speyer, who agreed to help Yerkes raise £5 million in capital for a new company, Underground Electric Railways of London Ltd, which would, in effect, take over the MDET. The capital structure of the company involved a complex hierarchy of shares, certificates, huge commissions to the bankers and other instruments which aroused the suspicion of the financial community. Sir Harry Haward, the formidable comptroller of the London County Council, investigated the arrangements but they proved impenetrable even to his experienced eye and to those of the members of the Royal Commission on London Traffic to whom he tried to explain them on 24 July 1903.[18] Most of the new company's shares were taken up by American and continental investors with British investors, wisely, taking up less than one-third of the half a million £10 shares. Yerkes himself subscribed for 32,000 shares.

ELECTRIFICATION

Yerkes now turned his attention to the project which had originally aroused his interest in the London Underground: the electrification of the District. In 1900 the Metropolitan Railway and the District sought tenders for the electrification of the Circle Line and in 1901 the two engineers they appointed to examine the proposals recommended a Hungarian company called Ganz, which offered a 3,000 volt alternating current system fed to the trains through overhead wires. Yerkes did not like the system, believing it to be unproven and possibly unsafe. He advocated a system using direct current carried through conductor rails, a system he knew to be practical from his American experience. The traditional hostility between the District and the Metropolitan[19] now resurfaced, the Metropolitan clinging to the Ganz system and denouncing Yerkes for opposing it in shareholders' meetings that were reminiscent of the earlier conflict between Edward Watkin and James Staats Forbes.[20]

The dispute rumbled on throughout the summer of 1901 with increasingly acrimonious exchanges in the columns of *The Times*,[21] in the course of which Yerkes offered to pay for the electrification of the Metropolitan in return for a royalty payment or, insultingly, to run the Metropolitan for the shareholders in return for a higher dividend than they had lately been receiving. In September a Board of Trade adjudicator ruled in favour of Yerkes. The Metropolitan, still sulking, turned down Yerkes' offer to supply them with electricity and built their own power station at Neasden.

In March 1902 Yerkes' group began to build its own power station at Lots Road, Chelsea,[22] a riverside site chosen because it offered ready access to barges which would bring in the huge quantities of coal which the station would consume. Its eight generators supplied current at 11,000 volts ac, which was converted at substations into 550–600 volts dc for all the company's lines. The scale and design of the plant offended the American artist James McNeill Whistler, who told the editor of the *Daily Express* that those responsible 'ought to be drawn and quartered'. Whistler, who died in 1903, would no doubt have been alarmed to know that during the Second World War some words of his were used on a poster called *The Proud City*, which featured the Lots Road power station as a heroic survivor of the Blitz: 'the poor buildings lose themselves in the dim sky and the tall chimneys become campanili'.[23] Multiple units were ordered from Britain, France and Belgium, the electric motors being supplied by British Thomson Houston. They entered service between Acton Town and Park Royal in June 1903 and began to operate on the Circle Line in conjunction with the Metropolitan trains in July 1905.

THE BAKERLOO REVIVED

Towards the end of 1901 Yerkes approached the Baker Street–Waterloo directors and offered, in effect, to buy out the London and Globe's shares provided that his syndicate had a majority on the Board. A deal was struck[24] and construction work resumed, additional powers being granted to extend the line south from Waterloo to what is now Lambeth North station. Yerkes ordered 108 multiple units from the USA which were assembled in Manchester and transferred by train and horse-drawn cart to the company's depot in Lambeth.

Yerkes' syndicate was responsible for a number of innovations, all of US origin, in its construction of the line. Signalling was automatic, using track circuits to set signals to 'danger' as trains passed and, at the same time, to raise a 'trainstop' arm which engaged a brake lever on any train which attempted to pass the signal: an early form of automatic braking. Signal-boxes were equipped with illuminated track diagrams which

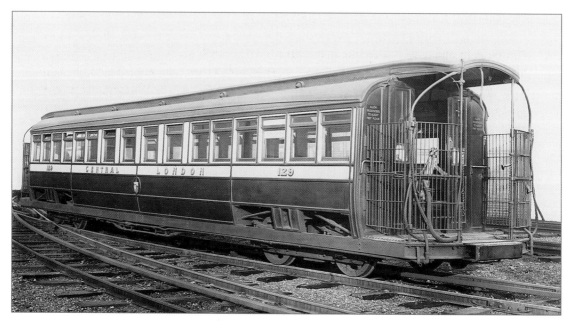

Early 'gate stock' of the kind used on London's deep-level tubes. It remained in use until the 1930s. (London's Transport Museum)

The red tiling of Chalk Farm station is highly characteristic of Leslie Green's designs for the Yerkes tubes. (London's Transport Museum)

showed signalmen where trains were. Yerkes also adopted a house style for station designs, devised by the company architect Leslie Green. Each station was two storeys high and faced with red, glazed terracotta bricks, a design that survives in many 'Yerkes' stations, notably Chalk Farm and Mornington Crescent. Patterned tiling schemes were also adapted for each station, a device which attracted favourable press comment and which may have encouraged the later enterprise of Frank Pick and Charles Holden.[25]

The line entered service on 10 March 1906,[26] its official name, the Baker Street and Waterloo Railway, having been sacrificed even before the official opening. On 7 March, three days before the opening, the *Evening News*, in a headline on its front page, referred to the 'Baker-Loo, London's latest Twopenny Tube', on which one of its reporters had travelled in a press preview of the new line. The name stuck – which is fortunate since it thereby forestalled less suitable alternatives, notably 'The Loo' which was proposed by *The Star*. Not everyone was satisfied. G.A. Nokes,[27] humourless editor of the *Railway Magazine*, was appalled when the company officially adopted the name in July 1906, complaining that 'for a railway to adopt its gutter title is not what we expect from a railway company.

English railway officers have more dignity than to act in this manner.' His implication was that rude Americans had no such scruples but his pleas were ignored. The brochure that accompanied the opening promoted the line as a unique north–south connection across the Metropolis, particularly emphasising the access to Lord's cricket ground. However, in the early days passenger traffic was disappointing and the management of the line had to take early remedial action. Train lengths were reduced and the twopenny flat fare was abandoned in favour of graduated fares related to distance travelled. Traffic began to recover and the line began to enjoy a modest prosperity.

THE PICCADILLY LINE

The Piccadilly Line began life as a project of the ailing Metropolitan District Railway, whose fluctuating fortunes were described in Chapter One. In 1896, in one of many attempts to improve its performance, its directors conceived a scheme for a deep-level tube between Earl's Court and Mansion House. The new line would run for much of its length beneath existing District tracks and would be operated by electric locomotives. The following year the District extended the plan by acquiring the rights to build another line between Brompton and Piccadilly Circus, together with a site for a power station at Lots Road, Chelsea. It is not clear how the directors of the District thought that their chronically unprofitable railway would ever have been able to raise the money to build this pipedream. The third element of the plan which eventually became the Piccadilly Line was the Great Northern and Strand Railway of 1898. This railway would run beneath Great Northern tracks between Finsbury Park and King's Cross and would run thence to Russell Square and Aldwych via Holborn. In 1901, as observed on p. 68, Charles Yerkes had acquired the District Railway and the rights to build these three railways which would link Hammersmith and Finsbury Park.

Following the opening of the Central London Railway in 1900 Parliament was besieged by a multitude of underground railway schemes. These were considered by two committees of the House of Lords: the Ribblesdale Committee, which was mostly concerned with north–south schemes, and the Windsor Committee, which adjudicated on east–west schemes. Lord Windsor's committee considered the Hammersmith to Finsbury Park scheme and they were no doubt impressed by the performance of Yerkes, who appeared before them and assured them of his disinterested motives in building the line, informing them, 'I have got to a time when I am not compelled to go into this business, but seeing the way things are in London I made up my mind this would be my last effort.'

He further reassured the committee members that he would purchase virtually all the line's equipment in Britain. This was a major public issue at this time as the Progressive party which dominated the London County Council was being accused of sacrificing British jobs to political dogma. He proceeded to buy most of the equipment abroad but

THE PICCADILLY LINE

The Great Northern, Piccadilly and Brompton Railway opened on 15 December 1906, having emerged from three rival schemes with the assistance of some astute and ruthless financial manoeuvring by the American financier C.T. Yerkes. Its first line ran from Hammersmith to Finsbury Park, an electric railway largely financed by Americans and using French and Hungarian rolling stock. A branch from Holborn to Strand followed in 1907 (renamed Aldwych in 1915 and closed in 1994). In 1930, in the face of opposition from the LNER, the owners of the line, the Underground Group, obtained an Act of Parliament authorising construction of a line beyond Finsbury Park to Cockfosters, which was reached in 1933. At the same time the line was extended west along tracks formerly operated by the District to Hounslow West (1933), South Harrow (1932) and Uxbridge (1933). The Hounslow branch was extended to Heathrow airport in 1977, an additional loop being added to serve Terminal 4 in 1986.

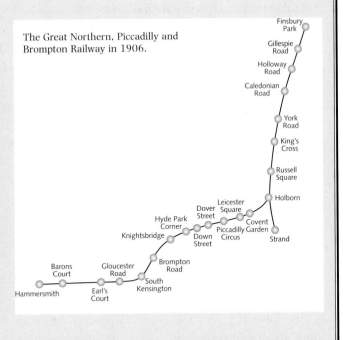

The Great Northern, Piccadilly and Brompton Railway in 1906.

was spared the need to explain this discrepancy by his untimely death. The committee was persuaded and in November 1902 the royal assent was given to the construction of the Great Northern, Piccadilly and Brompton Railway, joining up two of the earlier schemes.

The rival plan of J. Pierpont Morgan having been out-manoeuvred,[28] construction of the new railway began in the spring of 1902. Shafts were sunk into the London clay and tunnelling proceeded using a Price rotary excavator of the kind also used on the 'Hampstead' tube, with electrically powered knives cutting the clay and depositing it on a chute for removal. Some delay in the construction work was caused by the creation of the LCC's new thoroughfare, Kingsway, but by 15 December 1906 the line was ready to be opened. The first official train was started by Lloyd George, who was presented with a golden key for the purpose. This didn't work so a foreman's iron key was used instead.[29]

The twenty stations on the new line had been designed in the characteristic house style by the company's architect, Leslie Green, using ruby terracotta. Sixty electric lifts were supplied by the American Otis company and at Holloway Road station there was an early example of a moving stairway made from teak slats, described rather confusingly by the *Railway Times* as 'a double-spiral continuous-moving track, which travels at a hundred feet per minute and can take passengers up and down simultaneously'.[30] It never entered service and was later removed, some relics making their way to London's Transport Museum. The rolling stock, consisting of multiple units, was made in France and Hungary despite Yerkes' earlier assurances that he would buy in Britain. It consisted of traditional gate-end stock, painted crimson on the outside. Seats were upholstered in yellow rattan, derived from palm trees.

THE CHARING CROSS, EUSTON AND HAMPSTEAD RAILWAY

Meanwhile, Yerkes was busy building railways elsewhere, though his methods of raising finance for the purpose were to leave a disastrous legacy for his successors. The promoters of the Charing Cross, Euston and Hampstead Railway, authorised in 1893, had by 1900 had no success in raising capital to build it and no Whitaker Wright had come to 'rescue' the project. On 1 October 1900 a Yerkes-led syndicate which included Marshall Field, the Chicago store magnate, bought the Hampstead Railway from its promoters for £100,000. Yerkes became chairman and Robert Perks a director. Yerkes insisted on extending the proposed railway from Hampstead to Golders Green where cheap land was available for a depot. The Parliamentary Committee which considered the proposed extension was informed by one witness that Golders Green was: 'a district lying beyond Hampstead which has been almost unapproachable . . . excellent building land within twenty minutes of Charing Cross'.[31]

Yerkes knew from his experience in America that suburban railway lines were quickly followed by housing estates, with rich pickings for anyone astute enough to acquire the land in the meantime. The residents of Hampstead were alarmed at the proposed extension which would involve tunnelling beneath the Heath and were quick to articulate what they saw as their interests. W.J. Bull, MP for Hammersmith, succeeded in adding to the responsibilities of the committee examining the proposal by requiring them to establish whether the railway would damage the Heath on its journey to Golders Green by 'tapping its wells',[32] while on Christmas Day 1900 *The Times* ran a long article headed 'The Tunnel under Hampstead Heath', claiming:

> The heath has been hitherto considered sacred ground. . . . A great tube laid under the heath will, of course, act as a drain and it is quite likely that the grass and gorse and trees on the heath will suffer from lack of moisture.[33]

Tree roots would be disturbed by vibrations from passing trains while the prospect of Golders Green station on the edge of the heath appalled the writer: 'Picture the constant daily traffic over the greensward to and from the station.' Nevertheless Yerkes was granted his extension and tunnelling began in September 1903.

Having raised American finance to build the railway Yerkes then appointed American engineers to advise on its construction, though the principal innovation in the tunnelling was the work of the British engineer John Price, of the contractors Price and

THE PROUD CITY

CHELSEA POWER HOUSE FROM MEEK STREET

"...the poor buildings lose themselves in the dim sky, and the tall chimneys become campanili, and the warehouses are palaces in the night, and the whole city hangs in the heavens..."

James McNeill Whistler

Lots Road power station, as depicted in the Second World War poster, *The Proud City*. (London's Transport Museum)

An early advertisement for Underground travel, incorporating Edward Parrington's prize-winning slogan, for which the fourteen-year-old was paid £10. (London's Transport Museum)

Breach of copyright in Florence? This bizarre use of the roundel at Florence station, Italy, shows how well-known it has become. (Author)

Opposite: Not quite an A to Z of the LT roundel showing how it has developed over the course of a century. Some artistic licence has been used in its production, and some of the roundels shown have never actually been in use. (London's Transport Museum)

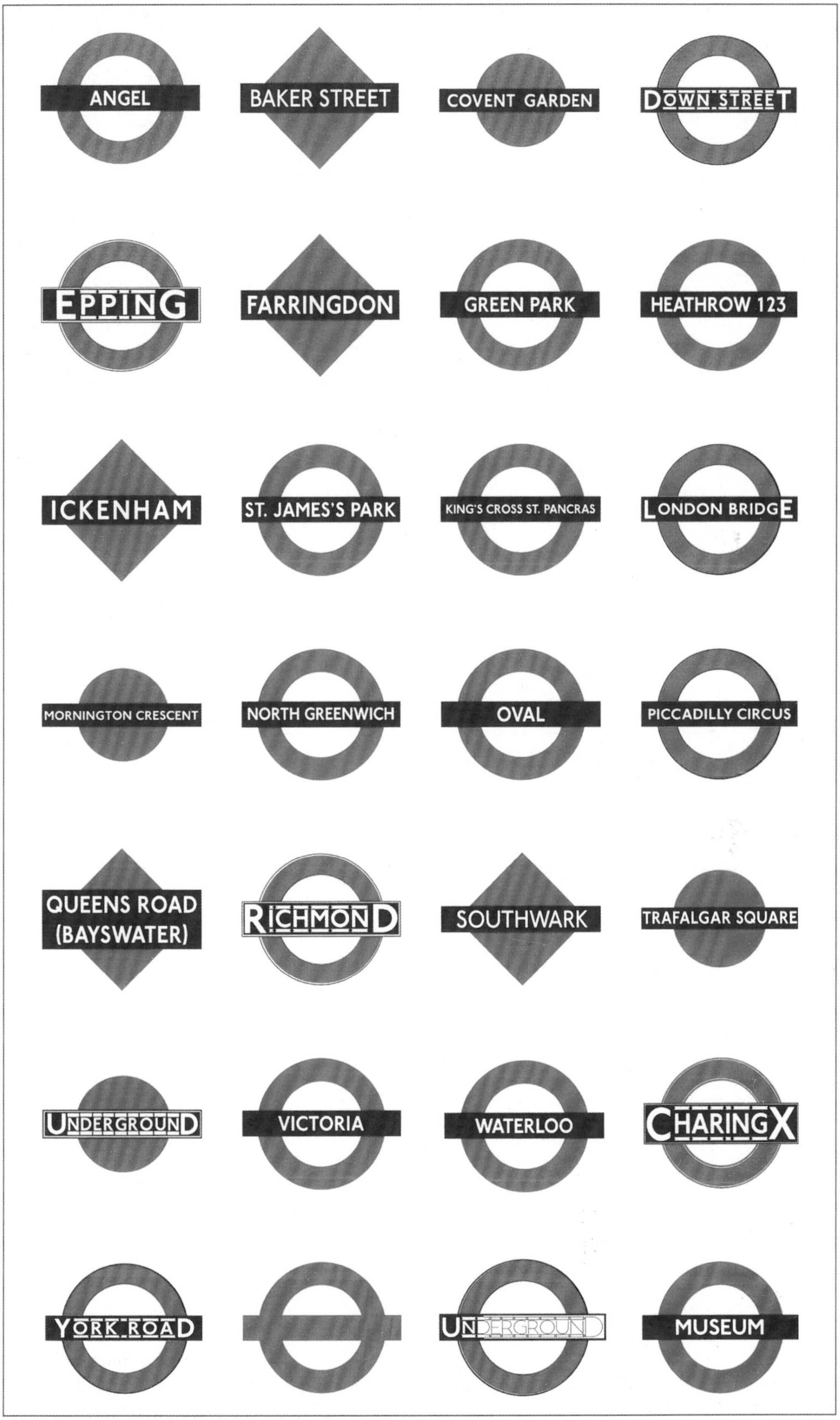

ANGEL

BAKER STREET

COVENT GARDEN

DOWN STREET

EPPING

FARRINGDON

GREEN PARK

HEATHROW 123

ICKENHAM

ST. JAMES'S PARK

KING'S CROSS ST. PANCRAS

LONDON BRIDGE

MORNINGTON CRESCENT

NORTH GREENWICH

OVAL

PICCADILLY CIRCUS

QUEENS ROAD (BAYSWATER)

RICHMOND

SOUTHWARK

TRAFALGAR SQUARE

UNDERGROUND

VICTORIA

WATERLOO

CHARING X

YORK ROAD

UNDERGROUND

MUSEUM

Numerous posters were produced promoting travel on the Underground for business and pleasure. (London's Transport Museum)

The great fares controversy of the early 1980s went all the way to the House of Lords. (London's Transport Museum)

THE CHARING CROSS, EUSTON AND HAMPSTEAD RAILWAY (CXEHR)

The line was originally authorised by an Act of 1893 but work on the CXEHR did not begin until 1903, using largely American finance, American engineers and American rolling stock brought in by C.T. Yerkes. It opened on 22 June 1907 from Charing Cross via Euston to Camden Town, where the line forked, proceeding north-east to Highgate (later renamed Archway) and north-west to rural Golders Green. The tunnels, at 11ft 8⅜in, were 18in wider than those of the City and South London Railway. In 1914 the line was extended south to the District Line's station, also called Charing Cross, which prompted the CXEHR to change its station's name to 'Strand' to avoid confusion. In 1924 the north-western branch was extended to Edgware and in the same year the line's owners, the Underground Group, built a link between Camden and Euston which connected it to another of the company's acquisitions, the City and South London Railway, thereby creating the Northern Line, though this name was not adopted until 1937. The extension from Archway to East Finchley was opened in 1939. High Barnet was reached in 1940 via LNER tracks and in May 1941 the network was completed by a short branch from Finchley to Mill Hill East in order to serve the nearby Inglis barracks. In 1979 Strand station was incorporated in the new Charing Cross station and the original Charing Cross station was renamed Embankment.

Reeves. His 'Price Rotary Excavator' incorporated electrically powered rotating knives within a tunnelling shield and this combination of technologies enabled the tunnels to be driven at unprecedented speed at greater depths than ever before,[34] though Greathead shields using manual labour continued to be used for difficult terrain. Rails were imported from the USA and rolling stock, in the form of multiple units, was built in the USA by the American Car and Foundry Company and shipped to Manchester where it was assembled and sent to the company's Golders Green depot by rail and road. These imports sparked off a controversy about the ability of British manufacturers to make things on time at competitive prices – a theme that was to become familiar as the century passed.

A CONVENIENT DISASTER

A particular problem attended the construction of the company's terminus at Charing Cross, which was to lie beneath the main line terminus of the South Eastern Railway. The latter, understandably, did not want construction works to impede access by road to its station so the new tube prepared plans to build its station from the bottom up, starting at platform level and excavating upwards until the booking hall was built beneath the main line station forecourt. The company was able to set aside this novel and hazardous plan when, on 5 December 1905, the main line station roof collapsed while it was being repaired. Three workmen were killed as the roof crashed on to the concourse and tracks, leaving the station wall leaning at a rakish angle over the nearby Players Theatre.[35] The station was closed for three months and the directors of the new tube seized the opportunity to persuade the directors of the South Eastern Railway to allow access to the station forecourt during the closure period. The underground station was then built by the conventional method of digging downwards rather than upwards. There were now three Charing Cross stations: the main line station; the new Hampstead

Line station; and the District Line station further to the south on the Victoria Embankment. This anomalous situation remained until 1914 when the Hampstead Line built an extension south to connect with the District Line station and, to avoid confusing its passengers, changed *its* station name to Strand. In 1979 the wheel turned again and Strand station, redeveloped, became 'Charing Cross' once again while the station to the south was given the more appropriate name 'Embankment'. As on the Bakerloo Line, surface stations were finished in a characteristic house style using glazed dark red terracotta, each station having its own distinctive tiling pattern. At Tottenham Court Road station (originally called Oxford Street) there was no space to build a booking hall on the surface so, as at Charing Cross, the booking hall was beneath the road, a pattern that was to become increasingly popular as the century progressed and land in the central area became prohibitively expensive.

LLOYD GEORGE RESISTS TEMPTATION

The new line was officially opened on 22 June 1907 and immediately became known as the Hampstead Tube. David Lloyd George, President of the Board of Trade, performed the ceremony by switching on the current with a golden key and then travelled to Golders Green and the second terminus at Archway.[36] At the banquet which followed he resisted the attempts of the railway's management to draw him into any undertakings to subsidise or regulate London's transport system to the advantage of the company. The chairman of the line, Sir George Gibb, commented ominously that 'companies could not go on losing money without serious consequences all round', while Sir Edgar Speyer, the chairman of the Underground Electric Railways Company which owned the line, pointed out that the main beneficiaries of railway investment were owners of properties along the line. Moreover:

> While other cities rendered active help in the provision of adequate transport facilities London stood alone in not assisting, by subsidy or otherwise, the enterprises which provided them.

Speyer invited municipal authorities to buy shares in the railway companies and urged Lloyd George to regulate competition between railway and bus operators. Lloyd George, shrewdly recognising the lobbying to which he was being subjected, replied that 'Sir Edgar Speyer had tried to lure him into some of the loveliest traps ever set for a Minister' but declined to give any assurances that any 'Socialistic legislation' would come to the rescue of the companies. The line was thrown open to the public for the rest of the day, free of charge, and *The Times* estimated that 127,000 people took advantage of the opportunity. In the years that followed the Hampstead Tube was popular with passengers though its success as an investment for its often suffering shareholders was influenced by the legacy of Yerkes, whose unorthodox financing arrangements cast a long shadow over his successors. If Yerkes had been an entirely honest, upright banker much of the underground system would probably never have been built.

DEATH OF THE TITAN

Yerkes did not live to see the opening of any of his tubes. In November 1905 he sailed to New York where he died on 29 December in the suitably resplendent setting of the Waldorf Astoria hotel. *The Times* carried an obituary the following day[37] in which it reminded its readers of the 'financial and practical abilities which he combined to a rare degree'. His legacies, both to his underground railways and to his heirs, were less certain. He had intended that his grand New York Mansion at 811 Fifth Avenue, with its collection of old masters including paintings by Rembrandt, Holbein and Raphael, should be left to the citizens of New York as a memorial to Yerkes. However, other claims were more pressing. One of these involved £160,000 owed to Underground Electric Railways, the final payment on the 32,000 shares which Yerkes had taken up when the company was launched. After much litigation his mansion, art collection and gold bedstead (formerly owned by the King of Belgium) were auctioned in April 1910 and two years later the Underground company finally received payment for its shares. On this occasion *The Times* was more sanguine,[38] describing the events in a moralising leading article as 'one of the ordinary hazards of the modern world in which speculators make money, buy art treasures lavishly and die in debt'. The shadow of Yerkes' financial manoeuvring continued to lie across the fortunes of his company for many years.

FINANCIAL ENGINEERING

Reference has already been made to the dubious methods by which Yerkes, assisted by Sir Edgar Speyer, had raised the initial £5 million to form Underground Electric Railways of London and the suspicions which they had aroused in the financial community.[39] In January 1903, as work proceeded on the electrification of the District Line and the construction of the three tubes, Yerkes had been faced with the need to raise more capital. An attempt to do so by selling £2 million of shares was badly received, barely 40 per cent of the offer being taken up. Yerkes therefore resorted to the ingenious device of offering £7 million of 'profit sharing notes'. They were to be released at a discount of 4 per cent (thereby supposedly giving an instant profit to the fortunate owners); they would bear interest at 5 per cent (substantially more than the dividends then being paid by underground railways) and were to be redeemed by 30 June 1908. By this time, it was confidently anticipated, the company's profits would enable this commitment to be met, a prediction based on forecasts of traffic and revenue made by an independent 'expert'. The security against which the certificates were issued consisted of existing shares in various undertakings owned by Underground Electric Railways. Since many of these were of doubtful value an additional inducement was offered in the form of an undertaking to share with certificate holders any profits arising from the sale of shares in any of the company's tubes.[40]

This extraordinary arrangement succeeded, with much of the stock again being taken up in the USA. In 1904 a further £775,000 of 4 per cent debentures were issued against the security of the Lots Road power station and in 1905 a final £2.5 million was raised from the sale of more debentures. Thus over £15 million had been raised since Yerkes and Speyer first launched the company to electrify the District, which was still losing money, and to finance three tubes which had not been built. As an exercise in raising finance it was magical but it burdened the forthcoming enterprise with some unsustainable commitments. These included annual interest payments approaching half a million pounds and an obligation to redeem £7 million of 'profit sharing notes' by 30 June 1908.

The ability to meet these commitments rested upon the belief that electric traction would prove to be much cheaper than steam, as well as cleaner; and upon some very optimistic forecasts of passenger revenue for the three tubes. The first hope was dashed by the cost of building and equipping the tubes since heavy interest payments on the capital invested cancelled out any savings from the use of electric traction. The forecast of passenger traffic revenue proved to be even more disastrous. Stephen Sellon, consultant engineer to the British Electric Traction Company and therefore an expert on tramways, had been employed by Yerkes to make estimates of likely revenue on the three tubes. He estimated that the Bakerloo could expect to carry 35 million passengers annually (the figure for the first full year of operation was 20.6 million); the Hampstead Railway could expect 50 million (it achieved 25.2 million); and the Piccadilly could expect 60 million (25.8 million). This gave a grand total for the three lines of 71.6 million passengers against Sellon's forecast of 145 million – less than half the volumes expected. More than twenty years passed before the three lines reached the levels forecast by Sellon. The situation was made even worse by the fact that average fares paid rarely reached the levels Sellon had forecast.[41] In addition, while the tubes were being built, a growing number of petrol-driven buses had been added to the trams which were picking up passengers and driving down fares.[42] Dividends were minimal or non-existent during the early years. Yerkes had tried cutting the fares but nothing could disguise the fact that the company was not making enough money to pay its debts.

YERKES' LEGACY

The task of dealing with Yerkes' disastrous legacy fell first upon his collaborator, Sir Edgar Speyer, who had helped Yerkes to raise the capital and who chaired the threatened company. To help him he recruited George Gibb, a university-educated Scottish lawyer who had been general manager of the North Eastern Railway since 1891. He was the first railway manager to recruit university graduates into the industry and the first to compile traffic statistics to identify profitable and unprofitable activities. He had experience of the electrification of railway services in Newcastle and he had been a member of the Royal Commission on London Traffic which sat between 1903 and 1905. Speyer approached Gibb in 1905 and on 1 January 1906, within three days of Yerkes' death, Gibb became deputy chairman and managing director of Underground Electric Railways of London at the enormous annual salary of £8,000. He brought with him Frank Pick, another lawyer from the North Eastern Railway, who was to be a dominant influence in the fortunes of London's transport for over thirty years.

Gibb quickly set about reversing some of Yerkes' fare reductions, which had cut revenue without noticeably increasing the number of passengers. Gibb also realised that he could make substantial economies in overheads by amalgamating the three tube lines into one company but when he proposed this sensible plan he alarmed the American shareholders who were still harbouring the illusion that they would make substantial capital gains by selling the shares in individual companies when the profits started to roll. In the meantime shares in the District had collapsed to a level at which the *Railway Times* described it as 'not very far removed from bankruptcy'.[43] At this point, in February 1907, the American shareholders moved to appoint as general manager Albert Stanley, from the New Jersey Tramways. Stanley succeeded Gibb as managing director in 1910.

In the meantime Speyer and Gibb faced a much more pressing problem bequeathed to them by Yerkes: the redemption of the £7 million of 'profit sharing notes' due on 30 June 1908 – whose profits had failed to materialise. Speyer first tried to sell the company to the London County Council, then dominated by the Progressive Party which was thought to be sympathetic to the idea of municipal ownership. On 6 April 1906 Speyer and Gibb went to share a no doubt frugal meal with the astringent Fabians Sidney and Beatrice Webb, at which Speyer broached the idea with the leader of the Progressives, T. McKinnon Wood. Beatrice recorded this early attempt at municipal socialism in her diary where she explained that her husband Sidney 'helped to bring Speyer and Wood together because he approves of the L.C.C. becoming a sleeping partner in London transport – eventually taking it over'.[44] She recorded Speyer as being 'almost gloomy' (he had good reason to be) and Gibb as 'a courtly official of great capacity and considerable charm' – a rare accolade from that unimpressionable lady.

This proposal came to nothing and, as the redemption date approached, the value of the £100 'profit-sharing notes' fell to £35 and Speyer brothers had to pay £175,000 interest on them from the bank's own resources to stave off the holders who were threatening bankruptcy proceedings. Eventually Speyer and Gibb put together a proposal to exchange the notes for a mixture of fixed interest bonds, due after twenty-five years on 1 January 1933, and a kind of preference share redeemable after forty years on 1 January 1948. Intensive and often acrimonious negotiations followed between shareholders' groups and panels of financial experts in London, Amsterdam and New York. Two tense Extraordinary General Meetings were held on 11 and 25 May 1908 as the deadline loomed[45] and Gibb was appointed to act as liquidator of the company. The scheme was finally accepted by 96 per cent of shareholders, the unfortunate owners of the profit sharing notes agreeing to the plan at the eleventh hour, on the date of redemption, 30 June 1908. They had little choice, the alternative being bankruptcy. Speyer addressed the meeting, pointing out that his own bank was the biggest loser as holder of many of the notes. At the board meeting on 30 July 1908 the directors, no doubt with relief, heard 'the solicitor reported that the court had, on 21 July 1908, stayed the liquidation of the company'.[46]

Sir Edgar Speyer was ill-rewarded for his services to the London Underground or for other philanthropic services to his adopted country. Besides his role in rescuing the Underground from bankruptcy he was a generous patron of the arts, subsidising the Whitechapel art gallery and the early promenade concerts at the Queen's Hall, as well as giving his support to medical charities. He was a fund-raiser and chief contributor to Captain Scott's Antarctic Expedition in 1910–12. In 1906 he had been created a baronet and in 1909 he was appointed to the Privy Council but none of these distinctions protected him from spiteful anti-German prejudice after the outbreak of the First World War. He was accused of trading with the enemy and, ludicrously, of signalling to German U-boats from his Norfolk home. He offered to resign his titles and offices but King George V declined his resignation assuring him, via Prime Minister Asquith, that 'these baseless and malignant imputations upon your loyalty' were no reason to resign. The charges against him were thrown out by every court to which they were taken but the campaign, involving some MPs, continued and Speyer was driven into exile. He lived for most of the remainder of his life in New York and died in 1932. He was not the only member of the Underground Group's senior management to be subjected to this form of persecution. In 1918 an independent MP called Pemberton Billing rose to ask a question in the House of Commons. Billing, a spiteful xenophobe, claimed to know of the existence of a 'Black Book' containing the names of 47,000 British perverts who were being blackmailed by the Germans, two of these security risks being Asquith, the former prime minister, and his wife Margot. On this occasion Billing's wrath was directed against Albert Stanley, who had been seconded from the Underground Group to become President of the Board of Trade during the war.[47] Billing addressed Bonar Law, Leader of the House:[48]

May I ask the Right Honourable gentleman whether he is prepared to state that the President of the Board of Trade is a German of the name of Nuttmeyer, whether the name Stanley has not been adopted since, and whether it is not the fact that he holds his position owing to the influence of a German Jew called Edgar Speyer who is now working out the damnation of this country in America.

LOST STATIONS: BRITISH MUSEUM

This station opened on 30 July 1900 as part of the new Central London Railway (Central Line), lying between the stations at Tottenham Court Road and Chancery Lane. When the Piccadilly Line opened in December 1906, Museum station found itself within a few yards of the new line's Holborn station but there was no subway to connect them. Eventually, work began in 1930 to turn the two stations into one and in September 1933 Central Line services transferred to the enlarged Holborn station and British Museum closed. Towards the end of its days an ancient Egyptian ghost was rumoured to haunt the station and a newspaper offered a reward to anyone prepared to spend a night on the station. The invitation was not taken up. The tiled walls of the station are still visible to passing trains just west of Holborn station.

Stanley, in a personal statement that was as dignified as Billing's was intemperate, explained that his family had lived in Derbyshire for generations; that they had no German connections; that his original name was Knattriess, an old English name that had been consistently mis-spelt and mis-pronounced during his time in America; and that this was the reason his father had adopted the name Stanley. His name changed again two years later when, despite Pemberton Billing, Stanley's wartime services were recognised in the 1920 New Year Honours list and he became Baron Ashfield of Southwell.

In 1910 George Gibb departed, no doubt with relief, to take a much lower paid job, at £3,000 a year, as chairman of the newly formed Road Board. He had survived the ordeals involved in dealing with the consequences of Yerkes' unorthodox practices in raising finance and left the company in much better condition than he found it. His successor was Albert Stanley.

CHAPTER FOUR
THE FIRST BARON ASHFIELD:
UNDERGROUND TO ANYWHERE

Of course it would not do to encourage this sort of thing, as I am a busy man.
(Albert Stanley, first Baron Ashfield, upon accepting an invitation to become
godfather to a baby girl born on a Bakerloo Line train)

The railway monopoly was assured by the unlucrative character of its capital
investment.
(Frank Pick, vice-chairman of London Transport, addressing the Institute of
Transport in 1939 on the difficulty of making underground railways pay)

THE INHERITANCE

When Albert Stanley became managing director of Underground Electric Railways in
1910, in succession to Gibb, he had three advantages which had been denied to his
predecessor. First, the capital reconstruction undertaken by Speyer and Gibb in such
fraught circumstances[1] had rescued the company from the prospect of liquidation. It
was still a poor investment for its long-suffering shareholders but it was no longer
operating under the perpetual threat of bankruptcy. Secondly, Stanley had been working
as general manager for two years and knew the company from the inside. He had had
the opportunity to observe the conditions in which the company was operating and the
effects of the sensible reforms introduced by Gibb which would form a blueprint for
the future. Gibb, by contrast, had been pitched straight from the well-ordered world of
the North Eastern Railway into the chaotic aftermath of Yerkes' sudden death. Finally,
Gibb had recruited a number of highly competent managers who, with Stanley himself,
were to form the bedrock of the group's future management.

A DECISION REVERSED

One of Stanley's first actions after he became managing director in May 1910 was to
push through the restructuring of the group which, when proposed by Gibb, had so

ASHFIELD, LORD (ALBERT H. STANLEY), 1874–1948

Chairman of the Underground Group and later chairman of the London Passenger Transport Board. Born Albert Knattriess, in Derby, he emigrated as a child to the USA with his parents and at the age of fourteen joined the Detroit Street Railway as a messenger boy. He rose rapidly and in 1903 became general manager of the New Jersey Tramways, his father having changed the family name to Stanley in 1897. In 1907 he returned to England to become general manager of the Underground Group at the behest of American shareholders who were dissatisfied with the group's financial performance following the death of C.T. Yerkes two years earlier. In 1910 Stanley succeeded George Gibb as managing director. Under his visionary leadership the Underground Group became the dominant force in London's transport system, owning most of the underground railways and many of the buses. In 1913 he became once again a British subject, was knighted in 1914, served as President of the Board of Trade in Lloyd George's wartime coalition (1916–19) and became Lord Ashfield in 1920, upon returning to the Underground Group. In 1933 he became the first chairman of the London Passenger Transport Board and briefly served on its successor, the British Transport Commission, in the months before his death in 1948. An effective and sometimes ruthless manager he was said to hold in reserve resignation letters from each of his chief officers, in case of need.

Albert Stanley, first Baron Ashfield, American tramway operator, British cabinet minister and creator of the twentieth-century underground railway network. (London's Transport Museum)

offended the American shareholders. It will be recalled[2] that Gibb had proposed to amalgamate the three separate tube lines – the Bakerloo, the Piccadilly and the Hampstead – into one group but the Americans had been so alarmed at the prospect of forfeiting capital gains on their (virtually worthless) shares that they had imported Stanley from New Jersey to keep an eye on Gibb. Stanley now pressed ahead with the very same proposals and on 1 January 1910 he became managing director of London Electric Railways, which managed the three tubes as one concern, with one board of directors and considerable savings in overheads. The sub-surface District Line remained under separate management. These changes were followed by the takeover of both the Central Line and the City and South London Railway. They were bought cheaply because their finances had been severely affected by competition from bus operators in the centre of London and neither had access to the more profitable suburban traffic. Both became part of the group on 1 January 1913. By this date, therefore, the Underground Group (or 'The Combine', as it was unaffectionately known) owned the whole of the London Underground system except the Waterloo and City Line (owned by the London and South Western Railway) and the Metropolitan which by 1913 itself owned the unloved Great Northern and City Railway. This pattern of ownership was to remain until 1933 when the Metropolitan was absorbed, protesting, into the London Passenger Transport Board. By 1912 the Combine also owned many of London's bus and tram companies, which enabled Stanley's management to coordinate policy on fares and mitigate the effects of cut-price competition in the central area which had been so harmful to the Central London Railway.

PROMOTING THE SERVICE

Having established a unified management structure, Stanley next turned his attention to promoting Underground travel. General managers' conferences had been instituted by Gibb in 1907, whereby representatives of all the Underground lines met at approximately monthly intervals to discuss and agree policies on a range of common interests from fares and through bookings to advertising, poster designs and charges for the recovery of lost umbrellas.[3] The days of Sir Edward Watkin and James Staats Forbes, when the District and Metropolitan operated in a state of unconcealed hostility, were consigned to the past.[4]

The early tubes had shown enterprise in promoting their services though each had acted independently, with little coordination of effort or policy. Each new line opened to a flurry of press publicity, ceremonial banquets, posters, maps and postcards. Stanley moved to coordinate all this activity to one common purpose. On 26 February 1908, while still general manager of the group reporting to Gibb, he chaired a general managers' meeting at St James's Park station at which all the lines were represented.[5] They debated whether they should adopt the name 'Underground', 'Tube' or 'Electric' as their common name for promotional purposes. Despite some reservations the name 'Underground' was chosen to be shown in white lettering of a specified size and typeface on a blue background: possibly the first 'corporate logo' to be adopted by such a group long before the term itself was coined. The design would appear on stations, posters, notices and tickets. The same meeting agreed to adopt a common illuminated map of the system, to be displayed at all stations, with each line picked out in a separate colour. Half a million copies of the map were printed for house-to-house distribution in the London area, much of the cost being borne by advertising. The eight lines represented at the meeting then agreed 'that a prize be offered, through the *Evening News*, of £10 for the best suggestion for the legend' (by which was meant the advertising slogan to appear on the maps). Despite the modest prize (£1.25 for each of the eight railways) the competition attracted numerous entries and at the next meeting, on 24 March 1908,[6] one hundred shortlisted suggestions were considered. Number 37 was selected:

Underground to Anywhere

Quickest Way   Cheapest Fare

The prize was duly awarded to the originator of the slogan who turned out to be a fourteen-year-old boy, Edwin Parrington. The announcement of the prize secured further coverage in the columns of the *Evening News*, a form of publicity which Stanley and his managers were very adept at exploiting. A competition in the same newspaper the previous year had produced a rather flamboyant logo for the Underground Group but this was soon replaced by the celebrated, and more restrained, bar and circle design.[7] A further promotional device took the form of a board game called *How to Get There*, in which players were required to move a train around a board, encountering hazards such as 'stop' signals and lost tickets. Some of the consequences were not anticipated, the *Railway Gazette* cruelly suggesting that the game should be modified to include such penalties as 'Breakdown on District; return on foot' or 'Polite conductor on Hampstead tube – miss eight moves through shock'.[8]

On other occasions the company's publicity was received with uncritical enthusiasm. Thus in October 1908 *The Times* lauded the introduction of strips of tickets sold at a very small discount[9] in the following terms:

> The Underground Company are willing to face the loss on the cheap strips if by their use delays at the booking offices can be avoided. The object of the underground lines is expressed by the words 'No waiting'. The lifts work in conjunction with the trains and the trains run at such frequent intervals that a passenger never has to wait above a few seconds.

Regular passengers must have had some difficulty recognising the service. Rarely can a company's public relations department have been so generously rewarded. Other favourable publicity occurred by chance. On the evening of 13 May 1924 a baby girl was born to Mrs Daisy Hammond on a Bakerloo Line train, an event which, one assumes, was neither organised not foreseen by the Underground's zealous publicity department. The *Evening Standard*, which reported the event the following day,[10] enquired whether Albert Stanley, now the first Baron Ashfield following his ennoblement in the new year's honours list of 1920, would become the child's godfather. He agreed, later adding 'Of course it would not do to encourage this sort of thing as I am a busy man.' The newspaper proposed the name *Louise Baker* for the baby but her parents were reported to have christened her **T**helma **U**rsula **B**eatrice **E**leanor. Alas, the story was too good to be true. On 31 July 2000 the object of the story, no longer a baby, appeared on a television programme to explain that she had been christened Mary Ashfield Eleanor. She added, ungratefully, that she didn't much like tube travel – but perhaps this is understandable given the circumstances of her birth.[11]

IMPROVING THE SERVICE

These ingenious and inexpensive devices for promoting Underground travel enjoyed some modest success. There was a steady increase in passengers carried and in receipts on all the tube lines from 1908 with the exception of the Central, which continued to languish in the face of competition from buses. By 1910 the Piccadilly, Hampstead and Bakerloo Lines were paying very modest dividends to their ordinary shareholders[12] and even the District was making a small profit, though not enough to reward its ever-patient shareholders with any dividend at all. Better financial performance would depend upon better services. Some improvements had already been made by the still-independent Metropolitan Railway. On 1 June 1910 the Metropolitan had introduced a Pullman service between Baker Street and Aylesbury, using two Pullman cars called *Mayflower* and *Galatea*. Breakfast, luncheon, afternoon tea and dinner were served, the last of these being on the service which departed from Baker Street at 11.35 p.m. for the benefit of theatre-goers. The Pullmans were never a commercial success but they survived the Metropolitan Railway itself and continued to be operated by the London Passenger Transport Board from 1933 until 1939 when they were withdrawn from service and converted into portable homes.[13] In February 1915, in an attempt to wrest some profit from the recently acquired Great Northern and City Tube, the Metropolitan introduced first-class travel to the line, the only such accommodation on a deep-level tube. The facility continued to be offered until March 1934.

Stanley and his team now set about providing better services on their network. The hourly frequency of peak hour trains on the busiest section of the District Line between South Kensington and Mansion House was increased from 24 in 1908 to 40 by December 1911.[14] Journey times were also reduced. The faster acceleration of electric trains enabled journey times round the Circle Line to be cut from 70 to 50 minutes while the journey from Hammersmith to Finsbury Park was reduced from 38 to 33 minutes. During peak hours some non-stop services were introduced and trains were lengthened.

At the same time station amenities were improved, a notable example being the installation of the world's first railway escalator at Earl's Court in October 1911,[15] though one had been in use at the nearby exhibition centre for some years.[16] The early escalators were known as 'shunt' escalators and passengers alighted by stepping sideways at the top or bottom. On the day of its inauguration the 'moving staircase' was welcomed by *The Times* in reassuring tones:[17]

> There need be no waiting on the part of the passenger for conveyance to or from the trains. He can step on to the stairlift at once, and be gently carried to his train. A boon that the mere man will also appreciate is the fact that he will not be prohibited from smoking, as in the lift, for the stairlift is made entirely of fireproof material.[18]

Another triumph for the public relations department.

Passengers were not so easily persuaded as was *The Times* correspondent and at first they showed a marked reluctance to use the moving stairway. On the first day of its operation a one-legged man called Bumper Harris was observed travelling up and down the new contraption and this sight may not have encouraged more nervous travellers to use it, though the missing leg had been lost in an earlier accident in the construction industry. Sadly there is no truth in the myth that he was paid by the management to ride up and down the escalators in order to demonstrate their safety, though this story ran for many years.[19] Large signs directed passengers to the moving staircase, urging them on with the words 'This way to the moving staircase, the only one in London now running'. By such enterprising methods customer resistance was overcome, further escalators were installed at other stations and Bumper Harris, and his wooden leg, passed into history. By the time the new device was installed at Paddington in 1913 it had become a selling point, Underground staff urging Great Western passengers on to the Bakerloo Line platforms by bawling through 'stentorphones' (early megaphones) *'This way to everywhere: moving staircase in operation; the world's wonder.'*[20]

Some cruder attempts were made to improve services at stations.[21] In December 1919 'hustlers' had been introduced to the District Line at Victoria to aid the prompt departure of trains. An employee stood on the platform with a stopwatch which he set going as soon as a train stopped. After thirty seconds he sounded a siren, which was the signal for the platform staff to close the doors and dispatch the train even if passengers were still attempting to board it. At Charing Cross, then the busiest station on the system, the company in 1921 installed a stentorphone (megaphone) which, during rush hours, bellowed instructions to passengers on the escalators: 'Please keep moving. If you must stand, stand on the right. Some are in a hurry. Don't impede them.' It must be assumed that passengers' reactions to this authoritarian device were more charitable than the company had a right to expect since a second stentorphone was installed at Oxford Circus shortly afterwards.

Ashfield's reaction to the increase in traffic that resulted from these measures was less enthusiastic than might have been expected. In 1924 he wrote a pamphlet which drew attention to the need for investment in London's tube network and the impossibility of obtaining the necessary funds without some regulation of competition. His analysis of the causes of overcrowding included some censorious judgements on the shopping and leisure habits of his fellow citizens: 'One contributory cause has been the emancipation of women, who are tending to travel as freely as men. . . . Another contributory cause is a greater addiction to pleasure.'[22]

EXTENSIONS

As amenities were improved at old stations, new stations and line extensions were added to the network. On 27 July 1912, shortly before its loss of independence to the Underground Group, the Central London Railway had extended from Bank to Liverpool Street, the Great Eastern allowing the construction of the Underground station beneath

UNDERGROUND ALCOHOL[23]

One of the less celebrated forms of 'addiction to pleasure' that the Underground allowed was the opportunity for out-of-hours drinking. At one time there were over thirty licensed buffets on Underground premises, many of them open for business when pubs were closed because of the restrictions on pub opening hours introduced in the First World War. Two bars were actually on the platforms. One, at Liverpool Street, on the eastbound Metropolitan Line, was known as 'Pat-Mac's Drinking Den' and survived until 1978. It is now a café called 'A Piece of Cake'. The other, on the westbound platform at Sloane Square, was called 'The Hole in the Wall'. It survived until 1985 and is now a convenience store called 'Treats'. They are both celebrated by Iris Murdoch in *A Word Child* (1975): 'After leaving the office I would travel either to Sloane Square or to Liverpool Street to have a drink in the station buffet. . . . Drinking there between six and seven in the shifting crowd of rush-hour travellers, one could feel on one's shoulders as a curiously soothing yoke the weariness of toiling London.' Baker Street also had a licensed buffet close to, but not on, the Metropolitan Line platforms. It was called 'Moriarty's Bar' after Sherlock Holmes's great adversary and is celebrated in verse in John Betjeman's poem, 'The Metropolitan Railway Baker Street Station Buffet'. Like the one at Sloane Square it is now a 'Treats' store. Mansion House station also had a bar close to the platforms in the early years of the twentieth century run by Spiers and Pond.

its terminus on the understanding that there would be no further expansion north or east which would compete with Great Eastern services. This would cause much controversy later. Stanley, however, had much more ambitious schemes in mind.

In the years that followed the First World War a number of parliamentary committees and commissions examined the problems of Metropolitan transport and commented, often scathingly, on its inadequacies,[24] though without suggesting any acceptable solution. At this time the London County Council, under the influence of the Progressive party, wanted to be the traffic authority for London while declining the opportunity to buy out the Underground Group[25] while the Metropolitan Railway, still independent, hovered on the sidelines. Underground railways were paying dividends less than the cost of capital[26] and the prospects of raising money for further investment were very poor.

In 1921 the deadlock was broken by a sudden rise in unemployment which embarrassed Lloyd George's coalition government. Such political alarms were to become an important feature of underground railway investment for the next half century. The Trade Facilities Act 1921 empowered the Treasury to underwrite capital sums for projects which would provide employment. On 26 October 1921 Ashfield presented to London MPs a £6 million plan which, he claimed, would provide 20,000 jobs for workers in steelmaking, construction and the manufacture of rolling stock. It included the connection of the Hampstead Tube to the City and South London, to create what became the Northern Line; the extension of the Hampstead to Edgware; and an order for new rolling stock. He told the MPs:

> Our people are depressed, they want something important, something dramatic, which would encourage them to look about and see in what way they can get the trade of the country going again.[27]

He and his spokesmen claimed that they were making the investment 'at the top of the market' and that, if they waited, they would get the job done for £4 million. In return they wanted protection for their buses from 'piratical adventurers' who took traffic from the best routes. It was not made clear how the onset of a depression represented 'the top of the market' or why the price would drop if they waited. However, the Treasury did agree to underwrite a slightly modified scheme to the value of £5 million.

THE NORTHERN LINE

In 1913 the Underground Group had purchased the City and South London Railway and made plans to link it with their Hampstead Tube to form what would eventually become the Northern Line. The customary shortage of finance, exacerbated by the exigencies of the First World War, ensured that no progress was made until capital became available through the Trade Facilities Act. Having raised cheap finance by this means the company began to extend the platforms on the City and South London and to enlarge the tunnels from their diameter of 10ft 2in to the 11ft 8in that prevailed on the rest of the system. Work was carried out at night and a special tunnelling shield was constructed which could be left in place during the day so that trains could continue to run through those parts of the tunnels where work was actually in progress. All proceeded smoothly until just after five o'clock on the afternoon of 27 November 1923 when, at the height of the evening rush hour, a train passing from Elephant and Castle to Borough station dislodged a plank of wood protecting the works and set off a series of accidents, each more threatening than the last.[28] Gravel, water and clay began to trickle and then pour on to the passing train, the driver of which made a dash through the deluge for Borough station and reached it just in time. A gas main then ruptured, causing, in the words of *The Times'* headline, an 'Alarming Gas Explosion' which sent flames leaping 40ft into the air and threatening to destroy the South Eastern Railway viaduct which stood nearby. In the meantime a crater had appeared in the roadway, 40ft deep, into which poured water from a ruptured main. This may have saved the day since escaping water doused the flames while police moved local inhabitants and shopkeepers away from the scene of devastation. Miraculously no one was killed, though much of the railway was closed while the damage was repaired.

THE *CANAILLE* OF HIGHGATE

Meanwhile a link was being created between the Hampstead Line station at Camden Town and the City and South London terminus at Euston. This opened on 20 April 1924, and thereby created the Northern Line though the name was not adopted until 1937. The first train through the link was driven by a sixteen-year-old boy called Anthony Bull, who later became vice-chairman of London Transport and, seventy-six

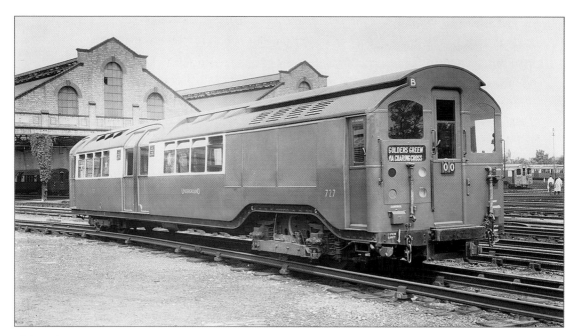

Sliding door stock, *c.* 1925. Note how much space is occupied by the electric motors. *See* p. 92. (London's Transport Museum)

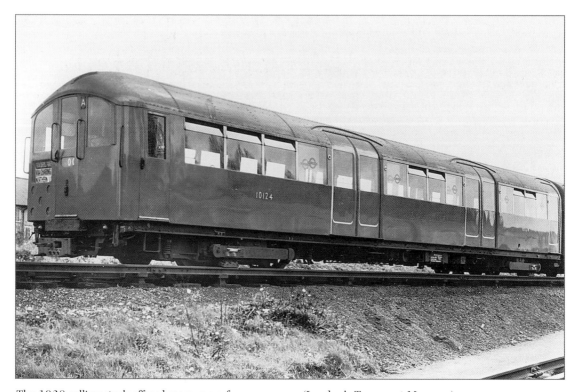

The 1938 rolling stock offered more room for passengers. (London's Transport Museum)

years later, gave an account of that and many other events in the history of the network to the author of this book.[29] In the meantime the old Hampstead tube was moving north to Edgware, which was reached in 1924. The railway, wishing to generate commuter traffic for its new line, printed posters urging citizens to move from the crowded inner suburbs to rural Edgware where they could be 'Master of a small House and a large Garden, with moderate conveniences joined to them'.[30] The housing developments at Edgware benefited the railway but enthusiasm in other quarters was more muted. In particular the residents of Hampstead, who had expressed deep misgivings about the railway when it was being built,[31] now objected to having to share it with their suburban brethren. On 28 February 1931, under the heading 'A grievance of Hampstead', a Mr W. Rushton wrote to complain that, since the extension of the line, 'The intelligentsia of Hampstead has the chagrin of witnessing the *canaille* of Highgate lolling at their ease while we have to hang on our straps. . . . Is it fair?'[32] Mr Rushton suggested no remedy for this grievous state of affairs.

UNDERGROUND TRAINS ON THE ISLE OF WIGHT

At one time the Isle of Wight had 55 miles of railway but by the 1960s the only remnant was the 8 mile stretch from Ryde Pier Head to Sandown and Shanklin. It was used during termtime by schoolchildren and for a few weekends each summer by holidaymakers arriving from the mainland, and the Minister of Transport insisted that the line be kept open for these uses. It was dependent upon ageing steam locomotives and rolling stock, some of which would have been recognised by Queen Victoria. The chief mechanical and electrical engineer of the Southern Region was becoming increasingly anxious about his ability to keep them running. The railway tunnels on the island were too small to accommodate main line gauge stock so British Rail bought from London Underground forty-three units of 1938 Standard Stock which were converted to run on the Island. The new service began in March 1967. In 1984 a further thirty-four units of 1938 stock were purchased. Visitors to the island arriving by ferry from Portsmouth are thus confronted by a bizarre spectacle. A London Underground tube train, clearly recognisable despite its colourful livery, awaits them at the end of the pier, ready to convey them to their holiday destinations. Some of the rolling stock has been in use for over sixty years yet the Isle of Wight Railway regularly heads the league tables for punctuality and reliability, an encouraging testimony to the skill and dedication of the engineers who converted them and those who continue to lavish tender loving care upon these memories of the age of Lord Ashfield and Frank Pick.

1938 Underground stock still in use on the Isle of Wight in the twenty-first century. (Author)

In addition, the Underground Group took advantage of the Trade Facilities Act to order new rolling stock. In 1919 it had placed with Cammell Laird a modest order for forty units equipped with air-operated doors instead of gate-end doors. On these new units only three train staff were required instead of eight: a driver, front guard and rear guard who operated the doors. Following the release of funds under the Trade Facilities Act the company invited six suppliers to tender for a modified version of the new stock. In the next seven years over 1,100 units were ordered, thus ending the era of the end doors and their gatemen (although they did survive on the Bakerloo Line until 1 March 1930). On this so-called 'Standard Stock' the electric motors occupied a considerable space located immediately behind the driver's cab (*see* p. 90). Another fifteen years passed before design improvements enabled the motors to be positioned directly beneath the carriages on the 1938 stock, thereby releasing much more space for passengers. The 1938 stock survived into the twenty-first century on the Isle of Wight (*see* panel on previous page).

MONEY AND POLITICS

These were substantial improvements but much remained to be done, particularly in connection with some serious bottlenecks which were beginning to embarrass MPs and councillors in north and east London. Further funds for investment had to be raised and some political obstacles had to be removed before these problems could be overcome. During his government service in the First World War Ashfield had gained some useful political contacts as well as lobbying skills which he now exercised in the interests of the Underground Group. As early as 1923, while the funds from the Trade Facilities Act were funding his investment programme, Ashfield told his shareholders that unrestrained competition in urban transport produced a poor service for passengers and poor returns for shareholders:

> Competition is a dangerous weapon. It may seem to offer immediate gains, but they are at the expense of future losses. . . . Competition weakens the undertakings so that the fresh capital required for progress cannot be obtained on reasonable terms. . . . Competition ends in obsolete vehicles being retained in service when they should have reached the scrap heap.[33]

At a time when there were over a hundred one-man bus operators in the capital, switching day by day between the most profitable routes, he called for a 'responsible judicial authority' which would be able to make judgements on London's transport needs and protect the capital from the worst effects of unbridled competition. The following year he issued a stark reminder of the record of underground railways in rewarding their investors:

It may be a great surprise to you to know that the underground railways in London have never been, in their whole career, a financial success. In other words they have failed to earn anything approaching a reasonable return upon the capital invested in them.

A year later, in 1925, in a speech clearly aimed at his former colleagues in the political establishment, he drew his shareholders' attention to the pressing transport needs of communities to the north and east of London which were then under investigation as a result of electoral pressure, but added 'to all these projects we must turn a deaf ear' while unrestrained competition produced poor returns. 'These projects' we will now examine.

LONDON TRAFFIC

The London Traffic Act of 1924 established a group with the cumbersome title the 'London and Home Counties Traffic Advisory Committee' to advise the recently created Ministry of Transport on transport facilities within an area bounded by St Albans, Gravesend, Dorking and Slough. It included representatives of local authorities, national government, police, transport unions and transport companies. It quickly identified serious inadequacies in rail transport to the north and east of London. A particular problem lay at Finsbury Park, where long-standing difficulties had been only partially eased by the services of the Great Northern and City Tube and the Piccadilly Line which had served the station since the early years of the century. In 1902 the Great Northern Railway, jealous of its suburban traffic, had secured an Act which effectively prevented the tubes from extending their services to the suburbs beyond. Passengers were obliged to transfer to buses, trams or the Great Northern services whose station was inconveniently situated in relation to the tubes.

In 1922 there began a campaign to overturn this veto. It was initiated by the Middlesex Federation of Ratepayers' Associations which, on 14 June 1923, presented a petition bearing thirty thousand signatures to the Minister of Transport. In the meantime the Great Northern had been absorbed by the London and North Eastern Railway (LNER) which was, on that very day, promoting a parliamentary bill to consolidate its powers.[34] The minister was warned that MPs for Middlesex constituencies had been asked to vote against the bill later that day unless the railway lifted its veto. The LNER clung to its veto and the bill passed, with 75 votes against it, but the skirmishes continued. The following year the MP for Tottenham described the embargo as 'a bargain made twenty-two years ago between two railway companies, neither of which now exists, to be used to deprive half a million people of reasonable travelling facilities for all eternity'.[35] The Member for Hornsey added that appalling conditions were being endured by passengers 'because the Great Northern Railway had wangled into the 1902 Bill the obnoxious clause which reserved for them the whole of the area as a sort of Tom Tiddler's Ground'.

In the meantime the Underground Group's formidable publicity department was also at work on the problem of the veto. Frank Pick, the company's assistant managing director, arranged for photographs of the rush-hour mayhem to be taken from the roof of an adjacent building and these were distributed to MPs and the press. The *Daily Mirror* told of rugby scrums to board buses and trams, nervous breakdowns and a haven for pickpockets.[36] Faced with this pressure the LNER, in the autumn of 1925, reluctantly conceded the lifting of the veto and the London and Home Counties Traffic Advisory Committee began an enquiry into the best ways of improving facilities in the stricken area. Frank Pick argued in his evidence that the extension of the Piccadilly Line to Manor House, or beyond to Southgate, would present no threat to LNER suburban traffic.[37] The main line railway should concentrate on its more profitable, longer-distance suburban traffic with its faster trains and leave the short-distance stopping services to the tubes, though he added that such a solution would only be possible if the Underground were protected from unbridled competition and thus able to offer a reasonable return to investors. The committee agreed and in its report of March 1926 recommended that the Piccadilly Line be extended to Southgate.

MONEY

The Underground Group immediately began to discuss with the Ministry of Transport the impossibility of its undertaking this electorally desirable project unless it was given some financial help. In the meantime, however, it began discreetly surveying the route, buying up parcels of land and obtaining permission for trial boring. In May 1929 the project was rescued by another unemployment crisis which, like that of 1921, prompted Ramsay Macdonald's Labour government to promote public works, this time through the Development (Loan Guarantees and Grants) Act 1929. This prompted Frank Pick to submit a more ambitious proposal, costing £13 million, which extended the Piccadilly Line beyond Southgate to Cockfosters. Pick also proposed to extend the Piccadilly Line in the west, alongside congested District Line tracks, to Hounslow and Uxbridge, and to reconstruct fifteen busy stations in the central area, equipping them with escalators rather than lifts.

The extension beyond Southgate to Cockfosters aroused renewed opposition from the LNER. Its general manager, Sir Ralph Wedgwood, told the committee investigating the plan that the proposal would have a disastrous effect upon his company's passenger traffic. He tried to buy off the committee with a vague assurance that the LNER would electrify its suburban services to Welwyn and Hertford. While applauding this worthy intention the committee elicited from him the admission that the LNER had little prospect of raising the finance to execute the plan. Frank Pick disingenuously informed the committee that the Piccadilly's extension had been carefully designed to bisect the LNER's routes and thus open up sparsely inhabited areas:

> We designed our railway to go as near as possible between the two lines of the L.N.E.R. so as to avoid, as far as we could, this allegation that we are competing with them . . . the moment you get past Wood Green there is an almost entire absence of development. The population of East Barnet is at the rate of half a person to the acre.

Armed, as he always was, with well-prepared statistical data, he argued that the Piccadilly Line was delivering to Finsbury Park, during the evening peak time, six hundred people in each train, 78 per cent of whom were then carried away in small buses and trams, adding 'You are ladling out traffic from a bucket and picking it up in a teacup.'

The committee approved Pick's plan and the royal assent was given on 4 June 1930. Work on the 7½ mile extension began in September and proceeded at an unprecedented pace. Twenty-two tunnelling shields were used from nine separate sites and huge steam-driven, six-wheeled road vehicles with solid tyres were used to cart away the spoil to dumps in the valley of the River Lea. Within two years the line was completed as far as Arnos Grove.

The Bauhaus comes to the Piccadilly Line: new shapes and new materials. *See* pp. 138 *et seq.* (London's Transport Museum)

Pick had also made some changes to the timetable which were designed to make the longer-distance services more attractive. Three stations in central London were closed (at Brompton Road, Down Street and York Road) so that trains would have longer runs between stops and thereby achieve an average speed of 25 miles per hour. Some tracks were realigned to permit faster running and station layouts were altered to facilitate interchanges between lines. The first train from the new extension left Arnos Grove at 5.23 a.m. on Monday, 19 September 1932. Thirty thousand free tickets had been distributed to residents along the line and the service was an immediate success. A month after the line opened Pick received a letter from the Federation of Ratepayers which had begun the campaign for the lifting of the LNER veto in 1923. It ended: 'Blessings have been showered upon your undertaking by thousands daily during the past month.' Nine months later, on 31 July 1933, the line opened to Cockfosters. Many of the stations on the line were outstanding examples of 1930s architecture, designed by one of its leading exponents, Charles Holden. These will be examined in Chapter Six.

TROUBLES IN THE NORTH

Following the creation of the Northern Line by the linking of the Hampstead Tube and the City and South London Railway,[38] the line was extended further into the suburbs, reaching Morden in September 1926, two years after it reached Edgware. Parts of the new tube, notably in the Tooting area, passed through waterlogged soil which made tunnelling by conventional methods very difficult. In these cases the tunnels and the shafts leading to them were sealed with airlocks and compressed air was pumped into the airtight chamber until the pressure was sufficient to hold the water at bay in the surrounding soil. Tunnelling then continued in this high-pressure atmosphere. This technique had been used at the turn of the century when building the Bakerloo Line through waterlogged gravel beneath the Thames between Charing Cross and Waterloo. It has harmful effects upon the tunnellers, who can suffer from 'the bends', a condition to which submariners are susceptible when escaping from submarines. These were casually described in an alarming account to the Institution of Civil Engineers in 1908, in which the consequences of the Bakerloo tunnelling in compressed air were described:

> The tunnel was being driven under a pressure of 35 pounds per square inch for a considerable distance [atmospheric pressure at sea level is 15lb psi]; a great deal of illness resulted among the men but *there were not many fatal cases* [author's emphasis!]. The air escaping through the gravelly bed of the river boiled three feet high above the surface. It came in the path of a race from Charing Cross to Putney and upset one of the competitors' boats.[39]

The speaker went on to comment on the compensation that had to be paid to the boat owner but appeared to accept the illness and mortality among the unfortunate tunnellers as a normal hazard. Compressed air tunnelling is now rarely used and is surrounded by stringent and costly regulations. Later, tunnelling through watery soil was done by freezing the water with liquid nitrogen, rendering the soil hard and solid enough for the tunnelling excavators to cut through it.

The Morden extension resulted from a compromise agreement with Sir Herbert Walker, the formidable general manager of the newly formed (1923) Southern Railway, who had initially opposed the invasion of what he regarded as his railway's exclusive commuter territory. His legacy is felt to this day as commuters south of the Thames are far more dependent on main line railways than are their fellows to the north, the incursions of the suburban Underground system being confined to Richmond, Wimbledon and Morden. In accordance with the hopes of its promoters, the Underground Group's Edgware and Morden extensions were followed by the rapid transformation of these rural communities into prosperous suburbs with a steady supply of the profitable, long-distance commuter traffic that the line needed. The population of the village of Morden, in Surrey, which entered the twentieth century with 960 inhabitants, reached 12,618 within five years of the line opening.

However, as the trains approached the centre of the metropolis they quickly became overcrowded, a fact recognised many years before as essential to the profitability of the lines. As Sir Edgar Speyer had commented upon the opening of the Piccadilly Line in 1906: 'Straphangers meant dividends and those who had a complaint to make would find their angry feelings greatly soothed if they became shareholders in the railway.'[40] Complaints as early as 1931 about the intelligentsia of Hampstead having to stand while the *canaille* of Highgate took their ease have already been noted.[41] The Metropolitan Railway, like the Underground Group, had made use of government support for railway projects by extending its services via a branch line to Stanmore in 1932. However, this measure met with little success owing to a peculiarity in the Acts of Parliament which governed the fares. Metropolitan fares from Stanmore were determined by an Act designed for main line railways while those offered from Edgware, via the Northern Line, were regulated by a separate Act for Underground fares, which were lower. So the Metropolitan's potential passengers took buses from Stanmore to Edgware, adding further to the congestion on the Northern Line. By the mid-1930s the columns of newspapers like *The Times* carried an almost continuous litany of correspondence about overcrowding and poor service. These complaints became particularly vehement late in 1935 when a series of letters to the newspaper described the horrors of travelling on the Hampstead branch of the line. A correspondent from the Vale of Health, Hampstead, complained[42] that he had been one of 88 passengers standing in a passenger car that he had boarded at Hampstead and in the days that followed other correspondents capped this claim. One asserted that, in the evening peak, on trains to Hampstead, standing passengers were 'not less than sixty in every compartment. This is double the complement. The discomfort is extreme, the air vitiated, everyone fatigued.'[43] The raised voices were not confined to the Northern Line, one contributor to the debate giving an account of the procedure he adopted when attempting to board a second Central Line train, when congested cars led to his being repulsed from the first:

> On several occasions I have been one of a bunch of rejects and have had to wait for another train. At such times one's only chance of adding to the crush inside was to judge the speed of approach and jockey for position near a door. Once there I admit things are much easier; one only has to adopt a passive stance and a wave of surging humanity does the rest.[44]

In the midst of this angry correspondence *The Times* published a letter from one M. du Plat Taylor suggesting that the situation could be alleviated by the installation of parcel racks in tube trains, though it was not entirely clear whether the racks were to contain parcels or prostrate passengers. Since his letter was written from the hallowed precincts of his London club, the Athenaeum, one may speculate that the gentleman travelled by taxi and not by tube.[45]

Some passengers did more than complain. They went on strike. In April 1937 there were reports of passengers staging 'sit-ins' on trains. *The Times* carried an account of an incident at Colindale station on the Northern Line.[46] A train full of Edgware-bound commuters, whose homeward journey had already been delayed, was terminated at Colindale, two stops short of its planned destination and the passengers were asked to alight. The passengers in one coach, enraged, shouted 'Stay in your seats and demand to be taken on to Edgware. We have had enough of this messing about with the line.' As the more timid passengers left the train the militants ignored all pleas from the station staff and all assurances that a following train was approaching which would take them on to Edgware. They were duly shunted into a siding. A few moments later the following train arrived, picked up the less obstreperous passengers and took them on to Edgware – while the awkward squad looked on from their siding as their former fellow-passengers waved them a friendly farewell.

THE LONDON PASSENGER TRANSPORT BOARD

Into this mayhem stepped the newly created London Passenger Transport Board. The Board had been conceived by Herbert Morrison, Minister of Transport in Ramsay Macdonald's second Labour government, as a body to be appointed (by Morrison) to manage all of London's bus and underground railway services, a more powerful instrument than the 'responsible judicial authority' which Ashfield had called for in 1923.[47] Under Morrison's proposal shareholders in existing bus and underground train companies would be compensated with stock in the new undertaking and some cash. Main line railways would not be part of the scheme though they would be subject to some regulatory control. Ashfield, who formed a strong rapport with Morrison after a shaky start, persuaded his shareholders to accept the deal, implying that a later Labour government with a larger majority might force the issue on less favourable terms. Metropolitan Railway shareholders followed suit rather more reluctantly. During the course of their investigation of the ownership of the Underground Group the civil servants of the Ministry of Transport unearthed some remnants of the Yerkes–Speyer legacy.[48] The controlling interest in the group was held by interest-bearing bonds whose true ownership was concealed by the fact that they were bearer bonds.[49] Many of these had been sold by Sir Edgar Speyer when he went to live in New York, the buyers being interests represented by Solomon Barnato Joel, diamond merchant, theatre and racehorse owner, cricket enthusiast and Derby winner. He was the nephew of Cecil Rhodes's partner Barney Barnato, whom he accompanied on the latter's fateful voyage to South Africa in 1897 when the uncle killed himself by jumping into the Atlantic as the ship approached Madeira. Thus the Underground's association with unconventional financiers, begun by Whitaker Wright,[50] continued until its last days as a private company.

The financial crisis which followed the Wall Street crash of 1929 then precipitated the fall of the Labour government and its replacement by the National government but the board survived Morrison's loss of office with only one significant change. Instead of being appointed by the minister, the Board would be chosen by independent trustees which would include the chairmen of the LCC, the Institute of Chartered Accountants, the Law Society and the Committee of London Clearing Banks. This would create an arm's-length relationship with government on the model of the BBC, which had been established the previous decade. Outright nationalisation and direct government control were not yet quite respectable.

To no one's surprise Ashfield was appointed chairman of the new board with Frank Pick as his vice-chairman and chief executive. The other five members were all part-time, representing national government, local government and trade unions. Pick, in a lecture which he delivered in 1933 at the London School of Economics on the role of the board, gave a surprisingly stern judgement on the new body:

> Power has been transferred, let me say it with bated breath, to a bureaucracy. In the escape from capitalist control, in the escape from political control, we have almost fallen into a dictatorship.

In another lecture, to the Institute of Transport, he described the difficulties involved in earning a reasonable return on investment in underground railways.[51] He explained that railways' operating costs absorbed 66 per cent of their revenue, leaving 34 per cent for overheads and profits. For buses, operating costs were much higher: about 85 per cent of their revenue. However, buses travelled on infrastructure provided by local authorities in their road building programmes so they required far less capital investment. Railways not only had to provide expensive tracks and stations (on which they paid rates), they also had an enormous burden of interest payments on the far greater capital investment they required. This problem had plagued the underground railways from the earliest years. It had almost bankrupted Yerkes' network and it continued to hang like a shadow over future investment proposals for the rest of the century and beyond. Pick explained to his audience that the London Passenger Transport Board had been given a bus monopoly in order to regulate destructive competition among rival bus operators but that this had scarcely been necessary in the case of the underground railways since 'the railway monopoly was assured by the unlucrative character of its capital investment'.

NORTH, EAST AND WEST

Frank Pick's reservations about the dictatorial character of his board's authority did not inhibit him, or Ashfield, from using it. As soon as the board took office on 1 July 1933, they began work on a programme to rationalise road services, to coordinate them with trains and to extend the underground railway system. Once again their plans were inhibited by difficulties in raising finance, and once again unemployment came to the rescue – for the third time. On 22 February 1935 Ashfield wrote to Leslie Hore-Belisha, Minister of Transport.[52] In the letter, marked 'most secret', he wrote: 'It is not necessary for me to remind you of the clamant demand from the travelling public for improved travelling facilities in the North Eastern and Eastern sectors of London,' and went on to propose a £30 million programme of improvements including Central Line extensions to Epping and Ruislip, the money to be 'provided' by the government. This ambiguous word, after three months of negotiation, was defined as another loan underwritten by the Treasury. On 5 June 1935 the Chancellor of the Exchequer Neville Chamberlain announced to the House of Commons a £40 million[53] five-year plan for the improvement of transport facilities in London. He emphasised the beneficial effects upon employment. Once again, Treasury guarantees would be given to enable transport undertakings to raise money at lower rates of interest than the markets would have otherwise required. The plan as originally announced by Chamberlain was modified in the years that followed but it enabled the London Passenger Transport Board to finance a significant extension of its services which would alleviate the problems which had occupied the columns of *The Times* for the previous five years.

The Northern Line was extended from Highgate (renamed Archway) to Barnet and Mill Hill. This new route was completed in 1941. The Bakerloo Line was extended to Finchley Road and took over the Metropolitan's services to Stanmore in 1939, at the

---

LOST STATIONS: SOUTH KENTISH TOWN

This station, between Camden Town and Kentish Town, was one of the original stations on the Hampstead Tube (later Northern Line) which opened in June 1907. It was designed by Leslie Green in his characteristic dark red terracotta. It was never busy and was closed 'temporarily' during a strike at the Lots Road power station in 1924. It never reopened and became more celebrated for events which allegedly occurred after the closure than it ever did as a working station. Its later fame derived from a persistent story that an absent-minded passenger had alighted at the dark, abandoned station when his train was stopped by a signal. He was allegedly marooned at the station until, after a week's lonely sojourn, he caught the attention of a passing driver by setting fire to some advertising posters. An even more improbable version, given currency in a broadcast by John Betjeman in a radio broadcast in January 1951, held that the castaway, an income tax inspector, was eventually rescued by a group of gangers who informed him that he was trespassing. As late as 1997 the story was the subject of a television programme but no one has ever identified the subject of this improbable tale. During the Second World War the station became an air raid shelter. All traces of the station below ground have vanished but the booking hall, at street level, is now an ugly feature of Kentish Town Road, occupied by a pawnbroker and a massage parlour with protective metal shutters disfigured by graffiti.

---

same time bringing its fares into line with those of the Northern Line from Edgware and thus ending the problems caused by 'bussing' to that overcrowded line.[54] The Central Line was to be extended alongside Great Western tracks to Ruislip in the west; and in the east it would pass over LNER tracks to Ongar and via a new tube line to Newbury Park. In addition, many stations would be modernised, platforms lengthened to accommodate longer trains and new rolling stock purchased. The 1938 rolling stock, taking advantage of improvements in technology, mounted the electric motors beneath the trains rather than behind the driver, thus releasing more space for passengers. This rolling stock remained in use for over fifty years and some units were later transferred to run the Isle of Wight Railway.

The plans were widely, though not universally, welcomed. The Federation of Ratepayers' Associations of Middlesex, which had been instrumental in enabling the Piccadilly Line to break the LNER's veto on extensions beyond Finsbury Park, now opposed the Northern Line's extensions unless service levels and capacity improved and the Stanmore/Edgware fares nonsense was resolved. Their secretary, who bore the unlikely name H. Bueno de Mesquita, made this clear in a letter to *The Times* which immediately elicited a reassuring reply from Frank Pick.[55] The Central Line extensions, begun in the 1930s, were not completed until after the Second World War, during which the partially completed Newbury Park extension played its own heroic role (as described in Chapter Seven).

CHAPTER FIVE
METROLAND AND ITS FAMILY

Great was our joy, Ronald Hughes Wright's and mine,
To travel by the Underground all day
Between the rush hours, so that very soon
There was no station, north to Finsbury Park
To Barking eastwards, Clapham Common south,
No temporary platform in the west
Among the Actons and the Ealings, where
We had not once alighted. *Metroland*
Beckoned us out to lanes in beechy Bucks . . .

(John Betjeman, from *Summoned by Bells*)

A model garden village, on which a number of semi-detached residences have been erected. Peace and quiet prevail, and the stretches of country around offer plenty of opportunity for invigorating exercise to those who are inclined to walking and cycling.

(An estate agent's description of Neasden in the 1920s)

A LITERARY HERITAGE

The word *Metro-land* (originally with a hyphen) entered the language in 1915 as an advertising slogan adopted by the Metropolitan Railway. It was designed to encourage travellers like the young John Betjeman and his friend to spend their leisure hours in the area served by the railway. An unlikely alliance between the advertising slogan and the future poet laureate ensured that *Metroland* came to symbolise the suburbs that sprang up in the first half of the twentieth century along the lines of the Metropolitan Railway, to accommodate the desires of middle-class commuters to own a house with a garden. Similar communities sprang up in the paths of other Underground railways for the same reasons. Metroland is celebrated in Betjeman's poetry, with Harrow and Chorleywood at its heart and Baker Street as its headquarters, the London hub of the Metropolitan Railway. Betjeman's friend, Evelyn Waugh, an early resident of the new suburb of

John Betjeman was Metroland's
most prominent advocate. (By
courtesy of the National Portrait
Gallery, London)

Golders Green, added the eccentric figure of Lady Metroland in *Vile Bodies* and *Decline and Fall*, while in more recent times Julian Barnes has celebrated the area in his novel *Metroland*. However, the origins of the residential areas spawned by the suburban railway network, and particularly by the Metropolitan Railway, were altogether more mundane. Sir Edward Watkin had been among the first to recognise that medium-distance suburban traffic was more likely to yield satisfactory profits to railway operators than short-distance traffic in the city centre, where underground railways faced intense competition not only from other railways but also from omnibus operators whose activities were subjected to the lightest of regulation. The land deals of the Metropolitan Railway must thus be seen as a device to generate railway passenger traffic rather than as a source of profit from speculation in land.

SURPLUS LAND

The Acts of Parliament by which railways were established conferred upon the railway companies the power to make compulsory purchases of lands over which they passed. On occasion the companies entered into voluntary agreements with powerful landowners, foregoing their powers of compulsory purchase and the legal obstacles these entailed in return for buying more land than they really needed. In 1904 Robert Perks told the Royal Commission on London Traffic that the Metropolitan Railway had in this way acquired substantial holdings of land adjacent to its line, much of it acquired as a result of parliamentary opposition to its proposed route.[1] In most cases, once the railway was built the company was obliged by statute to sell surplus land back to the original owners who would then profit from any increase in the value of the land which arose from the construction of the railway. However, thanks to some strong advocacy in Parliament by the supporters of the Metropolitan Railway, the Acts which had set up the company allowed it to retain such surplus land in its own possession.[2] In 1887 the Metropolitan reconstituted its finances, establishing its property interests as a separate enterprise from its railway operations, and in 1919 this emerged as a fully fledged property company, Metropolitan Country Estates Ltd, which was effectively under the control of the railway.

Other railways were not so fortunate. In 1905 the Royal Commission on London Transport, having listened to the evidence of Robert Perks and others, recommended that railway companies be allowed to buy land whose value might be increased by railway developments. This idea did not commend itself to MPs, who believed that a railway company's attention should be focused on running the trains and not distracted by other opportunities for profit.[3] The idea was dropped. Thirty-three years later the vice-chairman of the London Passenger Transport Board, Frank Pick, told the Barlow Commission[4] that the Board would be encouraged to build socially desirable but unprofitable new railways if it could subsidise them by dealings in land. One senses a note of indignation in his evidence:

> The moment an underground extension is projected the value of the land is at least doubled. When the railway is built and the stations are opened the land adjacent to the stations is at least quadrupled in value . . . in view of the difficulty of maintaining a public utility like the London Passenger Transport Board in a satisfactory condition from the receipts of fares there is every reason, in the interests of the public, why the Board should receive its appropriate share of the land values it helps to create. . . . The earnings of a Tube railway, even under favourable circumstances, are not sufficient to provide the interest and the sinking fund upon the capital invested.[5]

Pick argued that the London Passenger Transport Board, like the former Metropolitan Railway, should be permitted to acquire property adjacent to projected lines and use the profits from its development to invest in its railway services. This potentially valuable source of railway finance was once again not taken up. Profits from property development would go only to property developers. The benefit to railway companies would be confined to the extra journeys of those who travelled to and from the properties.

THE WATKIN TOWER

An early, and bizarre, attempt to generate passenger revenue from property development occurred in 1890, soon after the Metropolitan Railway took advantage of its unique opportunity to establish a property subsidiary within the Metropolitan family. The property company purchased 280 acres of land at Wembley Park, upon the initiative of Sir Edward Watkin, to increase the Metropolitan's passenger traffic. Watkin's attention had been caught by the success of the Eiffel Tower in attracting visitors to the Paris Exhibition of 1889. He dispatched a Metropolitan engineer to inspect the edifice and in July 1890 he informed his shareholders that the existence of such a tower adjacent to their railway would guarantee huge increases in passenger traffic, profits and dividends.[6] It was naturally to be expected that a London tower would be superior to a Parisian one so a 'Tower Company' was formed which chose Wembley as the site for a 1,000ft tower, 15ft higher than Gustave Eiffel's. Watkin informed his shareholders that 'the Tower company have selected a site adjacent to your railway, between Neasden and Harrow, upon which to erect their proposed Great Tower'. This convenient decision was no doubt influenced by the fact that Watkin was the Tower Company's biggest shareholder, though the Metropolitan Railway itself later bought £60,000 worth of its shares on Watkin's advice: advice which, a century later, would have brought down upon his head the wrath of the Financial Services Authority. Like his Manchester to Paris visions, the Tower attracted his critics, who were roundly abused. One shareholder, Dr Turle, who moved an amendment criticising the plan, was told by Watkin that 'his amendment was about the most foolish he had ever heard a shareholder raise'. The meeting was temporarily reduced to turmoil.[7]

A competition was held for designs and the results were announced in *The Times* on 18 June 1890, where many of the entries were described as 'wildly eccentric or extravagant, whilst others were marked by an entire absence of architectural merit'.[8] Watkin wanted Eiffel himself to supervise the building of the Tower, which would accommodate restaurants, dancing rooms, theatres, exhibitions and a Turkish bath but the Frenchman wisely declined. Construction of the winning design began and, by May 1896, had reached a stage at which visitors could be admitted. Despite Watkin's excited anticipation the event passed almost unnoticed except in the *Wealdstone, Harrow and Wembley Observer*, where the announcement of its opening on the Whitsun bank holiday competed for space in that obscure newspaper with the attractions of jugglers, conjurors and mind-readers in a nearby fête. The magistrates even refused it a licence to sell alcohol.[9] In the first year only 18,500 people came, in place of the expected hordes. Construction ceased. The fragment was blown up by its disappointed owners in 1907 and the site was given over to Wembley football stadium – which generated far more traffic for the Metropolitan Railway than the Tower had ever done. The Watkin Tower was a disappointment but it could not be said that its promoter lacked vision. Other more conventional developments quickly followed.

HAMPSTEAD GARDEN SUBURB

At the time when Yerkes was planning the construction of the Hampstead Tube to Golders Green,[10] agricultural land in the vicinity of the proposed railway began to increase rapidly in value as speculators, many of them rumoured to be American colleagues of Yerkes, saw the opportunities for profit arising from its development. In his evidence to the Royal Commission on London Transport in 1904 Robert Perks had revealed[11] that land in the Golders Green area had tripled in value to between £600 and £700 an acre as a result of the proposed railway line. At this time much of the land in Golders Green, on the northern edge of Hampstead Heath, was owned by Eton College, which had acquired it from Henry VIII in exchange for St James's Park. One of the residents, with a weekend cottage overlooking Hampstead Heath, was (later Dame) Henrietta Barnett who was unenthusiastic at the prospect of developments which might generate suburban housing on the Heath. She later described an encounter she and her husband had in 1896, when the Hampstead Tube existed only on paper.[12]

> In 1896 we went to Russia and on the ship we met a man who told us of the schemes of tube travelling of which we are all now cognisant; and that one of the plans was a station just by Wyldes [a farmhouse adjacent to the Heath]. It became therefore imperative to enlarge the Heath and a large Committee was got together whose object was to add eighty acres of open space to the historic Heath.

The identity of the fellow passenger who was so well acquainted with London tube projects is not clear. It may have been Yerkes himself, though there is no record of his having taken a ship to Russia in 1896, and if it was Yerkes one would have expected Henrietta Barnett to mention that he was American, which she omitted to do.

As a result of Henrietta Barnett's campaign 80 acres to the east of the proposed station were purchased for £43,241 16s 4d from Eton College and the land was presented to the London County Council as a permanent addition to Hampstead Heath. Henrietta's protective instincts were now turned to the remainder of the Eton College property, a further 243 acres, now evidently threatened by the prospective tube railway. Another committee was formed and over £200,000 raised, much of it from people who, in Henrietta's words 'loving beauty, grieved over the hideous methods usually pursued as London stretched out its arms into the suburbs'.[13] The remaining land was purchased and became the Hampstead Garden Suburb, designed as a community where different social classes could live together in harmony, in well-designed houses set among green spaces along tree-lined roads. The scheme attracted visits from royalty and the support of architects and planners as distinguished as Raymond Unwin and Sir Edwin Lutyens, though the latter's view of Henrietta was less than flattering: 'a nice woman but proud of being a Philistine – has no idea beyond a window box full of geraniums over which you can see a goose on the green'.

Hampstead Garden Suburb may have been saved from developers of a kind of whom Henrietta disapproved but other communities along the railway line developed according to more conventional commercial impulses. In 1906, the year before the Hampstead Tube opened, 14 houses were built in Golders Green. In the following eight years, up to the outbreak of the First World War, 3,179 houses were completed and Golders Green had changed from a hamlet to a suburb. One of the first houses in this new wave was built for Arthur Waugh, father of Evelyn Waugh. In September 1907, at the age of three, Evelyn Waugh moved with his family to 'Underhill', 145 North End Road,[14] and thus became the youngest member of one of Golders Green's first commuter families as his father travelled daily from the newly opened Golders Green station to the Covent Garden office of Chapman & Hall where he was managing director. Building resumed at the same pace when the war ended and the number of passengers using Golders Green station rose from just over a million in the year the Tube opened to over ten million by the outbreak of war.[15]

Evelyn Waugh, who would probably not want to be remembered as a member of one of Golders Green's first commuter families. (By courtesy of the Estate of Felix H. Man/The National Portrait Gallery, London)

HOMES FIT FOR HEROES

In 1918, as part of the demagogic election campaign which secured his coalition government an enormous parliamentary majority, Lloyd George declared that the task of the new government would be 'to make Britain a country fit for heroes to live in'. Heroes needed homes and during the war very few had been built. The demobilisation which followed the end of the war revealed a serious shortage of good housing, especially in London and the south-east. A short post-war boom ended in 1920 and the depression and unemployment which prompted the government to support the Edgware extension of the Northern Line[16] also saw a sharp drop in material prices and interest rates, which fell from 7 per cent to 2 per cent in little more than a year. In 1923 Bonar Law's Conservative administration offered cash payments of £75 to builders of medium-sized houses with bathrooms at a time when it cost about £500 to build such a house. This was the signal for the post-war housing boom which populated *Metroland* and the rest of suburban London. The Metropolitan Railway was quick to ensure that its surplus lands were used for the benefit of its passenger traffic. The initiative in the matter was taken by the company's general manager, Robert Selbie, who in November 1918 presented to the Board a scheme for estate development and drew to their attention the opportunities that would be presented by the imminent ending of the war and the demobilisation of the armed forces:

> in view of the large demand there will be for houses once Peace is declared and the Forces are demobilised, and also in view of the advertisement the districts served have received during the War, I am of the opinion that the scheme should be taken in hand forthwith.[17]

John Betjeman put the same point with greater style:

> We called you Metroland.
> We laid our schemes
> Lured by the lush brochure, down byways beckoned,
> To build at last the cottage of our dreams,
> A city clerk turned countryman again,
> And linked to the metropolis by train.[18]

Over the years that followed, Metropolitan Country Estates Ltd developed a dozen estates along its route and thereby created *Metro-land*, a term coined by the company in the form of a slogan – 'Live in Metro-land' – which was at one time embossed on the door handles of the company's carriages. The first development was at Pinner where the company built and rented out six-bedroom houses for £65 a year.

"IN METRO-LAND"
The Cedars Estate—Rickmansworth.

(Subsoil Gravel and Sand.)

100 Trains daily—25 minutes journey by Metropolitan Electric Service to Baker Street, and 'Through' City trains morning and evening.

OWING to the popularity of this charming Residential district, with its lovely views, healthy surroundings and exceptional train service for the business man, development on the Cedars Estate is being rigorously pursued, and new roads made to afford a selection of sites upon which prospective purchasers can build their homes.

IN order to assist those who cannot find a house to rent or who do not wish to disturb their capital, a system of purchase has been inaugurated whereby a nominal deposit is payable and the balance as rent, thereby placing the occupier in the position of ultimate Owner instead of a Tenant without interest in the property.

HOUSES
from
£1,075
to
£2,000

DEPOSITS
from
£75 *to* £200

Price £1,400 Freehold - Deposit £150

OTHER ESTATES—
KINGSBURY GARDEN VILLAGE, CHALK HILL ESTATE, WEMBLEY PARK, WEMBLEY PARK ESTATE, ELM GROVE ESTATE AND MANOR FARM ESTATE, RUISLIP. EASTCOTE HILL ESTATE, EASTCOTE, CECIL PARK ESTATE, and GRANGE ESTATES, PINNER.

Purchasers are offered BETTER TERMS than can be obtained elsewhere. "Where to Live" booklet can be obtained *free* from

H. GIBSON
GENERAL OFFICES,
BAKER STREET STATION, N.W.1.
RICKMANSWORTH 182.   LANGHAM 1130.   FREE

The allure of Metroland: an advertisement by the Metropolitan Railway's property company, 1927. (Author)

Although the Metropolitan Railway occasionally built, rented and sold houses on its own account the normal procedure was to lay out the land and then sell plots to speculative builders or private individuals wishing to design their own homes. The houses were mostly intended for the middle classes, with whom *Metroland* became almost synonymous. In Ruislip a 'palace in miniature' with two bedrooms was offered for £450 while at the luxurious Cedars Estate, Rickmansworth, houses were offered in 1927 at prices up to £2,000.[19] One advertisement assured readers that its serving hatch was sound-proofed so that servants in the kitchen would be unable to hear conversations in the dining room. Other communities were quickly developed following the acceptance of Selbie's plan. Wembley, Rickmansworth, Harrow and their surrounding communities were among the first, Harrow being described by the architect Sir Hugh Casson as: 'the capital city of Metroland – that strange Arcady that was the product, some fifty years ago, of a partnership between the Metropolitan Railway and the speculative builder'.[20] The speculative builders may have created Harrow as we know it but they knew their place. They did not intrude upon the Hill on which sat the school of Byron and Churchill, though they did presume to name some of their streets in the valley after Vaughan, Butler, Drury and other headmasters of the school.

SELLING THE HOMES TO THE HEROES

The Metropolitan Railway put its publicity department to work to encourage prospective purchasers. In 1915 it published a booklet called *Metro-land*, aimed at encouraging walkers and cyclists to take their exercise in the areas served by the railway.[21] From 1919 to 1932 *Metro-land* was published annually, the emphasis switching from leisure activities to the promotion of house purchases. Robert Selbie, the general manager, told the magazine *Modern Transport*[22] that 'Railway companies are trusted and not open to the suspicion that often attaches to the speculative builder.' A short essay on each community served by the railway was included but half of the content was devoted to advertisements from builders whose payments enabled the company to sell the 150-page booklet for twopence. Other inducements to live in Metroland took the form of a popular song called *My Little Metroland Home*, while another song urged people to buy houses on the Poplars estate, Ruislip; beginning with the immortal line 'Neath the shade of the Ruislip Poplars, it ended with the excruciating:

> It's a very short distance by rail on the Met
> And at the gate you'll find waiting, sweet Violet.

Neither this strained rhyme nor the accompanying Poplars Waltz made a permanent impact upon music or literature.

The speculative builders themselves showed considerable enterprise in marketing their homes. In 1908 the *Daily Mail* held its first Ideal Home Exhibition and builders were quick to recognise the opportunities it offered for them to advertise their new estates, both in the exhibition itself and in the catalogue. By the 1930s small 'villages' comprising homes of varying designs were a feature of the exhibition and these were followed by show houses erected on sites in central London. Places with large numbers of passing pedestrians were especially popular. Laing erected five houses in Oxford Street, close to Marble Arch, and a substantial residence was incongruously situated next door to a most unattractive tea room in front of King's Cross station. Free travel to developments by train, car, bus and even river steamer was offered to prospective purchasers, together with free light fittings, curtains and house removals once the purchase was completed. Occasionally a year's season ticket to London was offered upon completion of the purchase.

THE GARDEN CITY

Many of the communities which were created presented themselves as being modelled on the fashionable concept of the Garden City, as popularised by Ebenezer Howard at this time. The area around Northwood was originally promoted under the clumsy and

---

EBENEZER HOWARD AND THE GARDEN CITY MOVEMENT

Sir Ebenezer Howard (1850–1928) worked as a shorthand writer in a stockbroker's officer in the City of London before going to Chicago in 1872 where he came under the influence of the philosophers Ralph Waldo Emerson and Walt Whitman. In 1877 he returned to London and became a parliamentary reporter. In 1902 he published *Garden Cities of To-morrow* which advocated the building of small towns, where people would be furnished with allotments and would live close to their places of work. He called them 'garden cities' because of their close proximity to surrounding countryside. In 1902 he formed the Garden City Pioneer Company which raised money from investors on the principle that dividends on the capital would be limited to 4 per cent and surplus profits would be reinvested in amenities for the community. Lord Northcliffe was one of the subscribers and his *Daily Mail* encouraged other investors to support the construction of Letchworth Garden City, which Howard called 'a town designed for healthy living'. Welwyn Garden City followed in 1920 and Howard lived there for the rest of his life. From the start, shortage of finance meant that many houses were owned by their occupiers rather than by the community but Howard's ideas, though diluted, were admired and exerted considerable influence over town planning in the twentieth century both in Britain and overseas, where *Garden Cities of To-morrow* was translated into many languages. Howard was knighted in 1927. His ideas were particularly prominent during the time that *Metroland* was being created: hence the attachment of the suffix Garden Village or Garden City to many of the estates, though by urbanising the countryside they colonised, Metroland's communities may be said to have contravened Howard's principles.

---

unconvincing name *Ruislip-Northwood Garden City* until a newspaper competition produced the more attractive *Northwood Hills*. The prize cost the developer £5.

At Neasden, Kingsbury Garden Village, which was unusual in being intended primarily for working-class families, was described by an estate agent as:

> A model garden village, on which a number of semi-detached residences have been erected. Peace and quiet prevail, and the stretches of country around offer plenty of opportunity for invigorating exercise to those who are inclined to walking and cycling.[23]

The rickety wooden halt in the middle of fields at Rayners Lane had been opened in 1906 to provide a railway service to two sewage farms. In 1929 it was chosen as the site of Harrow Garden Village where the builder, E.S. Reid, assured prospective buyers:

> wherever you choose a house on this estate you may rest assured that you will be surrounded by other E.S. Reid houses and you may be sure that you will not have a nasty cheap mass-production house anywhere near you to lower the value of your property.

One can detect the black arts of estate agency being honed in these phrases but in those innocent days, when Metroland was introducing the idea of owner-occupation to millions of middle-class families for whom it would previously have been unattainable, the exhortations worked. They worked particularly quickly at Harrow Garden Village. In 1931 Reid celebrated the opening of the first phase of his development with a fireworks display to which prospective buyers could travel at specially reduced rates on

Rayners Lane temporary station, built to serve the sewage works, was 'all peace and quiet' in 1935, but by 1938 (below) things were very different. (London's Transport Museum)

Metropolitan trains. In the space of five years the number of passengers using Rayners Lane Halt increased from twenty-two thousand to four million and in 1938 the wooden halt, collapsing under the weight of traffic, was replaced by one of Charles Holden's classic designs. The slogan under which the houses were sold – 'Living in Rayners Lane would be all peace and quiet' – was tactfully acknowledged by the final issue of *Metroland*, in 1932, as no longer applicable: 'the quiet rustic beauty of old Rayners Lane is now a thing of the past'.

Other developments in the marketing of suburban housing began at the same time. By the 1920s pages devoted to property were a regular feature of the *Daily Express* with its *Modern Homes Guide*. In February 1923 the *Evening News* launched a weekly page of advertisements called *The Homeseeker's Guide*. The advertisements were often illustrated with small pictures of the desirable residences on offer and may be regarded as the precursors of the pages of estate agents' advertisements which are an inescapable feature of local newspapers in the twenty-first century. They carried alluring headlines such as 'Pack up Your Troubles' (a play on a First World War song which in this case encouraged readers to buy a house in Essex); 'Why Pay Rent?' (buy a house in Streatham) and 'Easy Terms can be Arranged' (for a house in Wembley Park costing £1,125).[24] Ten years later houses in Perivale, on the planned (but not yet completed) Central Line extension, were available for £690.

To novel methods of promotion were added new methods of financing house purchase. The extension of the idea of owner-occupation to groups who had previously rented property was an important ingredient in Metroland's success. Building societies had traditionally required a deposit of at least 20 per cent of the value of a house but in the 1920s this cautious arrangement was supplanted by the Builders' Pool System, whereby speculative builders effectively underwrote the borrower's mortgage by depositing with the building society a proportion of the house's purchase price. This enabled borrowers to obtain mortgages of as much as 95 per cent of the value of the houses they were buying. Thus houses in Rickmansworth were offered for as little as £25 deposit on houses costing between £1,000 and £2,000. For those unfamiliar with mortgages the scheme was described as follows: 'a system of purchase has been inaugurated whereby a nominal deposit is payable, and the balance as rent, thereby placing the occupier in the position of ultimate Owner instead of a Tenant'.[25] Special offers included surveys offered free of charge while the Metropolitan Railway encouraged the process by offering free first-class train travel at weekends for families visiting prospective homes in Metroland.

The estate agents had done their work. Between 1901 and 1937 the population of inner London declined by almost half a million while that of the suburbs grew by two-and-a-half million as *Metroland* and equivalent communities elsewhere on the network created a new style of suburban living characterised by middle-class, commuting owner-occupiers.[26] The figures in the following table show the growth in population of suburban communities between the years 1901 and 1931, all of them offering a good supply of profitable passengers:[27]

	1901 census	1931 census
Edgware	868	5,352
Harrow Weald	1,517	10,923
Kingsbury	757	16,636
Pinner	3,094	23,082
Ruislip	1,441	16,042
Wembley	3,753	48,561

CHILTERN COURT

Although the Metropolitan Railway's activities in the property market were mostly designed to increase the line's suburban passenger traffic, the management did not hesitate to profit directly from the development of the company's Baker Street headquarters when the opportunity presented itself. In January 1925 the enterprising Robert Selbie presented to the Board an ambitious plan to build half a million square feet of shops and luxury flats over the station, to be called Chiltern Court.[28] Harrods was invited to take space on three floors but when it turned down the opportunity, small shops were put there instead. The flats ranged from huge, ten-room Mansion Flats to three-room Bachelor Flats. Thirty small bedrooms for maids were also included. The development was prominently featured in the final edition of *Metro-land*, published in 1932, whose writer explained: 'The governing idea in the planning of the flats has been to secure quiet, unobtrusive luxury combined with the highest degree of comfort and convenience.' One suspects that these ringing phrases were the work of the company's estate agent, Mr Gibson, whose offices were at the company headquarters, also at Baker Street.

Among the first tenants were the authors Arnold Bennett and H.G. Wells, and the artist E. McKnight Kauffer, whose work in designing posters for the Underground railways is described in Chapter Six. As a gesture to what was supposed to be the real purpose of Metropolitan property development Selbie assured the Board that the wealthy tenants of the flats would be sure to use the railway to travel to their offices in the City and to their golf clubs and country homes at weekends. However, the rental income of over £40,000 a year on an investment of £500,000 must also have had its attractions since this was a far higher rate of return than could be made from running the railway. On the ground floor was the Chiltern Court restaurant, seating 250 diners, which was opened amid much splendour in November 1929. Complete with a musicians' gallery,

Chiltern Court, Baker Street, a fashionable London residence constructed by the Metropolitan Railway, and home to Arnold Bennett and H.G. Wells, among many others. (London's Transport Museum)

the building was designed by Charles Clark, architect to the Metropolitan Railway and one of Metroland's most important architects since he also designed houses built at Pinner in the first of the railway's developments. Chiltern Court remains one of the more attractive buildings in Marylebone.

METROLAND'S FAMILY

Other suburban communities sprang up at the same time, with similar characteristics and serving the same purpose for the Underground railway companies in generating medium-distance passenger traffic. A striking example, bordering Metroland, was Edgware.[29] This village had grown up as a staging post on Watling Street (now the A5) where northbound horse-drawn vehicles could stop for hay and water. The coming of the railways in the 1830s robbed it of much of this traffic and at the dawn of the twentieth century it had barely a thousand inhabitants, served by a Great Northern Railway branch line from Finsbury Park. In 1902 a Bill was proposed for an Edgware to Hampstead

Railway to link with the proposed Hampstead Tube. No progress had been made with the scheme when the Hampstead Tube opened in 1907 but this did not blind the enterprising estate agent and property developer George Cross to the potential profits if the tube were ever to be extended. In 1910 he opened an office in Edgware but the community continued to be served by its inadequate Great Northern branch line and the business failed to flourish.[30] Nevertheless in 1919, recognising that there would be a demand for housing following the ending of the First World War, he purchased 70 acres of poor farmland in Edgware, close to the village centre, at £175 an acre. The rural character of the area was such that, on his first visit to his new property, Cross narrowly escaped death at the hands of a shooting party in pursuit of partridges. Five years later, in August 1924, the Hampstead Tube opened its extension to Edgware and three months later Cross began to advertise three-bedroom semis for £1,100. Premises around the station he let to Sainsbury's, W.H. Smith and the Midland Bank. By the end of the following year he had disposed of virtually all his property at a profit of £56,000 – four times his initial outlay. An elderly lady who had inadvertently purchased a property close to the future Edgware station for £4,000 in 1921 was besieged by developers and sold it, reluctantly, for £29,000 shortly before the railway opened. Given that such profits could be made as a result of railway development one understands why Frank Pick, in his evidence to the Barlow Committee, had pleaded for some of the proceeds to be invested in railways.[31]

On 9 July 1926 the *Golders Green Gazette*, showing a friendly interest in the development of its northern neighbour, declared that Edgware was now a 'beautiful garden suburb, on a hillside facing south, protected from north winds and catching every gleam of sunshine'. By 1939 the population had reached 13,000 and Edgware had become the home of one of Britain's thriving Jewish communities who had followed the Northern Line out beyond the larger community of their co-religionists in Golders Green. A synagogue was opened in the 'beautiful garden suburb' of Edgware in 1934.

A Limit is Reached

An attempt to extend the line beyond Edgware met with fierce local resistance. In 1937 the London Passenger Transport Act authorised the extension of the Northern Line from Edgware to Bushey Heath and Aldenham, where the Board planned to build a new maintenance depot and sidings. This occurred at a time when the need to create a 'Green Belt' around London was being debated. Taking on the mantle of Henrietta Barnett in Hampstead the headmaster of Aldenham School, G.A. Riding, wrote to *The Times* suggesting that the real motive of the Board was not to build a depot but to create a new source of passengers:

> it is suspected that the 'development' of the whole area by the creation of a further 'dormitory' suburb is at least as important in the eyes of the board as the provision of

sheds and sidings for its rolling stock. . . . [The Board really wanted] to create artificial centres of population in the few precious and unspoilt areas around London under the pretence of 'serving' communities which either have no desire to be so served or do not exist.[32]

The Labour MP Philip Noel-Baker, better known for his work as a peace campaigner than for his views on underground railways, denounced the proposed extension in Parliament, declaring that:

It is proposed to destroy a piece of admirable country which cannot be replaced. . . . Already land values in this area have risen enormously since the plans of the London Passenger Transport Board were first divulged, and a rise in land values is always the surest sign of the jerrybuilders' wrath to come. All this is to be risked for the sake of a depot.[33]

He forecast 'ribbon development of the absolutely atrocious kind' but despite these pleas to exclude Metroland-style development from this part of Hertfordshire, work actually began on the extension and much of the depot at Aldenham was completed. During the war the depot was pressed into service as an aircraft factory and after 1945 it became a bus repair depot. It was never linked to the railway whose partly built tunnels, viaducts

The sad, graffiti-covered relics of the planned Northern Line extension in a field at Edgwarebury. (Author)

and signal-boxes were left to languish when work on them ceased at the outbreak of the Second World War. They remain to this day, graffitti-covered ruins, as a forlorn reminder of a railway that might have been. Edgware, with its flourishing Jewish community, has Hitler to thank for the fact that it remained the northern outpost of the Northern Line's version of Metroland, with the green belt on its doorstep.

THE GREEN BELT

In 1580 Elizabeth I issued a proclamation forbidding the construction of new buildings on a belt of land 3 miles wide around the City of London, the intention being to prevent the spread of plague. The effectiveness of this measure was severely compromised by the fact that dispensations could be granted in exchange for payments to the Crown – a source of revenue that was all too tempting for cash-strapped monarchs. For the next three centuries the idea of a green belt around London was in abeyance. In 1890 Lord Meath, chairman of the London County Council Parks Committee, returned from a visit to Chicago where he had been impressed by the broad open spaces of that windy lakeside city. In 1891 his committee was asked by the LCC to consider:

> the desirability of the Council drawing the attention of Parliament, by petition or otherwise, to the need for statutory control and direction as to the extension of building in the suburbs of the county of London and in the adjacent parts of the neighbouring counties, as affecting the health and sanitary condition generally of the metropolis.[34]

Nothing happened as a result of this strangulated prose. Thirty-three years passed before the council returned to the theme. In 1924, as the development of Metroland gathered pace, the LCC asked its town planning committee to consider 'whether or not the preservation of a green belt or unbuilt-on zone or zones within the bounds of or adjacent to Greater London is desirable and practicable and, if so, what steps can be taken to effect this'. This clumsy phraseology contains the first reference to the 'green belt'.

In the years that followed Raymond Unwin[35] produced two reports for the LCC which recommended that land devoted to playing fields and open spaces in the London area needed to be more than double the existing provision and that, to compensate for the lack of open spaces, a 'green girdle' of parkland should be created around the capital. The girdle would be about 5 miles wide and the outer boundary would pass close to Brentwood, Sevenoaks, Dorking, Slough and St Albans.[36] Acting upon these recommendations the Labour leader of the LCC, Herbert Morrison, made an offer to neighbouring councils that the LCC would share the cost of buying up land in the 'girdle' and preserve it against development, £2 million being set aside for this purpose. In little more than a year 30 square miles had been acquired by this means. In 1938 the Green Belt (London and Home Counties) Act gave statutory authority to the scheme, allowing councils to acquire land in the belt or to prohibit new development within it. This measure, in effect, set the boundary to Metroland and similar developments. Further refinements were incorporated in the Greater London Plan (1944) of Patrick Abercrombie, while the Town and Country Planning Act 1947, with its restrictions on development, secured the future of the green belt. The further expansion of London would leapfrog the green belt to new towns like Hemel Hempstead, Harlow, Stevenage and Crawley, well beyond the reach of the Underground.

THOMAS THE TANK ENGINE

In November 1935 the London Passenger Transport Board closed the Brill Tramway which linked Quainton Road to the hilltop village of Brill in the Vale of Aylesbury. In 1891 Sir Edward Watkin had acquired the Aylesbury and Buckingham Railway as part of his dream of creating a rail service from Manchester to Paris via a channel tunnel, with Quainton Road as the 'Clapham Junction' of the Watkin empire. The Brill Tramway

Quainton Road station, now a museum, was the 'Clapham Junction' of Sir Edward Watkin's dream. (Author)

Brill line locomotive, with chain drive. (London's Transport Museum)

Engine no. 23 with wagons & coaches on Brill Tramway. Note the prominent condenser pipe (*see* p. 18). (London's Transport Museum)

followed shortly afterwards. At Quainton Road, he vainly hoped, trains from every part of the kingdom would pass one another on their journeys to and from the continent.[37] The closure of this remote line prompted a flood of nostalgic correspondence to *The Times* from the local community.[38] This revealed that it had originally been planned by the Duke of Buckingham as the first stage of the Oxford and Aylesbury Tramroad, for the convenience of his tenants, to run from Aylesbury to a terminus at Magdalen Bridge, Oxford, though it never went beyond Brill. The carriages had been drawn at a speed of 4mph by a traction engine, shunting operations being carried out by a horse. In its final years it had been operated by one of Daniel Gooch's 'condenser engines', used by the Metropolitan in its early steam days.[39] The Metropolitan Railway used special milk vans to collect milk churns from the many farms in the area. A lady correspondent to *The Times* recalled that, when carriages came off the rails, farm labourers ran from neighbouring fields to help the passengers push them back on to the track. It is, perhaps, reassuring to reflect that this railway, which seems to belong to the pages of the Revd Awdry and the adventures of Thomas the Tank Engine, was once part of the Metropolitan Railway system: indeed it was the furthest outpost of Metroland.

CHAPTER SIX
LORENZO THE MAGNIFICENT: THE UNDERGROUND'S ARTISTIC HERITAGE

For he was, to add a last word, the greatest patron of the arts whom this century
has so far produced in England, and indeed the ideal patron of our age.

(Frank Pick, as described by Nikolaus Pevsner)

I have always kept in mind my own frailties – a short temper, impatience with fools,
quickness rather than thoroughness. I am a bad hand at the gracious word or
casual congratulation.

(Frank Pick, September 1939)

TEASPOONS TO TRAINS

In October 1978 the Victoria & Albert Museum mounted an exhibition called *Teaspoons
to Trains*. It was a celebration of the centenary of the birth of Frank Pick (1878–1941),
managing director of the Underground Group from 1928 and vice-chairman of the
London Passenger Transport Board from its formation in 1933. Never before or since
has the head of a commercial undertaking been honoured by such an exhibition. Frank
Pick's enlightened use of art and design in the service of commerce earned him the
accolade from one writer that he was 'the nearest approach to Lorenzo the Magnificent
that a modern democracy can achieve'.[1] In his introduction to the exhibition catalogue
Roy Strong, the director of the Victoria & Albert Museum, wrote of Pick that his view of
modern design was in harmony with that of the museum itself 'in his aspiration to the
highest design standards in public service and in his attention to detail. . . . Public
services, if guided by imagination of the type of Pick's era, could be responsible for a
much needed renaissance in design.'[2] He set design standards for London's transport
network that influenced his successors and sometimes inspired them to show enterprise
on their own account, as in the introduction of poetry and, more recently, of
mathematical concepts in posters on trains and stations. Nor was his influence confined
to the Underground. In his capacity as chairman of the Council for Art and Industry he

was called upon to advise on the furnishings, fittings and accoutrements of the *Queen Mary*, samples of which (including teaspoons) spent long periods in his office while he reflected upon their suitability. This chapter will consider the role of the London Underground in introducing good modern designs in art and architecture to the everyday lives of those who use its facilities.

PREDECESSORS

Pick's predecessors had already made some notable contributions to the London skyline and to the design of its Underground stations. Stations on the City and South London Railway had adopted a uniform design developed by the architect T.P. Figgis (1858–1948), a prominent member of the Victorian Arts and Crafts movement. Single-storey brick stations were surmounted by prominent domes which accommodated the lift mechanism. The station buildings on the Yerkes tubes had been designed by Leslie Green (1875–1908), whose premature death at the age of only thirty-three may have been hastened by the pressure of designing over fifty stations for the tubes under the direction of Yerkes himself, who insisted that each of his three lines (Bakerloo, Hampstead and Piccadilly) should have a distinct design while incorporating common features that would identify them as belonging to the Yerkes family: an early example of 'corporate identity' that was to become such a fashionable concept much later in the century. Single-storey stations were faced with dark red terracotta. Many of these survive, notably the one at Gloucester Road, now restored, where a comparison can be made between the red terracotta of the 1906 Yerkes Piccadilly Line station and the more restrained pale brickwork of the District Railway station, designed by John Fowler and opened in 1868, and now a listed building.[3] It would be difficult to describe the terracotta finish as beautiful: utilitarian might be more appropriate, though it clearly represents an attempt to find a house style. At platform level each line had a slightly different arrangement of coloured tiles which identified the separate lines and picked out the individual station name in large, dark tiling. Hyde Park Corner and Mornington Crescent remain good examples of this feature. Pick may thus be said to have inherited a tradition of industrial design but his own contributions far exceeded those of his flamboyant predecessor.

FRANK PICK (1878–1941)

Born in Spalding, Lincolnshire, the son of a draper, Frank Pick went to school in York. After training as a solicitor he joined the North Eastern Railway in York in 1902 and followed its general manager, George Gibb, when the latter joined the Underground company in 1907. In 1928 Pick became managing director of the Underground Group and, with Lord Ashfield (*see* panel on p. 83), was responsible for the dominant position

Frank Pick, Chief Executive and 'Lorenzo the Magnificent' of the underground. (London's Transport Museum)

which the Group assumed in London's transport network in the 1920s and 1930s. A shy, reserved and occasionally severe man, Pick worked exceptionally hard himself and expected the same of colleagues, who sometimes found him cold and intimidating. He kept two full-time secretaries busy but he also wrote letters to colleagues in his own hand, his striking green ink alerting the recipients to the identity of the writer and the need for a swift and convincing response. His personal assistant from 1936 to 1939 was Anthony Bull who, in 1924, had driven the first train through the Camden Loop linking the northern and southern branches of the Northern Line as described in Chapter Four.[4] Anthony Bull described Pick, for whom he clearly felt much affection, as 'A man of no social graces, a perfectionist',[5] and he compared Pick's management style with that of Lord Ashfield, his chairman. Ashfield was warm, worldly and sociable, at his ease among politicians and financiers yet able to exchange pleasantries with junior staff and put them at their ease. Pick was an austere, teetotal Quaker who described his recreations in *Who's Who?* as 'the wider aspects of transport and seeing the world'. Ashfield would sometimes tell his staff 'I'm going riding' and would spend an afternoon travelling on trains or buses, chatting to passengers and staff, listening to their opinions and complaints. Pick's visits were more like a military inspection. Every other Friday he would visit a garage, maintenance depot or other site to satisfy himself that everything was as he wished. If it wasn't, withering letters in green ink would swiftly follow. After one such visit he took his young assistant, Bull, to lunch at the Reform Club. He looked on disapprovingly as Bull ordered a Guinness. Putting down his glass of water he commented 'I don't know how you can drink something that looks so disgusting.' But Pick was aware of his shortcomings. In September 1939 he wrote to Anthony Bull:

> I have always kept in mind my own frailties – a short temper, impatience with fools, quickness rather than thoroughness. I am a bad hand at the gracious word or casual congratulation.[6]

Every month he went through the Underground Group's accounts, line by line, with the single exception of the telephone bill, explaining that 'The telephone is such an awful instrument I cannot believe anyone would use it unless it was absolutely essential.' He was vice-chairman of the London Passenger Transport Board upon its formation in 1933 and Director-General of the Ministry of Information in the early part of the Second World War before his untimely death. Appropriately, he made his home in Hampstead Garden Suburb, a community which flourished as a result of the extension of the Underground network.[7]

Pick insisted, publicly,[8] that his interest in art and design was purely that of the salesman who was trying to promote travel. One commentator has described the role of industrial design in Pick's eyes as one 'by which he aimed not only to make the traveller's journey as pleasant as possible but also to impress on the traveller's mind the remarkable efficiency of the whole system'.[9] However, Sir Nikolaus Pevsner has suggested that this posture was assumed for the benefit of Pick's shareholders and fellow directors and that his true interest ran much deeper.[10] Pevsner refers to the millions of people who were exposed in their daily travels by Underground to the work of design schools of which they had never heard. He writes:[11]

> it can safely be said that no exhibition of modern painting, no lecturing, no school teaching, can have had anything like so wide an effect on the educatable masses as the unceasing production and display of [Underground] posters over the years 1930–1940.

Frank Pick's interest in design can be traced with certainty to 1915 when his name was attached to a memorandum addressed to the President of the Board of Trade, drawing attention to the advances made by German industry as a result of improvements in quality and design under the influence of the *Werkbund* whose aim was the 'co-operation of art, industry and crafts in the ennoblement of commercial activity'.[12] Other signatories to the memorandum included Lord Aberconway (chairman of the Metropolitan Railway), Gordon Selfridge and H.G. Wells. There swiftly followed an exhibition in Goldsmiths' Hall, London, entitled *Exhibition of German and Austrian Articles typifying successful design*. The exhibition catalogue commended 'the founders of the modern movement in Germany' for eschewing unnecessary ornamentation and for promoting 'appropriateness, technical perfection and honest workmanship'. The exhibition itself and the praise bestowed on the exhibits are all the more remarkable in view of the anti-German sentiments that were sweeping the country at this early stage in the First World War.

In the month that the exhibition ended, May 1915, the Design and Industries Association (DIA) was formed, with Frank Pick as one of its founding members. The *Werkbund* repaid the earlier compliment by publishing an account of the DIA's foundation and its early projects. The first exhibition organised by the DIA opened at the Whitechapel Art Gallery in October 1915 and was on *Design and Workmanship in Printing*. In the years that followed Pick found time to contribute thoughtful articles to the DIA Yearbook on a matter as remote from Underground trains as 'Design in Cities' (1926–7 Yearbook) and in 1933 he gave a talk on the BBC on 'Modern Design', despite the fact that he had just become vice-chairman of the newly formed London Passenger Transport Board with the immediate task of sorting out the burdens inherited from over thirty years of unregulated competition. In the same year, despite his numerous other responsibilities, he had agreed to become chairman of the newly formed Council for Art and Industry, a forerunner of the Design Council. A bizarre episode resulted from a lecture Pick prepared in 1933 on street furniture. He asked the 25-year-old Anthony Bull, then an assistant in the Underground publicity office, to obtain photographs to illustrate the lecture. One such photograph, to illustrate 'Street Lighting for Pleasure', was to be of the Reeperbahn, the notorious red light district in Hamburg. Bull, who was about to take a holiday in Germany with a friend, duly visited the Reeperbahn and entered a bar that was displaying photographs of the lights. Two girls immediately planted themselves in the laps of the English visitors. The photographs were delivered to Pick but the austere Quaker was spared an account of the events which accompanied their taking.

In 1932 Pick became president of the Design and Industries Association and mounted an exhibition of well-designed British goods in the booking hall of Charing Cross (now Embankment) Underground station, where good design was exposed to the hundreds of thousands of passengers who used this busiest of stations. Further exhibitions followed and the tradition continued after Pick's death, with an exhibition in 1953 called *Register your Choice* inviting visitors to choose between a room furnished with DIA-approved designs and another equipped with popular best-sellers. Thirty thousand votes were cast, almost two-thirds of them for the DIA products. Given this consistent pattern of support, it may be concluded with some confidence that Pick's interest in good design went well beyond that required to sell tickets for trains. Pevsner suggests that Pick's credo was that of the DIA itself: 'fitness for purpose and simplicity are the key to good design'.

'TRAFFIC ALL DAY LONG'

In March 1908, as Speyer and Gibb struggled to save the company from liquidation,[14] Stanley, the general manager, called a meeting of his officers, including Frank Pick, and demanded from each of them a letter of resignation dated September 1908, six months later. The resignations would take effect if the fortunes of the company did not improve. The concentration of minds achieved by this brutal process had the required effect and in September 1908 Stanley was able to tell his anxious subordinates that the situation had improved to the point at which their resignations would not be put into effect, though some suspected that he kept the letters in his desk in case they were needed later.[15] Pick had long complained to Stanley about the poor quality of the company's publicity so in April 1909 Stanley appointed Pick to the newly created post of Traffic Development Officer, with responsibility for developing new lines and services and publicising existing ones. It is not clear why Stanley chose him for a task which was crucial for the future of the organisation but for which Pick's training as a solicitor gave him no relevant qualifications. The management of the Underground had long recognised that off-peak travel was critical to the profitable operation of a system with such a heavy burden of investment in fixed assets. In Ashfield's words, the system would 'need traffic all day long and not just at the tidal movements of business'.[16] Pick's previous employers, the North Eastern Railway, had used posters to promote travel to seaside resorts like Scarborough but Pick himself had no previous experience of publicity work and had to learn as he went. It is possible that Stanley appointed him to the post to stop his stream of complaints about the quality of the company's publicity: in effect calling his bluff. It was an inspired choice, though Pick was characteristically self-deprecatory in his account of his early work:

> After many fumbling experiments I arrived at some notion of what poster advertising ought to be. Everyone seemed quite pleased with what I did and I got a reputation that really sprang out of nothing.[17]

THE ART OF THE POSTER

Pick enjoyed some luck in his timing. The work of William Morris and the Kelmscott Press in the latter part of the nineteenth century had raised to a high level the standards of printing bold, clear designs on flat surfaces and Pick was able to put these techniques to work in designing posters which promoted both suburban living and leisure travel in areas served by the Underground. However, not everyone approved of the uses to which the new processes were being put. They had brought into existence an industry devoted to the advertising of everything from seaside resorts and soap to alcoholic drinks and quack medicines. William Morris himself wrote of the 'daily increasing hideousness of the posters' and railways both above and below ground were a particular object of criticism. Railways were attractive to advertisers in the days when mass-circulation newspapers were still building their circulation[18] because of the large numbers of potential consumers who converged on their stations; and the advertisements were attractive to the railways because of the additional revenue they brought. Consequently both the stations themselves and the roads leading to them became so plastered with posters that passengers had difficulty finding essential information like station names and route maps. In the words of Pick's biographer, stations 'had become a sort of breeding ground, disfiguring whole neighbourhoods with the ugly symptoms of their disease'.[19] So pervasive was the problem that, on the opening of the Bakerloo Line, a passenger wrote to *The Times* applauding the fact that it was possible 'to alight at the station required without having to hunt through all the soap, pills, whisky, milk etc. to find the name of the station', and commending the company for its restraint. Within weeks the Bakerloo Line was amply furnished with posters.

One of Pick's first priorities was to introduce some order to this confusion. Designated areas were set aside at station entrances for the company's route maps so that passengers always knew where to find these essential travel aids. Commercial advertising, from which the company derived substantial revenue, was confined to platforms and passages. Station walls were divided into units of standard size, based on the dimensions of a printer's double crown poster, 30in high by 20in wide. From 1908 the station names themselves were displayed on an early version of the famous bar and circle, the station name appearing in white lettering on a blue bar across a solid red disc at regular intervals on the station walls, thus breaking up the run of advertising material.[20]

Pick next turned his attention to the production of posters designed to encourage the off-peak leisure travel that the company's finances so badly needed. There were precedents for this. The Underground railways had long recognised the opportunities presented by special events such as exhibitions and athletic spectacles. In the nineteenth century the records of the Metropolitan and District Railways frequently contained optimistic assessments of the traffic to be generated by exhibitions at Earl's Court, Olympia and elsewhere. Particular hopes were attached to the Colonial and Indian Exhibition of 1886 which attracted 5.5 million visitors, and Barnum's circus which drew crowds to Olympia in 1888–9. A special extension to Wood Lane (White City) had been built by the Central Line in 1908 to accommodate visitors to the Franco-British Exhibition and later the same year the Olympic Games at the nearby White City stadium generated further traffic.[21]

UNDERGROUND TO ANYWHERE

Pick, however, did not want to depend upon occasional spectacular events organised by other people to generate traffic. He wanted posters which would put ideas for travel into the minds of potential customers for regular, even commonplace activities. In his own words, 'A poster must awaken a purpose in the mind, must stimulate a motive.' The earliest posters which he commissioned were from established commercial artists like John Hassall, who had already produced humorous advertising material for Colman's mustard, for the Great Northern Railway and for early vacuum cleaners. His design 'No need to ask a P'liceman' (1908) was one of the first that Pick commissioned and it made use of the advertising slogan for which fourteen-year-old Edwin Parrington had been paid £10.[22] The poster shows an Underground station booking hall, uncluttered by advertising material, a route map clearly displayed and the reassuring presence of a London bobby. It suggests a network offering a full range of cheap, safe, quick services. Many similar examples of 'generic' advertising for the network as a whole were used. They showed people of all ages and classes using the system, though top hats, smart gowns and exotic millinery were frequently featured – the implication being that if fashionable people were prepared to commit themselves to the Underground then it was suitable also for everyone else. Examples are shown in the colour section. For the same reason posters were produced showing works in progress: new lines being built, stations being modernised and new equipment being introduced.

SPECIAL EVENTS AND INTERESTING PLACES

A second category of poster promoted special occasions such as the annual air pageants at Hendon aerodrome which became a very popular spectacle in the years between the wars. In 1931 the event set a record for the number of passengers handled by a suburban station when 820 trains delivered 108,000 passengers in one day to the small station at Colindale near the end of the Northern Line. Sporting events also featured prominently in this category, including the boat race, tennis at Wimbledon and the Cup Final at Wembley, all of them accessible by Underground.

Some of the most interesting and imaginative posters featured not events but places, the aim being to arouse in the traveller's mind the desire to visit them at any time. Thus Mabel Lucie Attwell, best remembered as an illustrator of children's books like *Alice in Wonderland* and *Peter Pan*, designed posters to encourage parents and teachers to take children to Eastcote in the heart of still-rural Metroland in 1913. Destinations to which travellers were encouraged to travel in and around London included Hampstead Heath, Kew Gardens, museums, galleries and the royal parks, some of these posters being designed by artists like Rex Whistler.[23] The posters were sometimes accompanied by illustrated booklets which encouraged people to visit places of interest in and around

Posters like this encouraged people to use the Underground system for leisure as well as work. (London's Transport Museum)

London. Twenty-six such booklets were produced by the Underground's publicity department with titles like *City Churches*, *London's Markets* and *Epping Forest*. They were among the first such guides to London and were usually distributed free of charge.

UNDERGROUND ART

In his early days Pick experienced some difficulty in persuading serious artists to undertake commercial work. In 1912 he contacted an artist called Ernest Jackson, who had founded the Senefelder Club to encourage a higher standard of work in the developing art of lithographic printing. Jackson persuaded some fellow artists to produce a series of posters depicting aspects of life in the capital. Frank Brangwyn's *The Way of Business*, featuring also a quotation from the nineteenth-century chronicler Richard Jefferies on the work of London docks, appeared in 1913 and this was followed by A.S. Hartrick's *Folk-dancers*. Hartrick had worked in Paris and was a friend of Gauguin, Van Gogh and Toulouse-Lautrec, who had himself made the poster an acceptable artistic medium in France. The

Frank Brangwyn's poster was based on the work of the London docks. (London's Transport Museum)

poster designed for Pick was Hartrick's first excursion into commercial art. In 1914 the originals of these posters were acquired by the Victoria & Albert Museum.

Posters had thus become a respectable medium in much of the artistic community and from this time poster design began to attract artists of stature. Pick encouraged them to apply to their subjects styles and treatments not normally found in conventional advertising. The most prominent of these artists was an American called Edward McKnight Kauffer (1890–1954). In 1914 Kauffer passed through England on his way back to the United States from Paris. He was introduced to Frank Pick who was impressed by the quality of his work and asked him to produce some landscapes of the Surrey countryside. Kauffer postponed his return to America for twenty-six years and, during that period, turned entirely to commercial art, becoming the Underground Group's principal designer of posters as they became his principal source of income. His fellow artist Paul Nash (1889–1946), who himself designed posters for the Underground, wrote that Kauffer was

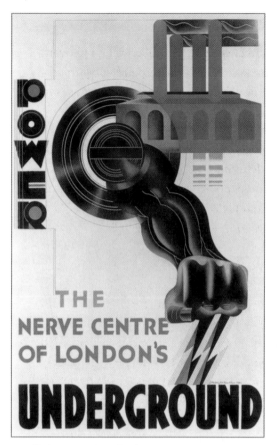

Kauffer's *Power*. (London's Transport Museum)

'responsible above anyone else for the change in attitude towards commercial art in this country'. His work penetrated fashionable society in the 1920s so that Charles Ryder, the narrator and central character of Evelyn Waugh's *Brideshead Revisited*, decorated his rooms at Oxford with Van Gogh's *Sunflowers* and a Kauffer poster. Kauffer's work has subsequently been the subject of exhibitions at the Museum of Modern Art in New York and the Victoria & Albert Museum.

Pick encouraged Kauffer to experiment with different styles and these are reflected in his later work. He was briefly associated with the vorticists. Their ideas (in the words of the poet Ezra Pound, 'the vortex is the point of maximum energy') may be detected in some of Kauffer's work of the 1920s and early 1930s such as *Power*. Other eminent artists employed by the Underground at this time and later included Paul Nash and Graham Sutherland, many of them earning their first commissions in this way. Nash also helped to design the textiles used in the 1938 tube stock, choosing colours and designs that would look well on surface trains in natural light and on underground trains in artificial light. Through the work of such artists thousands of travellers who would not have thought of visiting an art gallery were exposed to artists, designs and styles they would not otherwise have encountered. The tradition continued after Pick's death with Len Deighton, later better known as a novelist, producing a poster in 1957 while later artists felt sufficiently confident of the sophistication of Underground travellers to be able to make fun of some modern masters, even using a version of the Underground map for the purpose, as in the 'Tate' poster in the colour section.

In 1924 Kauffer wrote the definitive work on poster design, *The Art of the Poster*.[24] He dedicated it to Frank Pick, a reflection of Pick's central role in the development of this art form. In the same year the influential magazine *Studio*, declared 'This is the day of the poster' and wrote of Frank Pick that he had 'provided the mainspring for the modern British school which, but for London's Underground, might never have existed in its present form'. Nikolaus Pevsner, a man not given to over-statement when praising others, was even more emphatic, describing Pick as 'the greatest patron of the arts whom this century has so far produced in England, and indeed the ideal patron of our age'.[25]

A New Alphabet

In 1908 the various independent companies that constituted the Underground network had, after some debate, agreed to adopt the common name 'Underground' for purposes of promotion but they still employed a jumble of different typefaces, logos, signs and posters. Pick commissioned the well-known calligrapher Edward Johnston to design a new style of lettering to replace the 'grotesque' type which predominated on the network. Though plain, the grotesque style could be heavy and clumsy, especially in signs conveying a lot of information. The new lettering was to be bold, clear, modern and suitable for use on display material such as station names, direction signs and posters. Edward Johnston, who had originally studied medicine, had abandoned his medical career owing to illness and turned to calligraphy, making a study of lettering styles from the classical world. He set up an artistic community at Ditchling in Sussex, where he was joined by other artists. These included Eric Gill who later devised his own typeface (Gill Sans) based on Johnston's and who also produced some notable sculptures for the Underground headquarters at 55 Broadway. In 1906 Johnston had written an influential book called *Writing and Illuminating and Lettering* which may have caught Pick's attention. Johnston produced the first version of his new lettering, officially called *Underground Railway Block*, in 1916 and it was incorporated in Underground display material produced thereafter. He continued to work on it until 1929, producing versions for use in smaller font sizes though no font less than 36 point exists (½in) and it was not intended for use in large bodies of text. The font is clear, plain and based on simple geometrical forms such as squares and circles. A later version of the typeface, known as *New Johnston*, was developed in the 1980s. It is designed to be computer-typeset and is used in publicity brochures and other small fonts. Johnston also designed the revised Underground bar and circle logo and Pevsner suggests that Pick's influence was felt here. Pick had been impressed by the YMCA triangle and asked Johnston for something similar.[26]

Station Architecture

Pick's interest in stations was not confined to the posters that adorned them. He was interested in the buildings themselves and the equipment they contained. During the First World War Pick had become acquainted with an architect called Charles Holden (1875–1960), a fellow member of the Design and Industries Association. Holden, a fellow Quaker, was a quiet, ascetic teetotaller. Following the death of his mother and the bankruptcy of his father, he had studied architecture in Manchester and came to London in 1897 where he worked in a practice that specialised in designing hospitals. By the time he met Pick he had set up his own practice and had designed what is now Zimbabwe House, in the Strand, incorporating statues by Jacob Epstein (with whom he

Clapham Common station. Frank Pick: 'We are going to represent the Design and Industries Association gone mad'. (London's Transport Museum)

had also worked on designing the tomb of Oscar Wilde in Père Lachaise cemetery in Paris). An austere man, he twice refused a knighthood[27] on the grounds that architecture is, above all, teamwork and that it would therefore be wrong for him to be rewarded for achievements shared by others. Pick first employed Holden in redesigning the entrance to Westminster station and, when this trial was successful, he decided to commission Holden to build the new stations on the southern extension of the Northern Line between Clapham and Morden. Pick wanted a common design theme but most of the new stations were to be built on awkward corner sites, with intersections that varied from one site to another. If a common design were to be adopted it would have to be adjusted to each site. A mock-up was built in an engineering workshop at Earl's Court which was adjusted until Pick was satisfied. Pick wrote to one correspondent:

> We are going to build our stations upon the Morden extension railway to the most modern pattern. We are going to discard entirely all ornament. We are going to build in reinforced concrete. The station will be simply a hole in the wall. . . . We are going to represent the Design and Industries Association gone mad.

Holden's final design was a simple geometric pattern in reinforced concrete whose alignment could be adjusted to the needs of each site. He also made extensive use of glass to admit as much natural light as possible to the booking halls and platforms, a technique possibly derived from his experience in designing hospital wards and operating theatres. Some of these features are illustrated in the picture of Clapham Common station opposite. In the brochure which was produced for the opening of the Morden extension Pick asked: 'What is a station? An inviting doorway in an architectural setting that cannot be missed by the casual pedestrian.' All but one of the stations on the extension have since become listed buildings and one critic has described them as 'little masterpieces which reconcile discordant street lines and platform orientations by a precise, comprehensible geometry'.[28]

PICCADILLY CIRCUS

Holden's next commission was to reconstruct the booking hall and concourse at Piccadilly Circus, where the cramped surface buildings could not be extended because of the constraints of the sites on which they were built, hemmed in by expensive West End shops. The only solution was to build a new concourse beneath Piccadilly Circus itself and here Holden's task was as much logistical as architectural. The roads surrounding

The new Piccadilly Circus booking hall, 1938. (London's Transport Museum)

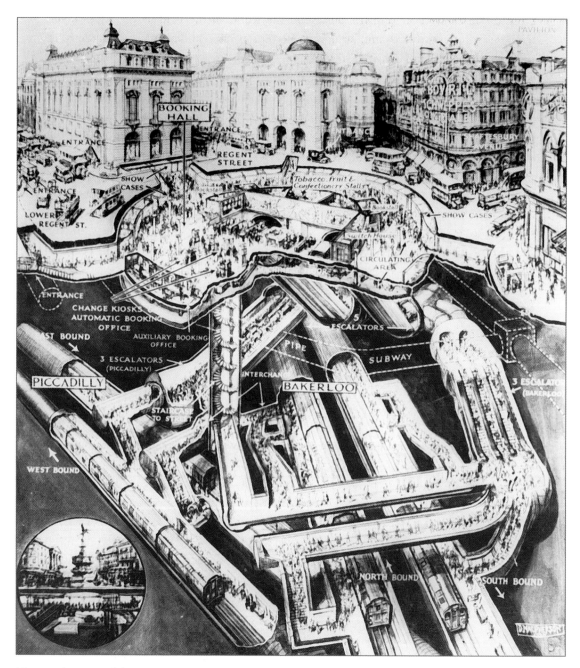

'Cutaway' picture of the new Piccadilly Circus. (London's Transport Museum)

the Eros statue were among the busiest in the world so the bold decision was taken temporarily to remove Eros and accommodate him in Victoria Embankment Gardens. In 1928 a shaft was sunk through the ground formerly occupied by the statue and the work of excavation and construction radiated from this point while road traffic continued to run on the roads, uninterrupted by the activity beneath. A subway then had to be built to accommodate the tangled skein of water pipes, waste pipes, gas mains and cables that pass beneath the circus and a main sewer had to be re-routed. Only when this preparatory work had been completed could the work of construction begin. The shaft beneath Eros was used to remove over 50,000 tons of clay and to introduce over a million bricks, together with over 6,000 tons of cement and cast-iron segments from which the concourse was built. When it opened on 10 December 1928, the public saw for the first time a huge elliptical space, 155ft by 144ft, immediately beneath the site of Eros who was shortly to be restored to his customary position. Shops, columns and ticket booths were framed in bronze and faced with marble. The new station reflected the grandeur of the surrounding streets. Both *The Times* and the *Illustrated London News* delivered generous verdicts on the new station. The latter included numerous photographs and diagrams of the luxurious fittings of the station and declared it to be 'the best in the world'.[29] The booking hall is now a grade 2 listed structure.

THE BAUHAUS AND BEYOND

In 1917 Ashfield and Pick had instituted a series of 'efficiency meetings' whose business was more inspiring than the dull title implies. Pick and other officers in turn made journeys to North America and Europe to study systems elsewhere in the hope that they would pick up ideas which would contribute to the running of London's transport. Following these visits papers were read to the 'efficiency meetings' which were attended by senior managers and their advisers. In June and July 1930 Pick, Holden and Bill Edwards, Lord Ashfield's personal assistant, spent seventeen days visiting Germany, Holland and Scandinavia and on their return presented a paper called *A Note on Contemporary Architecture in Northern Europe*. The paper is much more than a diary account of what they saw. It contains an analysis of developments in architecture in the Greek, Roman and Gothic periods and suggests that the development of new materials and techniques, notably the development of the steel skeleton or the reinforced concrete frame for large buildings, offered the first opportunity for major architectural innovations since the medieval ribbed vault and buttressed arch.[30] In particular the structural role of a wall was reduced so that it could become 'merely a covering' opening up the possibility of making extensive use of newly mass-produced materials like glass to admit light to Underground concourses and platforms. The report contains many photographs of good modern design in the countries visited and contains a clear

THE BAUHAUS

The Bauhaus school of applied art originated in Weimar in 1919, under the direction of the German architect Walter Gropius (1883–1969), who wished to bring together the ability of the artist to create beautiful, well-designed objects and the capacity of modern industries to produce them in large numbers at reasonable cost. These principles should be applied to any manufactured object, notably to textiles, furniture and buildings. Gropius regarded building ('Bau') as the highest form of artistic creation. The Bauhaus school attracted many prominent and talented contemporary artists and was associated with designs using primary colours and simple geometric shapes, notably squares, circles and triangles, which may be detected in Underground posters and architecture of the period. Gropius was known to Frank Pick who used him to help mount an exhibition on visual stimulation at County Hall in 1937 and Bauhaus ideas may be observed in the stations designed by Charles Holden for the Piccadilly Line in the 1930s following his tour of Germany and Scandinavia in Pick's company. The Nazis disapproved of the Bauhaus and closed it down in 1933, following which Gropius came to England.

statement of Pick's firmly held belief that 'fitness for purpose is a necessary attribute of all good design'.[31] At this time the ideas of the Bauhaus were at the height of their influence and although there is no specific reference to the movement in the report it may have been during this visit that Pick first met its founder, Walter Gropius. Pick certainly knew Gropius since he secured Gropius's help in mounting an exhibition at County Hall in 1937 and many of the stations designed by Holden in the 1930s exhibit Bauhaus influence, especially in their use of simple geometrical forms, circles and rectangles, in conjunction with modern materials, to achieve their effect.

The following year the Underground's chief architect, Stanley Heaps, undertook a similar continental tour though his report[32] was far less enthusiastic about what he had seen. He referred disparagingly to, 'the so-called modern Scandinavian types of Architecture in Germany, there being very few buildings of such extreme modern design in this country, for which I think we should be thankful'. Heaps's lack of enthusiasm for what he disparagingly called 'extreme modern design' may help to explain why Pick chose to employ Holden rather than Heaps to design the new stations on the Piccadilly extension to Cockfosters when the latter was built in the years that followed. Pick began cautiously. Shortly after they returned from their continental tour in 1930 he asked Holden to redesign Sudbury Town station at the western end of the Piccadilly Line. The old, low, shed-like station was demolished and replaced with a bold, rectangular brick structure, surmounted by a concrete cornice and flat roof – hallmarks of Holden's later work. Pevsner described the design[33] as 'a landmark not only in the history of Pick's work but also in that of modern English architecture'. It was one of the earliest examples of the continental style of architecture in England, in a setting where it was sure to be seen and used by multitudes of people quite unfamiliar with the style. Pick, however, could be a critical client. Though pleased with the architecture of the station he denounced the clutter that he perceived on the new station during his first visit, writing to the unfortunate engineer responsible: 'automatic machines have been dumped down and are now going to spoil the cleanness and clearness of the platforms

Golders Green appears as a rural idyll in this poster of the 1920s. (London's Transport Museum)

Gloucester Road station: Green's terracotta and Fowler's restrained brick stand side by side. (Dan Bernard)

THE TATE GALLERY
by Tube

Left and opposite page: Some of the promotional posters produced to encourage the travelling public to use the Underground for leisure activities. (London's Transport Museum)

THE TATE GALLERY

Weekdays 10 a.m. – 4 p.m.
Sundays 2 p.m. – 4 p.m.
Admission free *(Tuesdays and Wednesdays 6ᵈ)*

TRAFALGAR Sᴼ OR WESTMINSTER STN

thence by bus 32, 51ᵃ, 80, 88, 89, 180 or 181

LONDON MUSEUM

Mondays to Thursdays, & Saturdays 10 a.m. – 4 p.m.
Sundays and Fridays 2 p.m. – 4 p.m.
Admission free *(Tuesdays 1/ Wednesdays & Thursdays 6ᵈ)*

Sᵀ JAMES' PARK STATION

Thence a short and pleasant walk across Park

UNDERGROUND TO WOOD LANE

TO ANYWHERE

INTERNATIONAL
ADVERTISING EXHIBITION
AT THE WHITE CITY   NOV 29 TO DEC 4 1920

INCLUDING 13 TAX

This poster marked the opening of the Piccadilly Line extension to Heathrow. (London's Transport Museum)

Fly the Tube to Heathrow

Harry Beck's original map, with unfamiliar colours for lines. (London's Transport Museum)

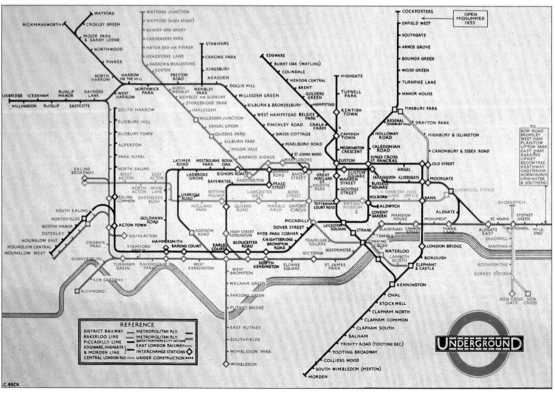

Sudbury Town station, object of Frank Pick's wrath. (London's Transport Museum)

. . . there seems to be a desire on the part of everyone to break up and destroy the tidiness of this station'. As a final, withering rebuke he concluded: 'I wish you to take no action to remedy the defects to which I have drawn attention in this memorandum. I wish Sudbury Town station to remain exactly as it is as a permanent memorial to the department that cannot do its work properly.'[34]

Pick immediately assumed the chairmanship of the committee concerned with the design of new stations to ensure that no similar outrages would be perpetrated on the remaining stations planned for the northern extension of the Piccadilly Line. Of the eight stations built on the extension five have achieved the status of listed buildings.[35] Pevsner's *Buildings of England* refers to 'the restrained Scandinavian modern of Charles Holden's stations of the Piccadilly Line' and particularly commends Arnos Grove for its 'circular ticket hall of great repose and dignity'.[36] This station, which is sometimes cited as the finest example of Holden's later style, is believed by some to be modelled on the Stockholm public library though there is no mention or illustration of the latter building in the report issued by Pick and Holden after they visited Sweden in 1930.[37]

NO. 55 BROADWAY

Charles Holden's most striking contribution to London Transport's architectural heritage lies in the company's headquarters at 55 Broadway, which he began to design in 1926

No. 55 Broadway: Holden's striking design and Epstein's controversial statues, 'not in any sense human, mere nightmares'. (London's Transport Museum)

and completed in 1929. The design was constrained by the irregular shape of the site (rather like a diamond with one end partly broken off) and by the fact that it lay across St James's Park Underground station on the District and Circle Lines. Holden designed a cruciform-shaped building in granite and Portland stone, with his customary generous use of glass to admit daylight to all offices. Offices in a central tower were not used until after 1945 owing to LCC fire regulations. No. 55 Broadway remains one of London's most outstanding buildings of the period and was the tallest office building in London when it opened in 1929. However, on its opening the merits of the architecture were lost in the fierce controversy arising from some of the sculptures which were carved out of the building's stonework. Eight sculptures of the winds by various sculptors (including Henry Moore and Eric Gill) aroused little comment but the full fury of the critics was turned on two sculptures representing Day and Night by Jacob Epstein. Epstein (1880–1959) was already a controversial figure. Born in New York to an orthodox Jewish family, he came to London in 1905 and was introduced to Charles Holden. In 1907 Holden invited him to create some sculptures for his British Medical Association building (now Zimbabwe House) in the Strand. The nudity of the sculptures aroused much satirical comment and derision and when the High Commission of Southern Rhodesia took over the building they vandalised the statues. In 1925 Epstein's statue in honour of the naturalist W.H. Hudson, unveiled in Hyde Park, aroused more controversy so, when it became known that he was again working with Holden at 55 Broadway, the critics and Philistines sharpened their faculties in readiness. The statues certainly succeeded in arousing the interest of the press and the public in a way that art rarely does. Newspapers as diverse as the *Daily Mirror*, *Daily Express*, *The Times*, *Manchester Guardian* and *Daily Telegraph* united in their condemnation of Night and Day on grounds which included obscenity, bestiality and cannibalism. A lecturer in art wrote to *The Times* to say of the statues that 'they are revolting. The figures are not Mongolian, as some have said, and not in any sense human, mere nightmares.'[38] This view was supported in the days that followed in letters and derisive cartoons, a particular fear being expressed that such statues might begin to appear in churches if no one put a stop to this sort of thing. In a more direct protest tar was hurled at the statue from a passing car. It was probably saved from a worse fate by the fact that, at a height of nearly 20ft above the ground, it was beyond the reach of the casual vandal. The architectural correspondent of *The Times* offered a more balanced judgement when he commented on the difficulties the sculptor faced in creating statues which suited the angular geometry of the building. He commended in particular Eric Gill's statues for achieving this and concluded that the statues:

> represent a serious attempt – almost the first that has been made in this country – to employ first-rate sculptors to decorate and complete a building in architectural terms and, with the reservations indicated, the attempt has been successful.[39]

Following some tense meetings of the directors,[40] at one of which Pick offered to resign,[41] the controversy subsided and the statues remain in place, noticed by very few of the multitudes who pass by. The building was awarded the London Architectural medal by the Royal Institute of British Architects in 1929. There was one final repercussion for Holden. When, in 1931, he was invited to design the building for the London University Senate House, Holden was forbidden to include any sculptures by Epstein. The building, which bears some resemblance in its design to 55 Broadway, has no external sculpture at all and many critics agree that it needs them.

The tradition of innovatory station design continued after the war. Holden's last station was Redbridge, on the Essex extension of the Central Line, which opened in December 1947 with its striking, circular glazed skylight. On the same day the nearby Gants Hall station opened, the magnificent barrel-vaulted lower concourse of which resembles that of the much grander Moscow Pushkinskaya station and probably resulted from a visit to the Moscow Metro made by Underground engineers when the first section of the Metro was opened in the 1930s. There existed at one time a proposal to twin the station named after Russia's greatest poet with the distinctly less celebrated Gants Hill. The visit to Moscow was made in return for a series of Soviet delegations which visited the London Underground while the Moscow system was being designed. In his memoirs the Soviet leader Nikita Khrushchev recorded that Stalin appointed him to oversee the

Gants Hill station's 'Moscow Pushkinskaya' concourse. (Author)

construction of the Moscow Metro in the 1930s because of his experience of the mining industry. Khrushchev persuaded Stalin to build the system following the London deep-tube model rather than the German 'cut-and-cover' model because the deep tubes would be better suited for use as air raid shelters.[42] Perhaps Khrushchev, in his memoirs, was laying claim to more foresight than he deserved but the Soviet visitors were so grateful for what they learned that Frank Pick was awarded the Honorary Badge of Merit by Stalin – an unusual distinction for a western company director from the communist dictator. Gants Hill's concourse is undoubtedly an impressive structure, if a little out of place on a suburban station whose passenger flows are well below the average for the system as a whole. It earned a Festival of Britain Award for Architectural Merit in 1951.

HARRY BECK'S MAP

The first map to show all the Underground railway lines[43] was published in 1908 as a component of the drive for a common marketing effort which also resulted in the adoption of the name Underground by all the participating companies.[44] Like later maps this one used colours to distinguish the separate lines, though the colours were different from those now familiar to users of the Underground. The major problem faced by those cartographers brave enough to attempt to create a unified map was the size of the system. Until 1935 the Metropolitan Railway ran trains to Quainton Road, in the Vale of Aylesbury, and on to Brill and Verney Junction. In the east the District Railway offered an electric service to Barking with onward steam services to Upminster and Southend. If these extremities were shown on one map then either the map was too large to be easily handled or the scale was so small that the closely spaced stations in central London were indistinguishable from one another. Two methods were employed to overcome this problem on early maps. Some simply omitted the outlying areas while others, produced from 1926 by an Underground Group draughtsman called F.H. Stingemore, compressed the more distant stations so that they appeared to be closer to one another than they really were. These early maps also omitted all reference to other features of the landscape, some of them even excluding the River Thames.

Harry Beck[45] (1901–74) joined the signal engineers' department of the Underground Group as a temporary junior draughtsman in 1925. His employment over the next six years was punctuated by dismissals prompted by economic crises of the kind that characterised the period and he was actually unemployed when, in 1931, he sketched in an exercise book a diagram which, after many additions and amendments, eventually became his famous schematic map of the Underground network. It was based on three design principles. First, the Central Line was used as a horizontal axis around which the map was built. Secondly, where lines intersected or where they diverged from a straight line, he used only 45 degree and 90 degree angles. Thirdly, in spacing the stations, no regard was paid to the true distance between them. In the centre of London stations are much more generously spaced than geography requires in order to give sufficient space for the insertion of station names. In the outer area stations are much closer to each other on the map than they are on the ground. The schematic map, with station names removed, is strongly reminiscent of an electrical wiring diagram and it is no coincidence that much of Beck's work, in the signal engineers' department, involved drafting just such diagrams for signalling circuits. If any proof were needed to confirm this suspicion, in March 1937 he produced a spoof version of his map for a London Transport staff magazine in which the references to a wiring diagram are explicit.

At first Frank Pick's publicity committee rejected the diagram, believing it to be too novel for the public to accept but the following year, 1932, they reconsidered it and decided to try it out. Some 750,000 copies of the map were ordered in January 1933, and any anxieties the management may have had about the wisdom of placing such a large order were removed when the following month they had to order another 100,000. The maps had been quickly taken up by an enthusiastic public not in the least perturbed by the innovative design. Its popularity was a happy augury for the new London Passenger Transport Board which took office in July of the same year, with Ashfield as chairman and Pick as vice-chairman. Any doubts which Pick had entertained were quickly overcome since, on 3 August, he wrote to the publicity officer: 'I confess that upon a large scale this looks very convenient and tidy and is a better map than any we have had so far.' By this time Harry Beck was once again a temporary employee of the Board, in which hazardous status he remained until 1937 when he was given a permanent post in the press advertising section. Since he had technically been a freelance designer when he submitted his map he was paid the princely fee of 5 guineas for the design, in return for which he assigned the priceless copyright to the Board.

Over the years that followed the map evolved. Clearer colours were adopted for the separate lines (the Central Line changed from orange to red in 1934) and Beck made further improvements to its layout, the Circle Line appearing for the first time as a separate unit in its bright yellow in 1949. In 1947 Harry Beck left London Transport to become an instructor at the London School of Printing and the Graphic Arts. His final years were clouded by a dispute with London Transport about modifications to his design. He believed he had made an agreement that any changes to the design would be made by him, so when a new version, designed by a publicity officer called Harold Hutchinson, appeared in 1960, Beck engaged in a long and angry correspondence with the company. The Hutchinson map did not long survive criticism but the argument was not resolved to Harry Beck's satisfaction and subsequent designs, incorporating the Victoria Line, the Jubilee Line and the Docklands Light Railway, were prepared by other artists. (The original 1933 design is shown on the front endpaper.)

Towards the end of his life Beck became rather bitter about this episode but his map remains one of the icons of twentieth-century industrial design. It has long outgrown its original purpose of helping travellers to find their way around London. It is printed on surfaces as diverse as aprons, computer mousemats and articles of clothing, souvenirs taken home by tourists from New York, Singapore and Sydney as evidence of their visits to England. Along with Tower Bridge and Big Ben it is the most widely recognised symbol of London. It has often been copied, not always successfully, by other transport systems, but it has never been equalled.

FRANK PICK'S FINAL DAYS

In his final years Frank Pick devoted much time to campaigning for improvements in design well beyond the realm of transport in his capacity as chairman of the Council for Art and Industry (CAI). In January 1937 he oversaw the production of a report entitled *Design and the Designer in Industry* and in June of the same year he persuaded the Building Centre, in New Bond Street, to lend its premises for an exhibition based on a CAI report called *The Working Class Home*, which demonstrated how well-designed domestic furniture and utensils could be brought within the purchasing power of a family of modest means. In the same year the CAI, under his chairmanship, organised the British pavilion at the Paris exhibition of industrial art. In 1941 Pick published a book of his own entitled *Britain Must Rebuild, a Policy for Regional Planning*,[46] which criticised what he branded the contemporary 'obsession for iron rod stiffening and cement filling' and the 'functionalism' prevalent in modern architecture (an extreme application of his own 'design for purpose' philosophy) on the grounds that it had failed to find a distinctive style:

> Before functionalism can take its place fully and gratefully as the current style of building it must learn what it is that it lacks to make it cultured. Its vitamin content is too low.

He also argued for the establishment of national parks and the protection of the countryside from urban sprawl: 'One garden city may be excellent, but a hundred of them set five miles apart would be repellent' – sincerely held but paradoxical views for one who had done more than most to create suburban London.

WINSTON CHURCHILL VS FRANK PICK

Pick, like many of his countrymen, had profound misgivings about Neville Chamberlain's Munich settlement, regarding Hitler as a dangerous madman. In 1938, as war approached, he was asked to promote the work of the Women's Royal Voluntary service (WRVS). He asked his young assistants, Anthony Bull and David McKenna, to find a suitable picture of a young woman to pose as a WRVS volunteer on a poster, telling them that she had to appear 'good-looking and courageous'. This mission they

The face looking out from the front window and lower panels of the recruiting bus is the only surviving record of the young German woman who unwittingly helped the Women's Royal Voluntary Service to recruit much-needed members as war approached. One assumes that the ensuing hostilities denied her the royalty payments she so richly deserved. (Reproduced by courtesy of the Women's Royal Voluntary Service)

accomplished with the help of a photographic agency. The poster was a success and the press wanted to know who the young woman was. Enquiries soon established that she was in fact an attractive young German from Hamburg. The press was fended off and this embarrassing fact was concealed until now. Unfortunately, the poster was lost when the remaining copies were 'pulped' during a wartime paper shortage, but a careful search of the WRVS archives has revealed a photograph of the unsuspecting Fraulein's poster on the side of a recruiting bus.[47]

Other war preparations proceeded more smoothly. Pick devised the plan to evacuate London which was put into action on 1 September 1939 as Germany attacked Poland. On that Friday he drove straight from his Hampstead home to Oakwood station on the Piccadilly Line to see children being transferred to main line trains which would take them away from London and danger. Satisfied that the operation was proceeding smoothly he boarded a train to 55 Broadway.[48] He never doubted the outcome of the war, writing to Anthony Bull[49] 'The war may shake our stability and daunt our ambition but a good peace will, with time, restore us and London to a better, finer, decenter basis'. When the war started the government assumed responsibility for running the railway system through the Railway Executive Committee and Pick took up posts in government but he never settled into wartime government as Ashfield had done. He wrote to Anthony Bull 'I fear my new venture may be hazardous. Political waters are full of wrecks and shoals'. How right he was. He was moved first to the Ministry of Transport and later to the Ministry of Information where his chief claim to fame was an encounter with Churchill in which Pick opposed the Prime Minister's proposal to drop leaflets on Germany spreading false news in order to discomfit the enemy. The following brief exchange then occurred at a meeting of the Political Warfare Executive:

> Churchill: Now Mr Pick, I understand you have been objecting to the dropping of the leaflets.
> Pick: Yes, Prime Minister, what is written on the leaflets is not wholly true and that is bad propaganda.
> Churchill: This is no time to be concerned with the niceties.
> Pick: Prime Minister, I have never told a lie in my life.
> Churchill: Yesterday the Germans shelled Dover with their long-range guns at Cape Gris Nez. This afternoon I shall be visiting Dover. I may be killed by a German shell. If so, it will be a great comfort to me to know that on the last day of my life I spoke with a man who had never told a lie in his life. Get out.

As Pick, red-faced, left the room, never to return, Churchill, in a deafening whisper, instructed his secretary John Colville 'Never let that impeccable busman darken my door again' – doubly insulting since Pick considered himself a railwayman rather than a busman.[50] Shortly afterwards the minister, Duff Cooper, dismissed Pick. He died of a cerebral haemorrhage the following year. In his will he made a bequest to the Victoria & Albert Museum.

POETRY ON THE UNDERGROUND[51]

The association of the Underground with art and design did not come to an end with the passing of Frank Pick. Station design, in particular, continued to reflect his legacy as described in Chapter Eight. But it also took other forms. In 1986 London Transport agreed to launch *Poetry on the Underground*, a selection of poems displayed on Underground trains and stations. A small grant was secured to pay for printing and displaying the posters. Each group of five or six poems included living authors as well as familiar names from the past like Shakespeare and Wordsworth. Poems selected have ranged from *Sumer is icumen in* by an anonymous thirteenth-century writer to Betjeman's *Summoned by Bells*. The British Presidency of the European Union was marked by a decision to publish poems from all fifteen European Union countries, one of the most moving being Primo Levi's *25 febbraio 1944*, which marked the date on which Levi, an Italian Jewish partisan, arrived at Auschwitz with 650 other prisoners. Three of them survived.

The poems have become an established feature of Underground train travel and other consequences followed their introduction. One of the first poems to be featured was Wordsworth's *Composed upon Westminster Bridge, September 3rd, 1802* ('Earth has not anything to show more fair') so on 3 September 1986, 184 years to the day after Wordsworth's composition, twenty people gathered at dawn on the bridge to read the poem. In 1996 the *Times Literary Supplement* sponsored a *Poems on the Underground Poetry Competition* which attracted over three thousand entries, many of them from abroad. Three of the entries were published.

One should not overlook the effect upon poets of knowing that their work is to be exposed to millions of Underground travellers. When Denise Leverton (1923–97), resident in the USA, heard that her poem *Living* had been selected for the Underground she wrote, 'I am totally thrilled by the idea of having a poem in the Tube. . . . Appearance in American trains and buses means nothing to me but London, ah, London, that's different.' The American poet X.J. Kennedy wrote that the appearance on the Underground of his poem *To Someone Who Insisted I Look Up Someone* 'delighted me more than if the Swedish Academy had handed me the Nobel Prize'. The idea of poetry on underground railways has since been adopted by many other cities, including New York, Paris, Athens, Shanghai and Moscow. *Poems on the Underground* is published annually by Cassell. The Sydney Olympics in 2000 coincided with the appearance of *Australian Poetry on the Underground*.

MATHS ON THE UNDERGROUND

In May 1992 the International Mathematical Union, with the support of UNESCO, declared that the year 2000 would be World Mathematical Year, one of its objectives being to raise the profile of mathematics as a subject relevant to the new century. To this end a team at the Isaac Newton Institute for Mathematical Sciences in Cambridge undertook to design a series of twelve posters, to be displayed month by month on Underground trains, following the precedent set by the poems. The posters aim to arouse interest, to intrigue and to explain the relevance of mathematical concepts to laymen. Thus the catastrophe theory is illustrated by the behaviour of a melting iceberg under the headline 'Maths is cool'; chaos theory is related to weather forecasts; and 'Maths takes off' heads a poster about aerodynamics. The *Guardian* welcomed the initiative, observing that:

> *Poems on the Underground* is one of those rare initiatives that has subtly, if marginally, improved the quality of commuters' lives. . . . Britain has lagged behind countries like

Maths on the Underground: one of twelve posters from the Isaac Newton Institute, Cambridge, for World Mathematical Year 2000. (Courtesy of the Isaac Newton Institute. Iceberg photograph: British Antarctic Survey)

Japan and Germany in understanding clearly that Mathematics is the foundation of modern industry. It remains to be seen whether puzzles and other devices printed on posters on the tube will do the trick but we have to start somewhere.[52]

Frank Pick would surely have approved of the addition of these two later art forms to his own visual legacy.

CHAPTER SEVEN
THE UNDERGROUND AT WAR: 1914–18; 1939–45

Underground stations cannot be used as air raid shelters.
  (Notice posted at Underground stations at the outbreak of the Second World War)

Vibration due to heavy gunfire or other causes will be felt much less if you do not lie with your head against the wall.
  (Advice from *De Profundis*, bulletin of the Swiss Cottage Underground station air raid shelterers, September 1940)

In both world wars the Underground railways played roles far greater than had been planned. It had been anticipated that the network would move civilians and troops around the capital and this was especially important during the Second World War when the streets above were ravaged by bombing. However, the role with which they are most often associated was one which they assumed, at first, with reluctance: that of providing air raid shelters for the population of London as well as accommodating some critical war industries.

NO GUNPOWDER PLOT

The First World War began with a comical incident reminiscent of the exploits of Guy Fawkes. G.A. Sekon, editor of the *Railway and Travel Monthly* had suggested that caches of armaments, explosives and German spies might lie concealed in disused tube tunnels, ready for use when hostilities began. A careful search by the police in the first week of August 1914 of the disused section of the City and South London Railway between King William Street and Borough stations revealed no lurking Guy Fawkes figures and the scare abated. Some more practical steps were taken to prepare the railways for war. The first was the establishment of the 'Common Fund', a revenue pooling agreement whereby the tubes, the District Railway and the London General Omnibus Company (each of these was still a separate company with different shareholders) paid surplus revenue into a common fund. 'Surplus' revenue was defined as that which remained after payment of working expenses, interest on loan stock and dividends on some preference shares. This pool of surplus revenue was then shared out among the members, with 32 per cent going to the buses and the remaining 68 per cent to the various Underground railway companies for reinvestment and dividends. Through bookings which involved a passenger using the services of more than one of the companies had previously been the subject of complex and costly internal accounting arrangements whereby the price of a ticket was shared out among the companies carrying the passenger. This process now ceased and the new arrangement presaged those which would apply when unitary management arrived in the form of the London Passenger Transport Board in 1933. The Metropolitan Railway, as ever, remained outside the pool.

The network made a further contribution to the war effort by releasing Albert Stanley and Frank Pick for war service. In December 1916 Stanley became President of the Board of Trade in Lloyd George's coalition government, entering Parliament for Ashton-under-Lyne in place of the sitting member – the newspaper magnate Max Aitken, proprietor of the *Daily Express* and *Sunday Express*. Aitken, a friend of Stanley, went to the House of Lords as Lord Beaverbrook, under which title he achieved fame in the Second World War as Minister of Aircraft Production during the Battle of Britain. The following year Frank Pick was seconded to a department of the Board of Trade to devise a coal rationing scheme which ensured that, during the final winter of the war, no householders went without coal. Both men returned to the Underground in 1919.

AIR RAIDS

Zeppelin raids on Belgium had occurred in the first month of the war but it was not until January 1915 that Kaiser Wilhelm II sanctioned raids on England, with the condition that they were confined to military targets. These no doubt noble intentions were frustrated by the crudity of the navigational and bomb-aiming devices available to the pilots. Bombs fell on the outskirts of London for the first time on 31 May 1915 and the Underground made it known that its stations would be available as shelters to those who were caught in the streets when an air raid began. At first casualties were negligible but in the late summer of 1917 a sustained air attack on London began, with six raids in the course of a month. This was very modest compared to the onslaught which London suffered in the Second World War but the new and unwelcome experience prompted many Londoners to arrive at Underground stations not when raids began but in anticipation of them.[1] The *Railway Gazette* commented loftily that 'During the air raid on Monday evening the platforms of the Tube railways in all parts of London were crowded with men, women and children, a feature being the large number of pet dogs which accompanied their owners into safety.'[2] They came to take up semipermanent residence either on the station platforms or, sometimes, on the trains themselves, endless journeys around the Circle Line being particularly favoured as a refuge from the bombs.[3] Consequently, from 28 September 1917 citizens were denied access to Underground stations unless they carried tickets, this rule being relaxed only if the sirens sounded an air raid warning. That same evening the sound of sirens caused a panic at Liverpool Street station among what the *Railway Gazette* disapprovingly called 'people of the poorer classes, mostly aliens, woman and children', in which one lady was trampled to death. A final sequence of raids in February 1918 prompted as many as 300,000 people to seek shelter in the tubes on a single night – almost twice the number recorded in the much worse conditions of the Blitz twenty-two years later. The uncompleted Post Office Railway[4] became the temporary home of the Elgin Marbles and other treasures from the British Museum.

WOMEN ON THE UNDERGROUND

The war brought a further change as many male staff were called up for military service. Between 30 per cent and 50 per cent of the staff of the companies were lost in this way, among them the fictional Jack Firebrace of Sebastian Faulks's *Birdsong*,[5] employed for his tunnelling skills to burrow beneath the German trenches on the Western Front. Faced with the acute shortage of manpower the Underground agreed with the trade unions that women could be employed, on a temporary basis, at the same rates of pay as men doing the same work: a point of great significance fifty years before the Equal Pay Act. On 6 June 1915 Maida Vale station opened on the new Bakerloo extension to Queen's Park. It was the first station on the network to be run entirely by women, though they did share a male stationmaster with three neighbouring stations. The *Railway Gazette*, a periodical not noted for its progressive attitudes, conceded that this was 'preferable to employing hobbledehoys'. As the war continued women penetrated other parts of the network, replacing gatemen on trains in 1917 though drivers and guards were invariably male.

By the end of the war the Underground railways were enjoying a period of rare prosperity. Traffic increased by over 60 per cent and fares were increased, with government approval, by 30–50 per cent. In 1918, for the first time, all the companies paid dividends on all their shares, except the long-suffering holders of the District ordinary shares who continued in the long tradition of receiving no dividend at all.[6] With that exception the Underground railways, and their shareholders, had a good war.

THE SECOND WORLD WAR: 'THE BOMBER WILL ALWAYS GET THROUGH'

In the evening of 27 September 1938 six Underground stations on either side of the Thames were closed for 'urgent structural works', to the consternation of passengers.

During the First World War London Transport took on women staff for the first time; it was 'preferable to employing hobbledehoys', according to one journalist. (London's Transport Museum)

Bakerloo and Northern Line trains ceased to run beneath the river. As Neville Chamberlain visited Hitler at Munich to make his ill-fated 'peace for our time', the London Passenger Transport Board was sealing off the lines beneath the river with concrete plugs to prevent the flooding of the system which, it was feared, would result from the destruction caused by imminent and overwhelming air raids on the capital. In the 1930s the destruction of the undefended Basque city of Guernica and the gloomy assurances of Stanley Baldwin that 'the bomber will always get through'[7] had created a widespread assumption that large cities like London were helpless in the face of aerial bombardment which would consequently result in wholesale destruction and enormous casualties. As early as 1924 the Committee of Imperial Defence had identified the deep-tube railways as uniquely invulnerable to air attack and therefore an essential artery in keeping the capital going in the face of such a threat. Mathematical formulae, based hazily on the supposed effects of bombing in the First World War, were used to calculate that fifty casualties would result from each ton of explosives dropped, of which almost one-third would be fatalities. In a heavy raid 700 tons of bombs would be dropped, resulting in 35,000 casualties, including 10,000 dead. The tubes would therefore be needed to evacuate the daily toll of dead and injured.[8] For this reason the system had to be kept free of people wishing to escape the bombing. Their use as air raid shelters was to be absolutely forbidden. There was also a belief in some quarters that the civilian population, paralysed by fear, would disappear underground and refuse to emerge, preferring a troglodytic existence to the hazards of bombing, with disastrous effects upon war production.

After Neville Chamberlain returned from Munich with his infamous piece of paper the train services were restored, the Underground's concrete plugs were removed and installed in their place were electrically operated metal floodgates which could be activated from a control centre at Leicester Square station. In 1944, when V2 rockets fell on the capital, the Underground management feared that one of these missiles might land in the Thames, penetrate one of the tubes beneath the river and flood the system over a wide area with appalling casualties. Ground radar was therefore directed at the launch sites and, as soon as it became clear that London was the target, the Underground control centre was warned via a direct telephone link. The centre then had four minutes to clear the tubes of trains in transit beneath the river and close the floodgates. It was an anxious time but no catastrophic strike occurred.[9]

On Friday, 1 September 1939, the day Germany invaded Poland, Underground trains, following Frank Pick's plan, carried some two hundred thousand children to outer suburban stations where they boarded main line services to the West Country and other places of refuge. The evacuation plan was carried out under clear skies and not, as had been anticipated, in the face of relentless bombardment. When the bombers failed to appear the evacuees started to drift back so the exercise had to be repeated nine months later when France fell and the Battle of Britain began.

In the meantime the government assumed control of the railway network for the duration of the war, authority being exercised through a Railway Executive Committee which consisted of representatives of the four main line railways and of the London Passenger Transport Board. A new revenue pooling arrangement was made whereby the government paid London Transport an annual sum of £4,835,705. As the war progressed and the Underground assumed a greater share of the burden of transporting Londoners around the ravaged capital this sum became steadily less adequate to replace its bombed, damaged and over-worked facilities while the Treasury's coffers filled with the surplus receipts earned by the network.[10]

SHELTERING IN THE TUBES

In accordance with the 1924 recommendations of the Committee of Imperial Defence, posters were exhibited at Underground stations explaining that they were not to be used as shelters. They read:

A children's Christmas party at Holborn station. (Hulton Getty)

The Luftwaffe fails to distract these Londoners from their game of dominoes in an Underground station. The chocolate vending machine behind them is presumably empty, owing to rationing. (Hulton Getty)

> The public are informed that, in order to operate the railways for essential movement, Underground stations cannot be used as air-raid shelters. In any event a number of stations would have to be cleared for safety in certain contingencies.[11]

It is not clear whether the last sentence, referring to 'certain contingencies', was meant simply as an additional discouragement to those tempted to shelter in the stations or whether it referred to the more specific uses which had been assigned to certain stations, as explained below.[12] At first the prohibition was accepted without complaint. During the period of the phoney war the Luftwaffe stayed away and in the early phases of the Battle of Britain they concentrated their attacks on the protective ring of RAF fighter stations in the countryside around London. The population busied themselves assembling their Morrison and Anderson air raid shelters.[13] On 24 August 1940 a German bomber, lost and separated from its squadron, jettisoned its bombs over what it believed to be open country. The bombs struck the medieval church of St Giles Without Cripplegate in the heart of the City of London. Churchill ordered an immediate retaliatory raid on Berlin. Hitler, enraged, redirected the Luftwaffe's bombers to an attack on London. Thus began the Blitz and thus also began the nightly invasion of the tube stations by Londoners wishing to escape the bombs. The first incursion occurred at Liverpool Street station on the night of 8 September, when a huge crowd gathered and forced their way past the hapless officials, police and soldiers who were supposed to stop them entering. Commenting on the incident *Picture Post* declared: 'London decided how the tube stations were to be used.'

At the end of September the government, recognising a *fait accompli*, decided to take the situation in hand. First they counted the sleeping Londoners, estimating that there were 177,500 in the stations on 27 September 1940. This figure was little more than half the numbers recorded in the far less threatening circumstances of the First World War. The difference no doubt partly reflects the greater preparation for the second war, with many purpose-built public and private shelters built in advance. Nevertheless it does suggest a greater degree of stoicism in the second war, with most Londoners sleeping in their own beds regardless of the bombs. Those sleeping in the tubes had no sanitation, organisation or supervision. Herbert Morrison, original architect of the London Passenger Transport Board,[14] now Home Secretary, was given the task of imposing some order on this confused situation. Shelter wardens were appointed and lavatories were installed, compressed air being used to blast the contents up to the public sewers. A ticketing system was introduced, with admission to the stations starting after 4 p.m. Some 'spivs' made a dishonest living queueing for tickets and then selling them to shelterers for half a crown each.[15] To prevent this abuse London Transport issued 'season tickets' for regular users to occupy particular platform spaces.[16] Special trains called Tube Refreshments Specials, provisioned by J. Lyons and Co., called at the stations in the small hours, delivering containers holding 7 tons of hot food and 2,400 gallons of tea, cocoa and milk, and removing the previous night's empties.

In many places the tube shelters became an established feature of community life. On fifty-two stations libraries were organised by the regular users while ENSA (the Entertainments National Service Association) provided entertainment. Some of these were broadcast, the first of them featuring George Formby, with ukelele and piano, perilously seated on a platform specially erected above the tracks of one of the deep-level tubes.[17] The Council for the Encouragement of Music and the Arts (CEMA) sent people into the shelters with gramophones and recordings of classical music but on one such visit the ungrateful occupants complained that the music made it hard to hear the bombs. Film shows were arranged in many shelters and an amateur theatrical company toured the stations with a production of Chekhov's *The Bear*. Chess, dominoes and darts were popular games for shelterers and an inter-shelter darts league was formed to compete for a trophy as the bombs fell in the streets above. Children's play centres were set up at Elephant and Castle and Gloucester Road stations. The LCC organised 200 evening classes on subjects ranging from current affairs to dressmaking, pedal-operated sewing machines being moved into stations for the purpose. On one occasion a bulkier piece of equipment was surreptitiously moved in. The writer Constantine Fitzgibbon, an eyewitness, recorded the warden at Bethnal Green as saying:

> unbeknown to me they moved in a piano . . . of course the first I'd heard of it was when they'd all come out of the pubs and it was a proper bedlam . . . I might tell you we had some lively times, mouth-organs in one shelter, the piano in the other.[18]

Tube shelter life became a recognised spectacle. Fitzgibbon recorded:

> Some people from the West End used to go sightseeing to this and other shelters even as before the war they would make up jolly parties to visit Chinatown. Needless to say, slumming of this sort was not at all popular with the shelterers and at least one party of sightseers was roughly handled before being ejected.

A study of life in the tube shelters was undertaken by Mass Observation[19] at one central London station on 25 September 1940 at the height of the Blitz. The station was opened to shelterers at 4 p.m. and by 7.10 p.m. a thousand people were distributed around the platforms, passages and stairways though it was 9 p.m. before the last arrivals reached the station. They took the least favoured positions on the escalators or in the entrance hall where protection was minimal. Most were 'regulars' on familiar terms with one another, who engaged in casual gossip and repaid debts of cigarettes or food incurred on previous visits. Many played games, cards being especially popular, while envoys occasionally ventured to the surface to bring back reports of the mayhem on the streets above. Children were persuaded, with difficulty, to go to bed, bribes in the form of sweets being used to secure their cooperation. Gradually the adults settled down to sleep, interrupted by exchanges like the following, initiated by an irascible lady whose sleeping place was close to the lavatory:

> 'Seventy-eight people want to go to the lavatory.'
> 'Can't you shut up, you bleeding little hypocrite?'
> 'I want to go to sleep and these people keep on going to the lavatory.'

Silence then ensued but it is perhaps not surprising that sleep was a scarce commodity, averaging 4½ hours per night for men and 3½ hours for women. At 5.15 a.m., after the All Clear was sounded, people started to leave and by 7 a.m. the station was empty.

A reassuring sign for Londoners during
the Blitz. (Author)

A total of 36 doctors and 200 nurses set up medical posts in the stations to attend to
the sick. A particular problem arose from mosquito bites, the insects being stirred from
hibernation by the unexpected warmth provided by the crowded platforms. The
mosquitoes were soon joined by a plague of head-lice. Occasionally babies were born in
the stations. Three-tier bunk beds were installed with space for 22,000 people to sleep in
comfort, though these encountered resistance from some of the more lively shelterers
who objected to the fact that the bunks reduced the space available for dancing and card
games. For this reason they were actually removed from two stations.

In some shelters management committees were elected with chairman, secretary and
minutes of proceedings. Rules were established for reserving spaces, playing music and
games, cleanliness and other matters which the regular users thought important.
Women were observed cleaning the areas around their allocated spaces as they would
previously have cleaned their living rooms or scrubbed their front steps. Raffles were
held and funds raised for children's Christmas parties, eleven thousand Christmas
presents being distributed at Christmas 1940. Some of the more ambitious shelters
published their own newspapers, one of the funniest being produced by the group who

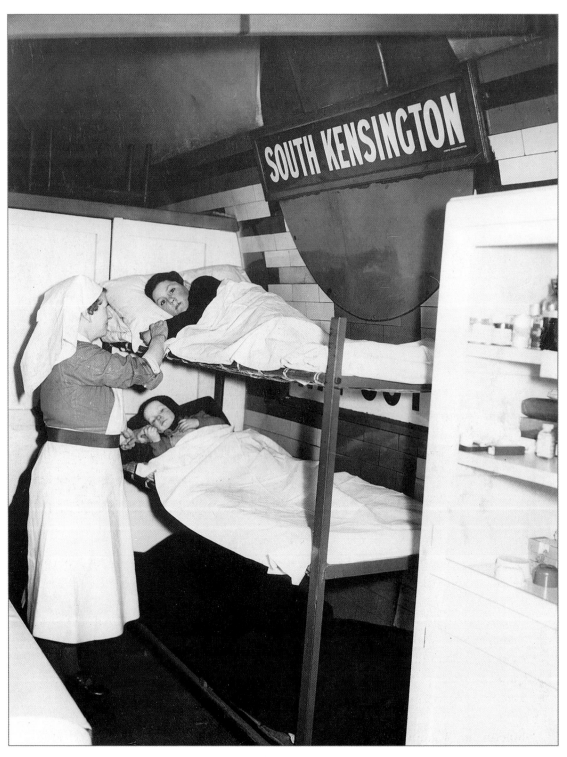

A nurse settles two children in her 'sick bay' at South Kensington station as the bombs fall overhead.

A sister and a nurse prepare for the night's work at an Underground station. (Hulton Getty)

used Swiss Cottage Underground station. It was called *De Profundis* ('From the Depths') and Bulletin no. 1 began:

> Greetings to our nightly companions, our temporary cave dwellers, our sleeping companions, somnambulists, snorers, chatterers and all who inhabit the Swiss Cottage station of the Bakerloo from dusk to dawn. This is the first in a series of announcements, issued in the name of co-operation, so that we may find what comfort and amenities there may be in this our nightly place of refuge.

Bulletin no. 2 gave some practical tips immodestly entitled 'Expert Advice' and suggesting: 'Vibration due to heavy gunfire or other causes will be felt much less if you do not lie with your head against the wall.'[20]

All seventy-nine deep-level tube stations were eventually opened as shelters and, in addition, unused and partly built new tunnels were made available for the purpose. The Holborn to Aldwych branch, which had been closed for the duration of the war; the disused King William Street to Borough branch of the former City and South London Railway; the new and as yet unopened stations between Liverpool Street and Bethnal Green; the disused British Museum station; and the partly built tube station at Highgate: all these were brought into use as shelters for 17,000 people. Once again the Elgin Marbles and other treasures from the British Museum took up residence in the Underground railway network, this time in one of the Aldwych branch tunnels.

DEATH IN THE TUBES

Those who sought shelter were not always safe. The first serious incident occurred at Trafalgar Square station[21] on 12 October 1940 when seven shelterers were killed by a bomb which landed at the top of Whitehall and penetrated the roadway above the station. On the following day a bomb struck Bounds Green station on the Piccadilly Line. The nature of the casualties here made this a particularly tragic episode. Sixteen of the dead were Belgian refugees who had fled from their country at the time of the Dunkirk evacuation and had created a Belgian enclave at one end of the platform. On this particular evening they had welcomed three English people who had been bombed out of two homes. All nineteen were killed. The others sheltering in the station were phlegmatic about the disaster. An elderly lady, surveying the carnage, declared 'We'll sleep well tonight. At least there'll be no trains coming through.'[22] The next night, on 14 October, a much worse incident occurred at Balham station on the Northern Line, when a bomb burst a water main and sent tons of water and debris down to the platforms, killing 68 out of 600 who were seeking shelter. The worst incident of all was a tragic accident at Bethnal Green station on the evening of 3 March 1943. An orderly queue waiting to enter the station during a distant and minor raid turned to chaos when a young mother holding a baby lost her footing in the dark and fell down the stairs. In the ensuing panic the woman survived but 173 people were trampled, crushed or suffocated to death. The incident was for a time kept from the public but one consequence was the installation of better lighting at the entrances to tube shelters.

LIFE IN THE TUBES

Many contemporary accounts describe the experience of the tube shelterers. The diplomat Harold Nicolson recorded the disapproving verdict of his housekeeper, Mrs Groves, who used a tube shelter only once, explaining her reservations about the other occupants: 'Greeks, they were, sir, by the look of them. I never did hold with foreigners.'[23] More surprisingly George Orwell, observing a disproportionate number of

SITE OF THE WORST CIVILIAN DISASTER
OF THE SECOND WORLD WAR

IN MEMORY OF
173 MEN, WOMEN AND CHILDREN
WHO LOST THEIR LIVES ON THE
EVENING OF WEDNESDAY 3RD MARCH 1943
DESCENDING THESE STEPS TO BETHNAL GREEN
UNDERGROUND AIR RAID SHELTER

NOT FORGOTTEN

Bethnal Green station, scene of a tragic accident which killed 173 Londoners. (Author)

non-Anglo-Saxon refugees in the tubes, appeared to endorse the xenophobic view of an anonymous friend that 'foreigners are more frightened than English people during the raids. It is not their war and therefore they have nothing to sustain them.'[24] However, Orwell also delivered more favourable judgements. He commented on the orderliness of the shelters, on their 'cleanly, normal, domesticated air. Especially the young married couples, the sort of homely, cautious types that would probably be buying their houses from a building society, tucked up together under pink counterpanes.'[25] Yet he shared official concerns about the effect upon morale and production of a population that was adjusting too readily to this subterranean existence:

> The Tube stations don't now stink to any extent, the new metal bunks are quite good and the people one sees there . . . seem contented and normal in all ways – but this is just what disquiets me. What is one to think of people who go on living this sub-human life night after night . . . taking it all for granted and having great fun riding round and round the Inner Circle.[26]

Leonard and Virginia Woolf described a friendly encounter over a cup of tea with two strangers in a south London shelter on their way from their cottage in Rodwell, Sussex, to Bloomsbury. In his autobiography Leonard Woolf gave a graphic description of a shelter in Russell Square Underground station:

In the worst days of the Blitz I passed through Russell Square Underground station on my way to or from my house in Mecklenburgh Square . . . dozens of men, women and children [were] on mattresses wrapped in sheets and blankets and lying side by side all the way down the platform as if they were sardines in a gigantic tin.[27]

One must not exaggerate. At the height of the Blitz it is estimated that only about 4 per cent of Londoners were sheltering in the tubes, the great majority preferring to sleep in their own homes or garden shelters regardless of the hazards of bombing. Nevertheless those who used the tube shelters were often the most vulnerable: those living in the central, most bombed areas, without garden shelters (or gardens) of their own, working in the factories or docks by day and able to seek refuge in the tubes by night. In these ways what had begun as a rebellion against a government prohibition became the tube system's special contribution to the war effort. Londoners who would otherwise have been vulnerable to bombing during the Blitz that lasted until the summer of 1941 were not only protected, but were also undisturbed by the noise of the bombing and thus able to have a night's sleep before returning to their war work during the daytime. In June 1941, as the Luftwaffe turned its attention to the Russian campaign, the Blitz abated and the numbers sheltering in the tubes steadily fell. In April 1943 Mass Observation conducted another study of tube life and reported that some families had established themselves permanently in the shelters, having abandoned their homes altogether. Children almost three years old had never spent a night at home and new, friendly relationships had been formed with new, like-minded neighbours.[28] This was the 'troglodytic' mentality that the government had feared but it was confined to about 6,000 people. There was a further invasion of the tubes in 1944 when the V1 and V2 rockets began to fall on London and on VE night there were still 12,000 people sleeping in the shelters, many of them homeless families who had been bombed out of their houses. London Bridge Underground station alone accommodated 134 homeless families from Southwark at the end of the war.[29]

ILLUSTRIOUS OCCUPANTS

As war approached, government officials had considered what steps should be taken to provide secure accommodation for public bodies in the event of war. In March 1939 Frank Pick offered the disued Down Street station between Hyde Park Corner and Green Park as accommodation for the Railway Executive Committee, which would assume responsibility for running the railway network in the event of war. This station had opened in March 1907 and suffered from the fact that it was only about 600 yards from the more popular Hyde Park Corner and Dover Street (later renamed Green Park) stations on either side. Renaming it Down Street (Mayfair) didn't provide the required stimulus to traffic and it was closed in May 1932. Following Pick's offer the passageways leading to

The disused Down Street station, once a temporary home for the war cabinet, now a convenience store in the heart of Mayfair. (London's Transport Museum)

the platforms were fitted out for emergency use with offices, bathrooms and lavatories – which remain there. None of the facilities is visible from passing trains because of a brick partition erected to conceal them, and the work was carried out at night so that it could not be observed from passing trains that might contain German spies. The offices were used during the war by the Railway Executive Committee and sometimes by the war cabinet, Churchill himself on occasion walking across Green Park to this unconventional meeting-place. Down Street's entrance building remains, an incongruous feature of this most fashionable quarter of London. Its neighbours include the Albany, the Cavalry and Guards Club and the Athenaeum Hotel, in which company the dark red terracotta ticket hall, now occupied by a convenience store, looks distinctly out of place. Similar suites were established at six other Underground stations, with accommodation for 350 people. One of them, the disused Brompton Road station, became the headquarters of the anti-aircraft batteries which protected London.[30] Brompton Road's surface buildings also survive, an incongruous neighbour to Brompton Oratory.

DEEP SHELTERS

As the Battle of Britain ended and the Blitz on London took its nightly toll, Home Secretary Herbert Morrison announced on the BBC on 3 November 1940 that 'a new system of tunnels linked to the London tubes should be bored'. These were to contain sleeping accommodation for 64,000 people. The reason for this decision is not entirely clear, since by this date the government was resigned to the fact that Londoners were firmly and contentedly settled in the tube stations. Some writers[31] have suggested that the decision was influenced by tales of 'Hitler's terror weapons', involving rockets, germ warfare, atom bombs and other threats frequently featured in the popular press as war approached. Accordingly the shelters were possibly designed to house essential government departments in the face of such horrors. Construction began almost immediately and eight were eventually ready for use in 1942 when *The Engineer* reported that:[32]

> Eight new tube shelters in the London area are now so nearly completed that in an emergency they could be brought into use without delay . . . constructed in such positions that they can become part of new tube railways that may be driven below London when the war is over.

In 1936 a delegation from London Transport had visited New York to study that city's Rapid Transit System, opened in 1932. The network provided a fast tube service to run alongside the traditional slow service stopping at all stations. In the late 1930s J.P. Thomas, the Board's general manager for railways, developed a plan for a similar network of lines beneath London, one of them running parallel to the Northern Line on which overcrowding was the subject of bitter complaint at the time.[33] It is certainly true that seven of the shelters were built beneath the Northern Line adjacent to stations at Clapham South, Clapham Common, Clapham North, Stockwell, Goodge Street, Camden Town and Belsize Park. Moreover J.P. Thomas was brought out of retirement to supervise their construction. The shelters took the form of tunnels, each about 1,200ft long, with a diameter of 16ft 6in, almost one-and-a-half times the size of the tubes. With additional tunnelling after the war the shelters could quite easily have been linked to form an express train service of the kind that New York had, so there seems no doubt that this was an example of long-term planning coupled to the exigencies of war. The eighth shelter was built at Chancery Lane. The location of the Northern Line shelters may be recognised by the large brick structures which still stand at the entrance to the shafts leading down to the tunnels.

These deep shelters were never used to house government departments, even when the V1 and V2 rockets began to fall on London in 1944 but they found a wide variety of uses. The one at Chancery Lane was commandeered by the nearby Public Record Office as a document store while that at Clapham Common was used by the Admiralty for the same purpose. The other shelters at Clapham, Stockwell and Camden Town were used

Entrance to one of the 'deep shelters' planned by Herbert Morrison and still a curious feature of the Belsize Park skyline. (Author)

by the War Office to accommodate soldiers passing through London on their way to the south coast and the beaches of Normandy. In 1942 the Goodge Street shelter became Eisenhower's headquarters, where he planned the Normandy invasion before moving to an advance headquarters in Hampshire, so for over a year that unremarkable London station witnessed a steady flow of generals, admirals and air marshals, including Montgomery and Eisenhower, as preparations for D-Day advanced. A scrambler telephone was installed on which Eisenhower spoke regularly to Churchill. It remained the centre of the communications network for the high command, operating every hour of every day. On D-Day three telephone lines were established between Goodge Street and the three British and Canadian beaches, Juno, Sword and Gold. Goodge Street thus received the first reports of the drama unfolding on the Normandy beaches, and as the allied armies advanced Goodge Street's telephone lines followed close behind, a line to Berlin itself being opened as the war ended. After the war the Clapham Common shelter took its place in a small incident of English social history.

THE *EMPIRE WINDRUSH*

In June 1948, as the SS *Empire Windrush* approached Tilbury with 510 immigrants from the West Indies, the government dithered about what to do with them. There was wild talk of sending the destroyer HMS *Sheffield* to turn back the boat and speculation that the Caribbean visitors would not see out the English winter. Eventually, having recognised that as Commonwealth citizens they could not be refused entry, the Home Office sent a former RAF policeman called Baron Baker, who was active in community affairs, to meet the ship and it was he who suggested that the Clapham Common deep shelter be used to house the visitors. Almost half of them moved in and made their way in the days that followed to the nearest labour exchange in Coldharbour Lane, Brixton. Thus was the Afro-Caribbean community of Brixton born.[34]

'PADDOCK' AND THE STATION THAT NEVER WAS

In his account of the war Churchill refers to the need for secure accommodation for government departments in the following terms:

> it was necessary to construct all kinds of strongholds under or above ground from which the Executive, with its thousands of officials, could carry out their duties. A citadel for the War Cabinet had already been prepared near Hampstead, with offices and bedrooms, and wired and fortified telecommunications. This was called 'Paddock'.[35]

Churchill goes on to describe how the Cabinet used it, for the first and only time, on 29 September 1940, holding a meeting 'far from the light of day'. It is known that such refuges existed in several places and 'Paddock' has been identified by some authorities with the shelter beneath the Post Office Research Station at Dollis Hill. However, it is unlikely that Churchill would have confused Dollis Hill and Hampstead so it is possible that 'Paddock' was North End station on the Northern Line between Hampstead and Golders Green. Yerkes' Hampstead Tube had always intended to build a station here, close to Wyldes Farm in Golders Green. During her successful campaign to acquire 80 acres of land around Wyldes Farm as an extension to Hampstead Heath, Henrietta Barnett had announced that she welcomed the station as a means by which Londoners could gain access to the Heath for recreation. However, her success in preventing housing development on the nearby land that she had added to the Heath made the station unattractive to the Yerkes group which built the line. While they would no doubt have welcomed the leisure travellers whom Henrietta wished to encourage they also needed a steady flow of commuters from local dwellings if the station were to pay its way. The station tunnels and platforms were already built when the decision was taken to abandon the station, which thus never opened. This station certainly fits Churchill's description of Paddock as 'near Hampstead . . . far from the light of day'. Further evidence was found by Peter Laurie when he was researching his book *Beneath the City Streets*. He was contacted by a man who had been on Home Guard sentry duty near the station in 1940 'when Mr Churchill popped out of the ground at my feet'.[36] Presumably this was on the day of the Cabinet meeting to which Churchill referred. Above the site of the station is a small white building whose notice proclaims that it is an electrical installation but which is in fact an emergency exit from the platforms beneath. This is perhaps the exit from which Churchill emerged beside the startled sentry. Since the war the station facilities have been used to store engineers' materials and a house, 1 Hampstead Way, has been built on the site of the unbuilt booking hall. The station is referred to by Underground staff as 'The Bull and Bush', the nearby pub made famous in a music-hall song. It is the only station on the system which was built but never opened.

KEEPING LONDON MOVING

While it fulfilled its role of sheltering the government hierarchy, officials and ordinary Londoners from the falling bombs, the Underground was also expected to continue its customary duty of moving citizens around the capital. The problems it faced were manifold but two in particular deserve examination. The first concerned damage to rolling stock. Out of a fleet of 3,869 railway cars 19 were completely destroyed by direct

Bank station after a direct hit. (London's Transport Museum)

hits and 1,050 were damaged – almost 30 per cent of the total.[37] The second problem concerned disruption to services when the stations and tracks were hit. A striking example may be found in the great fire bomb attack on the night of 29/30 December 1940. Long sections of the Northern Line, Central Line and District Line were impassable, eight stations in central London were closed and seven more seriously damaged. The Thames floodgates were closed, preventing trains from passing beneath the river. Twelve days later, on 11 January 1941, eleven stations were struck, the worst casualty being Bank, where the roadway collapsed into the concourse beneath. A train had entered the station as the bomb exploded and the blast blew the driver off his seat. The 'dead man's handle' mechanism quickly stopped the train – but not before it had run down some passengers who had themselves been blasted off the platforms into its path. In all, fifty-six people were killed. A huge hole in the roadway above was temporarily spanned by a Bailey bridge erected by Royal New Zealand Engineers.

Unexploded bombs often presented the greatest problems. On the night of 11 January one fell on Hyde Park Corner station, stopping the trains until the bomb was made safe. Stations which had the misfortune to be sited close to the front line RAF fighter stations were particularly vulnerable. Colindale station, on the Northern Line, was hit twice in September 1940 by bombs no doubt intended for nearby RAF Hendon while another fell near the railway between Hendon and Brent in the same month and failed to explode. For fourteen days the service was suspended and when the bomb, to the relief of Underground staff, did finally explode, it did no damage to the track.

There was a tendency to downplay these dramatic events. *The Times*, describing the fire raid of 11 January, emphasised that the fires were quickly brought under control and that most services were restored within forty-eight hours. The London Passenger Transport Board's daily reports recorded the disasters which struck them with laconic understatement. Thus after the first fire raid it reported, on 30 December:

> As a result of the intense attack last night traffic conditions in the central London area this morning are bad . . . the Northern City Line is closed to traffic . . . a train was set on fire west of Aldersgate station but was subsequently extinguished, with no casualties . . . the number of shelterers at Tube stations on Saturday night was roundly 89,000.[38]

The following day they reported: 'no fresh damage was caused during this period; there was no enemy activity in the Board's area . . . the District Line was re-opened between Charing Cross and Mansion House'. Such phrases conceal the frantic activity that lay behind them as the Board's staff, aided by firemen, police, service personnel and medical staff, laboured throughout the nights amid falling bombs to rescue casualties, recover corpses, repair bomb damage and maintain some semblance of a service to keep the beleaguered capital alive. Buses were worse affected as they were often unable to negotiate roads damaged or blocked by fallen buildings, so more passengers than ever crowded on to the trains. As in the First World War much of the work was done by women. By the end of the war 16,500 women were on the Board's payroll, working on stations, in signal-boxes and in maintenance depots. In all, 181 Underground staff were killed on duty and 1,867 seriously injured.[39]

WAGING WAR

Besides offering shelter to Londoners and keeping the capital moving, the Underground and its staff made some notable contributions to the military campaigns. Early in the war communities had been encouraged by Ashfield's old friend Lord Beaverbrook, Minister of Aircraft Production, to raise money to pay for fighter aircraft, these being the most visible symbol of Britain's defiance of the Nazis. In 1942 a cheque was handed over for the first of two Spitfires financed by London Transport's staff. They flew into battle

London Transport's Spitfire, with the RAF roundels on the wings and the London Transport roundels on the fuselage. (London's Transport Museum)

bearing the RAF roundels on their wings and the London Transport roundel on their fuselages. During the Battle of Britain 400 engineering staff were released from the network to service and repair Hurricanes damaged in the battle. By such means the RAF had more serviceable planes at the end of the battle than they had at the beginning. At the same time Underground facilities normally devoted to building and maintaining rolling stock were converted to more warlike purposes. In 1941 the London Aircraft Production Group was set up, managed by London Transport and including four other organisations involved in engineering and coach-building. Over the next four years 710 Halifax heavy bombers were assembled in the Aldenham maintenance depot which had been built for the planned (but never completed) extension of the Northern Line.[40] A few London Transport engineers had spent a short time at a Handley Page aircraft factory but with these exceptions the Halifaxes were built by a workforce with no previous experience of aircraft production. In fact, 80 per cent of them had no experience of engineering and half of the workforce were women.

At Acton rolling stock maintenance depot Sherman tanks were overhauled and some were converted to special uses, such as the waterproofed 'swimming tanks'. These were to be launched into deep water from landing craft to accompany the first British and Canadian infantry as they stormed the Normandy beaches, thereby helping to reduce the casualties on those beaches to well below the levels that had been feared (and fewer than those suffered by the Americans who did not use such devices). Acton also adapted tanks for bridge-laying, which proved critical in the break-out after the landings. At Earl's Court station the subway leading to the exhibition hall was converted into an aircraft components factory in 1942, the labour provided by London Transport volunteers working when their shifts had ended. However, the most extraordinary improvisation was that which occurred in the completed but as yet unused new section of the Central Line between Leytonstone and Gants Hill. This 5 mile section of tunnel was taken over by the Plessey company and turned into the world's longest factory, where 300,000 square feet of floor space employed 2,000 workers, day and night, manufacturing components for Churchill tanks, Spitfires, Lancasters and Halifaxes. The peculiar shape of the factory necessitated the installation of a narrow-gauge railway to convey components and materials. At the end of the war the production line was removed from the tunnels and installed in a factory in Ilford where, having been sold to the former foe in the form of the German company Siemens, it survived into the twenty-first century.

One contribution to the war effort may have been less conventional. Underground managers had long been concerned at the loss of rubber grips suspended from the ceilings of railway cars for the use of standing passengers, or 'straphangers'. It was believed that criminals removed them to use as coshes. The losses, however, were given a more heroic aspect when, in 1943, London Transport's publicity department announced that one of them had been found in a street in Algiers, having been used in a raid by commandos of the infant SAS. Was this true? We will never know.

Plessey aircraft components being made in unfinished railway tunnels at Leytonstone; the factory was later relocated in Ilford and sold to Siemens. (London's Transport Museum)

THE WORLD'S MOST EXEMPLARY (AND HATED) PASSENGER

Not all of London Transport's wartime efforts were received with undiluted enthusiasm. One of its more irritating productions was *Billy Brown, The World's Most Exemplary Passenger*, a character created by a cartoonist called David Langdon. Billy appeared in *Billy's Bulletin*, a series of posters presented to look like a newspaper, from which Billy delivered unctuous homilies to fellow travellers, often in excruciating rhymes. For example:

> **To-day's Good Deed**:
> When you travel to and fro
> On a line you really know,
> Remember those who aren't so sure
> And haven't been that way before.
> Do your good deed for the day,
> Tell them the stations on the way.

LORDS STATION: A CASUALTY OF WAR

In April 1868 St John's Wood Road station opened on the Metropolitan and St John's Wood Railway which ran from Baker Street to Swiss Cottage. It was convenient for the nearby Lords cricket ground and in the summer months it was found necessary to erect a temporary ticket office within the famous ground itself to supplement the small one at the station. At other times the station was not much used. In 1925 the station, by then part of the Metropolitan Line, was replaced by a new one, designed by C.W. Clark, the architect of Chiltern Court. It was renamed St John's Wood. In 1932 the legendary Arsenal manager Herbert Chapman had persuaded the Underground Group to change the name of Gillespie Road station to Arsenal in honour of the club, then at the height of its fame. Following this precedent in 1936 the Marylebone Cricket Club suggested that the St John's Wood station name be changed to Lords, and this took place on 11 June 1939. However, in November of the same year the Bakerloo extension to Stanmore opened (now the Jubilee Line), with its own St John's Wood station and the nearby Lords station was closed for the duration of the war as an economy measure. It never reopened, so Lords had its own station for only five months.

It was not made clear how these hapless passengers would be recognised or how they might react to being accosted in this way by a stranger following Billy's example. Billy was not always so sympathetic to his fellow passengers, as is shown by a *Stop Press* announcement headed **Significant Incident** which reported: 'At Bow Street Police Court to-day Billy Brown was commended by magistrates for frustrating attempt by passenger on Underground to smoke in car labelled "no smoking".' It was not explained how Billy 'frustrated' the delinquent passenger. He would surely have been too well-behaved to use a water pistol, even when so severely provoked. The *Daily Mail* spoke for many when it wrote:

> Some day very soon, by heck,
> Billy Brown, I'll wring your neck.

POSTSCRIPT

As the war ended the Underground railway could look back with some satisfaction at the previous six years. It had sheltered London's citizens, the nation's art treasures and, on occasion, its government. Its staff and its maintenance depots had not only kept the capital moving but had supplied its fighting services with equipment vital to the war effort. Its stations, tracks and rolling stock bore the scars of war and were in urgent need of renewal. It also needed new managers. Frank Pick had died in 1941 and Ashfield, aged seventy-one as the war ended, was overdue for retirement. In 1945, with the election of a Labour government sympathetic towards public services and investment, London Transport's managers must have felt confident that they faced a period of sympathetic, stable management and a generous flow of investment in public transport. They were to be sorely disappointed.

CHAPTER EIGHT
THE POST-WAR UNDERGROUND

By the end of the decade the Chairman was 'banging the table' and insisting that the work must be done. But as he had to work through the Commission the sound must have been muffled by the time it reached the Ministry. . . . London Transport took every step within their power to press the scheme upon the authorities concerned.

(The Select Committee on Nationalised Industries, 1965, commenting on the ten-year delay in constructing the much-needed Victoria Line)

Men who had worked hard all their lives, often in difficult conditions and with irregular working hours, under the impression that they were helping to provide a valuable service to the community, suddenly felt that they were being branded as wasters and parasites.

(Paul Garbutt, former London Transport Chief Secretary, in *London Transport and the Politicians*, 1985)

I'll take the government to court.

(Ken Livingstone, Mayor of London, 2001)

THE WARS OF THE ROSES

Between the end of the Second World War in 1945 and the establishment of London Regional Transport in 1984, the Underground was to undergo five changes in regime, each of them conditioned by political, social and financial agendas that arose from national and local politics. It must have been a turbulent time, somewhat reminiscent of the Wars of the Roses. By contrast, the long reign of Ashfield and Pick must have seemed a haven of tranquillity.

As the network enters the twenty-first century in the throes of further changes in organisation – accompanied by debates on the merits of public-private partnerships, semi-privatisation and transfer of control to the new mayor of London – there are reasons to fear that the network's management will continue to be distracted by issues which have little to do with running the services. But there are also some reasons for hope.

POST-WAR RECOVERY

As the war ended the battered system resumed something like a normal service. Bunks, lavatories and bombed-out families were removed from the station platforms and the Aldwych branch, having disposed of the Elgin Marbles and other refugees, was reopened to traffic.[1] For the moment the London Passenger Transport Board continued to manage the system, with Ashfield as chairman, though it was clear that this was a temporary arrangement. In November 1946 Attlee's Labour government introduced a Transport Bill which led to the establishment, in January 1948, of the British Transport Commission. This body was to assume the enormous task of determining policy and, most significantly, investment priorities, for all major forms of inland transport: the newly nationalised railways; inland waterways and docks; road passenger and freight transport; hotels formerly owned by the railways; and the activities of the former London Passenger Transport Board – that is the provision of bus and underground train services in London. Stockholders of all these undertakings were bought out at the prevailing market prices. From now on the network was wholly publicly owned. The British Transport Commission was one of the most conspicuous examples of the prevailing confidence in 'big government'. Big government, having won the war through centralised planning and government intervention, proposed to manage the peacetime economy in the same way. Unfortunately, big government was not equipped with big investment funds for the tasks that lay ahead.

The Commission appointed a number of subordinate executives to handle the day-to-day running of its various undertakings on its behalf. One of these was the London Transport Executive,[2] chaired by Lord Latham when Ashfield became a member of the Commission itself, though Ashfield died in 1948 within months of taking office. Latham had succeeded Herbert Morrison as leader of the LCC in 1940 and had been a member of the London Passenger Transport Board since 1935, so he was well acquainted with London and its transport needs. The London Transport Executive also contained several other former board members. This continuity of personnel may have eased the network through this first change of management but any potential advantage from this source was more than offset by the fact that London's transport needs assumed a low priority in the face of the Commission's other responsibilities. The Commission retained for itself a number of powers which were critical to the future of the network. In particular the London Transport Executive had to submit to the Commission any proposals for changes in fares policy; and, crucially, it had to submit for approval any proposals for capital expenditure in excess of £50,000. Even in 1948 £50,000 wasn't very much. To put the figure into context, the New Works Programme of the 1930s had been estimated to cost over £30 million. So the Executive could carry out a modest station refurbishment or replace a few lifts with escalators, but an order for much-needed new rolling stock to replace war damage, or the construction or extension of a line, would require the approval of the Commission. In turn, the Commission had to submit its capital investment proposals to the Ministry of Transport and the Treasury. And the First Lord of the Treasury, Clement Attlee, had many other things on his mind. This was the period of savage post-war austerity, of forced devaluation and shortages of everything. In 1946 bread was rationed, as it had not been even during the darkest days of the war, and scarce national resources had to be allocated between the tasks of replacing bombed houses, reconverting factories from making tanks and aeroplanes to making cars and refrigerators, creating the National Health Service, and retraining demobilised servicemen to follow careers as teachers, engineers and other peacetime occupations.

In the circumstances it is not surprising that investment in London's transport facilities in the decade after the war was negligible. It is, perhaps, remarkable that any improvements at all were made, the most notable being the opening of the Central Line extensions to Epping and Hainault in the east and West Ruislip in the west. It says much for the inadequacy of the steam service from Essex into Liverpool Street that the Minister of Transport, Alfred Barnes, was easily persuaded that the first sections should be completed in December 1946 despite the scarcity of steel for the rails. The tunnels had been completed before the war and, as indicated in Chapter Seven, had housed the Plessey company's aircraft components factory during the conflict. The production lines were removed and resited in a factory in the middle of Ilford. Ironically the factory survived into the twenty-first century under German ownership: Siemens. The new lines were opened progressively for train services between 1946 and 1949. The ceremony which marked the opening of the line as far as Leytonstone, in May 1947, was touched by farce. The chairman of the London Transport Executive, Lord Latham, was noted for his diminutive stature and for the flat monotone in which he delivered his speeches. At the ceremony, which took place at a pub called the Green Man, he delivered a speech of twice the expected length from behind a large lectern which concealed his small frame except for a barely detectable wisp of protruding hair. The thirsty journalists in attendance were thus entertained by an endless, monotonous drone apparently emanating from the lectern itself.[3]

An examination of the annual reports of the British Transport Commission and of London Transport reveals just how little was invested in the network in the decade which followed the war. Thus the Commission's report 'London Transport in 1953'[4] reveals that during that year only £300,000 was spent on new capital investment while the following year the figure of £406,000 was offset by £195,000 of surplus property sales. The investment was confined to such projects as realigned track layouts, refurbished stations and the occasional new escalator. After 1954 the reports do not identify new investment, probably because it was so low, but by examining the balance sheets for the period one can detect that, for the period 1954–9, the value of the Underground's fixed assets in track, signalling, buildings and rolling stock increased by less than 5 per cent *before depreciation*, which suggests that the assets were being run down rather than built up.[5] At the same time the Executive was commenting on the relentless increases in wages caused by shortage of labour in London and its powerlessness to raise fares without the authority of the Commission. The only capital expenditure proposal of any consequence to be authorised in the 1950s was the electrification of the Metropolitan Line north of Rickmansworth at a cost of £3.5 million. This was completed in 1960 and the last steam-hauled passenger train on the Underground ran on 11 September 1961. After 1959 the capital investment situation improved slightly as new rolling stock was authorised to replace the run-down cars on the Piccadilly and Central Lines.

The lack of investment was not caused by lack of understanding or sympathy on the part of the network's masters, the British Transport Commission. It was simply that the Commission's priorities when allocating its meagre investment funds lay with the main line railway network, where wartime damage substantially exceeded that inflicted on the Underground. In its first report, for 1948, the Commission commented on the need for railway improvements in London: 'If the planning needs of the Metropolis make such facilities essential, the labour and material which will be required must be found from sources additional to those at present available to the Commission.' They recognised the need. They just didn't have the money.

A New Regime

In 1951 Churchill replaced Attlee as prime minister and in 1953 his Conservative government appointed a committee headed by Paul Chambers, chairman of ICI, to examine the activities of London Transport. At the same time the British Transport Commission was reorganised and some of its activities sold off. Henceforward the Commission was to manage directly all the undertakings for which it was responsible, like the railways and waterways, with no intervening executives. The only exception was London Transport. London Transport retained its own executive, which was henceforth appointed directly by the Minister of Transport though nominally still responsible to the Commission. This second change in the management of the network since 1945 created an anomalous situation whereby the Commission was theoretically responsible for the London Transport Executive without having any real authority over its members, though it still had to provide the network's investment funds. In 1953 the Commission had acquired a new chairman,[6] the distinguished soldier and industrialist General Sir Brian Robertson (1896–1974). Robertson had worked logistical miracles for the Eighth Army in the desert campaigns for that most exacting taskmaster General Montgomery, and had been concerned with the post-war restoration of the German rail network. However, in deciding investment priorities among the various undertakings for which he was responsible London Transport's case cannot have been helped by its anomalous position.

The awkward nature of the relationship was underlined in the 1955 report of the Chambers committee which suggested that the Commission should either run London Transport itself or hand it over to the minister.[7] However, the committee was very complimentary about the management of London Transport itself, using such phrases as: 'so far as safety is concerned the standards maintained by London Transport are very high indeed . . . the standards of punctuality on London Transport's railways are excellent . . . London has one of the best passenger transport systems in the world.' It strongly recommended investment in a new route proposed by London Transport, later to become the Victoria Line:

> Although the proposed railway may not in the near future pay its way directly we are of the opinion that the indirect advantages to London Transport and to London's economy as a whole are so important that this project should not be abandoned or postponed because on the basis of direct revenue or direct expenditure it appears to be unprofitable.

Rarely has a nationalised undertaking received such praise. Paradoxically, Lord Latham, chairman of the Executive, to whom was due much of the credit for the Chambers Committee's favourable verdict, had resigned in protest when it was appointed, to be replaced by the polymath Sir John Elliot, journalist, author of historical works on the French Revolution and the First World War, and railwayman of many years' experience. Sir John Elliot (1898–1988) was the son of R.D. Blumenfeld, editor of the *Daily Express*, who in 1887 had predicted that underground railways wouldn't last (*see* panel on p. 24). Elliot followed his father into journalism, became assistant editor of the *Evening Standard* and adopted his mother's surname of Elliot on Lord Beaverbrook's advice. In 1925 he joined the Southern Railway and became public relations assistant to the general manager, Sir Herbert Walker. After 1948 he occupied a number of senior management positions in the nationalised railway industry, becoming chairman of the London Transport Executive in 1953. Unfortunately his wide connections both within the railway industry and outside it gave him no more access to investment funds than his predecessor had enjoyed. His frustrations, and those of the network as a whole at this time, are well illustrated by the saga of the Victoria Line.

The need for an underground rail link between the north-eastern suburbs of London and Westminster had been recognised as long ago as 1894. In that year the London, Walthamstow and Epping Forest Railway was put forward for parliamentary approval but no capital could be raised for it and the project lapsed. In 1946 a committee headed by Sir Charles Inglis (1875–1952), a former professor of engineering from Cambridge with much experience of railway work, proposed a network of one hundred miles of new tube railways crossing London. They would be built to accommodate main line gauge trains and would reduce or eliminate the need for the Southern Railway's congested

THE VICTORIA LINE

ROUTE 8 – ROUTE C – THE VICTORIA LINE

The Victoria Line was the first major cross-London tube line since the opening of the Piccadilly Line in December 1906. It was originally proposed by the Railway (London Plan) working party in 1952 but the necessary expenditure was not authorised by the Treasury until 1962, the more attractive 'Victoria Line' designation having become attached to the project in 1953. It runs underground throughout its length, the only line to do so with the exception of the Waterloo and City Line which finally became part of the Underground in 1994. The first section, from Walthamstow Central to Highbury and Islington, opened to passengers in September 1968 and the official opening was performed by the Queen on 7 March 1969 when the line had reached Victoria. The extension south of the river to Brixton opened in July 1971. It was the first Underground line to be justified on the basis of cost benefit analysis rather than the cruder financial criteria which had applied in the days of the earlier entrepreneurs. It was also the first to adopt a form of Automatic Train Operation whereby the driver starts the train and operates the doors while the train's speed and braking are governed automatically by pulses from trackside equipment. The Victoria Line was also the first to experiment with the use of automatic ticket barriers.

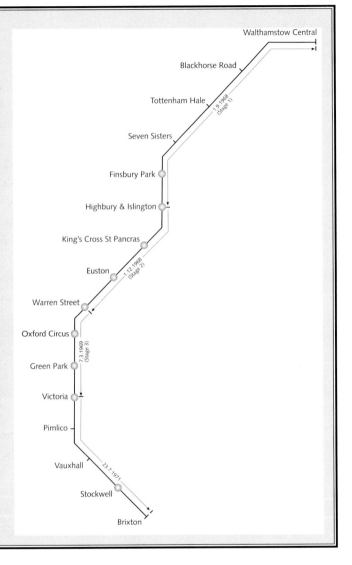

The Victoria Line, 1971.

termini north of the Thames at Charing Cross, Cannon Street, Holborn Viaduct and Blackfriars.[8] This would have pleased the LCC architects who at this time were campaigning for the demolition of the railway bridges across the river because, according to contemporary architectural fashion, they were regarded as unsightly. One of the committee's proposals, unromantically described as 'Route 8', was for a link from Finsbury Park to East Croydon via Victoria.[9] The London Transport Executive quickly recognised the advantages of such a line, crossing London from north-east to south-west. It would give better access to the West End for off-peak theatre and shopping traffic and it would pick up main line passengers from King's Cross, St Pancras, Euston and Victoria. It would further relieve congestion in the north-eastern suburbs around

Finsbury Park. The Executive accordingly developed the idea so that it ran from Walthamstow to Brixton, calling at the four main line termini en route. 'Route 8' became, in London Transport's planning schedules, the equally unalluring 'Route C' and from 1952 the Executive began to campaign vigorously for it.

In 1955 parliamentary authority was secured for Route C, a measure no doubt helped by the Chambers Committee's endorsement of the management, and the line, earlier that year. In the meantime a more attractive name had been found for the new line. At one point the name 'KingVic' was suggested, to indicate the link between King's Cross and Victoria, on the lines of the 'Bakerloo' half a century earlier. Eventually the name 'Victoria Line' was proposed by David McKenna, London Transport's chief commercial and public relations officer, early in 1953[10] and Sir John Elliot used the new name in an address to the Institute of Transport on 5 December 1955. Authority to spend the money, however, proved very difficult to obtain. From 1955 onwards each London Transport annual report contains a section headed 'The Victoria Line'. Plans were prepared, research undertaken, designs completed and trial borings made. Yet no line was actually built. In its report for 1955 the British Transport Commission wrote of the Victoria Line:

> In the present economic situation no starting date for its construction has been fixed but the Executive are convinced that this new tube railway is a traffic facility which is essential for the capital and that it will have to be provided sooner or later.[11]

The 'present economic situation' consisted of a booming economy, with post-war rationing finally abolished; a general election recently won by the Conservatives under their new and popular leader Anthony Eden; and a main line railway modernisation programme authorised the same year by the Minister of Transport. It is hard to imagine more favourable circumstances. In 1956 some money was released to enable experimental tunnelling to take place but another three years elapsed before the Underground was allowed to spend it. In January 1960 they began to construct a mile-long tunnel north of Finsbury Park to test two new tunnelling shield designs and to evaluate the advantages of cast-iron against concrete tunnel linings. This work was finished in July 1961 but another year elapsed before further work was authorised.

In 1965 a Parliamentary Select Committee cast some light on the reasons for the endless delays which attended the construction of the line. In the words of the Committee describing the frustration of the chairman Sir John Elliot in his dealings with the British Transport Commission and the Ministry of Transport:

> by the end of the decade [1959] the Chairman was 'banging the table' and insisting that the work must be done. But as he had to work through the Commission the sound must have been muffled by the time it reached the Ministry.[12]

The Committee concluded: 'For this delay Your Committee exonerate London Transport. They took every step within their power to press the scheme upon the authorities concerned.'

The 'authorities' were more than a match for Sir John Elliot when they wanted to procrastinate. In 1959, after one delay had followed another for four years, the Executive was asked to ascertain whether the £55 million which the line was estimated to cost 'would pay a better dividend were it spent on off-street parking or some other project'.[13] There is no record of the reaction to this suggestion of the 'table-banging' Sir John Elliot, though his regime at this time did enjoy its lighter moments. Many of them were associated with John Cliff, the Board member responsible for industrial relations. Cliff, a former Leeds tram driver, had been a member of the original London Passenger Transport Board since 1933. In the 1950s, despite his small stature, many of his colleagues found him intimidating and occasionally incomprehensible by virtue of his thick Yorkshire accent. On one occasion, after Cliff had spent a heavy morning negotiating with trade unions, Sir John Elliot summoned an engineer called Joe Manser to his office to discuss some technical matter. Upon entering, Manser was surprised to see Cliff supine on the carpet in front of the chairman's desk, either dead or asleep. Seeing the startled Manser, Cliff sat up, head on elbow, and reassured him: 'It's all right, Manser. I've 'ad a 'ard morning's negotiations and t'chairman's given me permission to 'ave a sleep on 'is carpet.' He rose to his feet and left the room as Elliot raised his eyes to the ceiling.[14]

The Victoria Line was eventually rescued by two factors. One, the spectre of unemployment, was familiar to Underground railway managers. The other was a new way of appraising projects using the techniques of cost benefit analysis. This latter concept had been developed by two academics, C.D. Foster from Oxford University and M.E. Beesley of the London School of Economics. In 1962 they presented to the Royal Statistical Society a paper on the subject, relating it to the Victoria Line.[15] The paper was followed up by articles in *The Times*. In the first article, headlined 'A Search for Principles' they argued:

> There is at present a double standard for road and rail investment. The Ministry of Transport and the Treasury do not – because they cannot – expect road investment to pay. But they now require rail investment to pay.

Earlier calculations of the line's financial performance estimated that, without fare increases, the new line would generate an operating surplus of about £250,000 a year which would be insufficient to pay even the interest charges on the capital cost of over £50 million. The return on investment would be negative. As with the tubes built by Yerkes and others the immense capital cost of boring tunnels beneath London could not be met by revenue earned from fares. Few doubted that the line would bring great benefits to the capital but accountants and economists alike struggled in vain to make a financial case for it.

Foster and Beesley took a radically different approach. They agreed that the revenue gained by the line itself would never give an adequate return on investment. 'Social need' they dismissed as too vague a concept to use. But they went on to argue that other benefits ought to be credited to the line. Thus others who did not use the line itself would benefit from it. These included motorists, who would travel faster and more cheaply along streets that were less congested as a result of the line opening. In fact Foster and Beesley estimated that 35 per cent of the benefits would accrue to motorists for this reason. Travellers on other lines would travel more quickly and more comfortably when other passengers switched to the new line. If a value of 7s 6d an hour was placed on the time of a working traveller, and 5s an hour on the time of a leisure traveller, this could then be built into the equation as well. On this basis the Victoria Line, they triumphantly announced, would give a return on capital of over 11 per cent – a very satisfactory return in that era of low inflation. This argument, which was to feature in future proposals for investment in urban transport, provided the theoretical justification for the new line but the impetus was imparted by a much older problem which had underpinned the New Works programmes of the 1920s and the 1930s. In 1962 the government became concerned about rising unemployment. It was suggested that the Victoria Line would not only boost employment in London but that tunnel segments could be ordered from north-eastern England, bringing much-needed jobs to that area. Ashfield and Pick would certainly have recognised these arguments. Yet again Keynesian economic remedies had done more for metropolitan public transport than any number of careful studies of transport needs had done. The government go-ahead was finally given on 20 August 1962.

BUILDING THE VICTORIA LINE

The Victoria Line had two unique characteristics which made its construction peculiarly difficult. First, it is the only line which runs underground for its entire length (except the Waterloo and City Line's shuttle service), all of which thus had to be bored through strata ranging from London clay to waterlogged gravel. Secondly, all of its original fifteen stations have interchanges either with other tubes or with main line stations, meaning that each station had to be carefully designed to make these connections as convenient as possible.[17] Three of the stations which the line served were among the busiest on the network, starting with Victoria itself (busiest of all), Oxford Circus (2nd) and King's Cross (4th). The rebuilding of Oxford Circus was particularly difficult. In September 1962, within a month of the line being authorised, work began on charting the cobweb of pipes and mains in the vicinity of the station. Nine months was spent re-routing these. As with the reconstruction of Piccadilly Circus station in 1928,[18] a new circular concourse and booking hall was built beneath the Circus but on this occasion there was no conveniently placed Eros statue whose temporary removal would give access to the space beneath. Instead, during the August bank holiday in 1963 the 'Oxford Circus Umbrella' was erected: a 2,500 square yard steel deck over which traffic passed for almost five years while the station was rebuilt beneath it. Nearby a concrete raft was built beneath the basement of the Peter Robinson department store to shield the tunnels of the Victoria Line on their way towards Green Park.

New Shields, Awkward Terrain and Awkward Ghosts

Both the new types of tunnelling equipment which had been tested on the trial bores in 1956[19] were used in the work. The Kinnear-Moodie 'drum digger' was equipped with knives which were mounted on one drum which rotated inside another, the spoil being drawn away on conveyor belts. An alternative design, developed by McAlpine, had the knives attached to a central shaft. In 1965 the McAlpine machine set a new record of 470ft of tunnel bored in one week.[20] The later extension of the line south of the Thames to Brixton brought problems which Marc Brunel would have recognised as he created the first Thames tunnel: badly waterlogged soil.[21] Rotary excavators were abandoned in favour of traditional Greathead shields using manual labour. Besides the waterlogged soil other hazards encountered by the tunnellers included some fifty-million-year-old fossils, now in the Natural History Museum, and a collection of human remains buried in a plague pit, the latter supposedly accompanied by a ghostly presence. Beneath King's Cross station the new line had to thread its way through the existing network of subterranean railway services[22] as well as the usual sewers, water mains, electricity and gas pipes. No ghosts were reported from this site so it must be assumed that the tunnellers sensitively avoided disturbing the grave of Boadicea, reputedly buried beneath platform ten of the main line station.[23] In the vicinity of the line's new station at Vauxhall the ground was so waterlogged that it had to be frozen before it could be excavated. This was done by inserting tubes carrying liquid nitrogen at a temperature of about −200 degrees centigrade.

New Trains, New Tickets, New Signals

The first section of the Victoria Line, between Walthamstow and Highbury, opened without ceremony on 1 September 1968 but the official opening had to wait until the queen started the first train to Victoria on 7 March 1969. The Brixton extension followed in 1971. Not everyone was impressed. *The Observer* commented rather grumpily on the 'lavatorial' character of the station decor but the line was popular from its first days and within little more than a year was carrying 229 million passengers, 35 per cent more than had been anticipated in the original plans. It had cost about £90 million to build, against the original 1955 estimate of £50 million, though the thirteen-year delay had brought with it inflation of 60 per cent, and the remainder of the overspend could be accounted for by the late decision to build the Brixton extension which cost £16 million. The line's early passengers would have seen at least one innovation in the design of the line. They would all have noticed the yellow, iron-oxide-coated tickets which activated automatic barriers to enter and leave the platforms. They were accompanied by the installation of many automatic ticket-issuing machines. The aim of the new system was to reduce the number of staff required to issue and collect tickets at a time of chronic labour shortage, and to cut down on fare evasion which cost the network more than £10 million a year. The technology was new and the system was later withdrawn but it may be regarded as a precursor of the later, and successful, Underground Ticketing System which is now installed throughout the network.

A second and less obvious innovation was the absence of a guard on the trains, each train being operated by one person only under the Automatic Train Operation (ATO) system. The operator's job was to open and close the doors and operate the 'start' mechanism when the train was ready to leave a station. Trackside sensors fed information to a control mechanism on the train and governed its running speed as well as stopping it in stations. This was the first such system on a major railway anywhere in the world and to make it work the Underground's visionary chief signal engineer, Robert Dell, had to bully the Westinghouse company into making equipment that it had thought to be impossible.[24] Trains were, for the first time, provided with communication systems so that in an emergency the operators could communicate with the control centre. The Victoria Line was the first major addition to the network in the central area for over sixty years and, significantly, it was the first to be built for social rather than supposedly commercial reasons. This, in varying forms, was to be the pattern for the future.

ANOTHER NEW REGIME: THE LONDON TRANSPORT BOARD

The authorisation to build the Victoria Line in August 1962 coincided with the Underground's third change of regime since the war. In the same month the Transport Act 1962 received the royal assent. The British Transport Commission was abolished and the new London Transport Board created, appointed by and reporting directly to the Minister of Transport. It foreshadowed a period of political involvement in London's transport which shows no sign of ending. During the seven years (1963–70) before London Transport was handed over to the Greater London Council the Board succeeded in gaining government approval, and an indication of financial support, for the extension of the Piccadilly Line to serve Heathrow airport. It was attractive to the Underground because an extension of a little over 3 miles from the existing station at Hounslow West would carry passengers from the airport a much longer distance into central London, producing a lot of additional revenue for 3 miles of railway. The government was persuaded to back the London Transport proposal in preference to a surface rail link from Victoria because many of the passengers arriving at Heathrow would want to be taken to hotels in central London which were directly served by the Piccadilly Line. There would be no need for airline passengers burdened with heavy luggage to change en route. Work began in 1971 and the extension was opened by the queen in December 1977, new stock having been ordered for the line which differed from the standard in having more space for airline passengers' luggage, though the luggage was the cause of further overcrowding during the commuting peaks. In 1986 the line was extended in the form of a loop to serve the new terminal 4.

Managing the Rush Hour

One of the Board's main preoccupations during the seven years it spent reporting to the Minister of Transport concerned the problems it encountered in managing economically the movement of millions of workers to and from offices in central London over relatively short periods in the morning and evening peaks. The problem was not new. Sir Edgar Speyer had told his shareholders that standing passengers in the peak periods meant dividends[25] but the rebuilding of bomb-shattered London in the years after the war witnessed an enormous growth in office space in the central area which was mostly occupied between the hours of nine and five. Factories, on the other hand, operating over longer hours with shift systems which gave a more even flow of workers, were moving to industrial estates like those on the Great West Road and Eastern Avenue where land was cheaper and freight transport facilities more suited to factory operations. Between 1955 and 1964 the number of people employed in London in manufacturing food, drink, tobacco and clothing fell by 23 per cent while the numbers employed in insurance, banking and finance grew by 24 per cent.[26] Thus in 1945 77 million square feet of office space was recorded in central London while by 1961 the figure had reached 168 million square feet, more than twice as much.[27] Outside the weekday peak hours, half of London Transport's rolling stock lay idle, a poor use of expensive assets. One attempt to combat this problem took the form of Office Development Permits, introduced in 1964, by which the newly created Greater London Council was able to control the building of offices exceeding 3,000 square feet in size. Other initiatives tried to alleviate the problem by altering hours of work. Thus the indecorously titled *Campaign for Staggered Hours of Work in Central London* gloomily informed the Minister of Transport in 1949 that companies were firmly resistant to starting work before 8 a.m. or finishing after 6 p.m. and that the best they could suggest was that the government should oblige the civil service to work in this way. Nothing more was heard of this suggestion.[28]

Few of these commuters wanted to work for London Transport. Unsocial hours and public sector pay levels were unattractive to most at a time when unemployment was

---

NEW BRITONS

The London Underground has some claims to distinction in the development of Britain's post-war multi-racial society. As observed earlier (pp. 167–8) the deep-level tube shelter built during the war at Clapham Common was the origin of Brixton's West Indian community and in 1956 London Transport, seriously short of workers, sent a recruitment officer and a medical officer to Barbados where they recruited seventy station staff. By 1968 40 per cent of applicants for non-clerical jobs were from non-whites. In 1975 a study of 'Race and Labour in London Transport'[31] offered some intriguing insights into the impact of these new Britons on the culture of the organisation. Many of them became train guards whose duties, according to ancient custom, included making tea for their drivers. But in the words of one interviewee 'it irks them to make tea when they don't drink tea'. There was, however, widespread agreement that the newcomers were good workers. London Transport changed some of its selection tests to ensure that applicants were not at a disadvantage through their ethnic background though the changes were too late for the author and television presenter Clive James, whose memoirs record that in the early 1960s he applied for the post of guard on the Underground but failed the psychological test, a failure he attributed to the fact that he was a 'congenital dreamer'.[32] In the late 1980s the management began a drive to increase the number of managers selected from ethnic minorities, the proportion increasing from 3 per cent to 15 per cent in 1989/90. As the Underground entered the new century 32 per cent of its workforce was non-white (figures supplied by Terry Day, London Underground).

---

almost non-existent. A series of pay increases, often accompanied by little or no productivity growth in the face of trade union opposition, created further financial pressures. Recruitment drives in the Caribbean and the Irish Republic alleviated the problems but services were regularly cancelled because of staff shortages, making the system worse. At the same time the growth of television and car ownership made it harder for the network to fill its trains outside the peak period, as Frank Pick had done, by promoting leisure travel. In the meantime passenger numbers fell slowly but steadily from the mid-1950s[29] and the system moved inexorably into deficit. The government, wishing to keep inflation under control and to please commuters, imposed a 'fares freeze' in May 1965 and made a compensatory grant to London Transport of £4 million. The following year this rose to £6 million. Barbara Castle decided to hand the problem to the Greater London Council even though a government White Paper published in the summer of 1968 declared that 'Judged against transport undertakings abroad which provide a similarly comprehensive range of services London Transport have done well.'[30]

THE GREATER LONDON COUNCIL TAKES OVER

In 1967 Barbara Castle, Harold Wilson's lively Minister of Transport, negotiated with Desmond Plummer, Conservative leader of the GLC, the transfer to the GLC of responsibility for London Transport. In a process similar to that by which the Labour stalwart Herbert Morrison had negotiated with Ashfield, these two unlikely collaborators reached agreement. Desmond Plummer drove a hard bargain whereby the whole of London Transport's capital debt of £270 million was written off by the government, leaving its balance sheet unencumbered by its history.[33] In addition the government agreed to fund a major programme of works to strengthen the sub-surface Circle Line roof where it ran beneath roads. The London Underground had passed to its fourth post-war master, the Greater London Council.

The relationship started promisingly. The 1968 Transport Act had permitted the government to make capital grants for new investment and London Transport was an early beneficiary, gaining £13.5 million from this source in the years 1968–9. Likewise the GLC contributed 25 per cent of the capital cost of the Heathrow extension, the government contributed 25 per cent and the rest was found from the network's own resources. The GLC appointed a competent industrialist and civil servant, Sir Richard Way, to run the network and supported him. In 1971 when the Jubilee Line was authorised the government contributed 75 per cent of the capital cost and the GLC the remaining 25 per cent. A £275 million package was agreed, extending over twenty years, to refurbish stations, with emphasis on the thirty stations which between them handle 50 per cent of passenger movements.[34] The Council made it clear that its aim was to win passengers for public transport: 'If a bus or rail passenger is once lost unnecessarily to the private car or to his own two feet he is unlikely ever to return.' Extensive research had been undertaken into policies elsewhere and the Council even considered the option of free travel on the tubes, based on practice in Munich, but decided that in a city the size of London this would be far too costly.[35] Fares should be set with this in mind, consistent with the network meeting reasonable financial targets. The management of the network itself was surprisingly muted in this debate. Commenting in their 1971 report on the debate over subsidies the directors wrote: 'This is a matter of politics and financial policy on which it would be improper for the Executive to adopt any stance or to express any views.' It is hard to imagine Lord Ashfield showing such restraint. Nevertheless in the light of later events the 1970s came to look like a golden age.

The honeymoon did not last long. In 1973 the Labour party won control of the GLC as the country, and the world, entered upon a period of economic turmoil. The price of

---

THE JUBILEE LINE

The Jubilee Line, like its older sister the Victoria Line, was originally conceived in 1948 and given the name 'Route F'. It was authorised in 1971 as the 'Fleet Line' because its original intention was to run beneath Fleet Street and across the valley of the River Fleet into the City via Ludgate Hill. The name 'Jubilee Line' was adopted by the Conservatives as a campaigning slogan during the GLC elections of 1977, the year of the Queen's silver jubilee. It was opened in 1979 between Charing Cross and Baker Street and also took over the Stanmore branch of the overcrowded Bakerloo Line (*see* panel on p. 65). The original idea of a route into the City was abandoned in 1980 in favour of a route south of the Thames, an area poorly served by the Underground. The resulting extension runs via Waterloo to Docklands, serving the Millennium Dome at North Greenwich en route. The line was an early beneficiary of the new system of capital grants made possible by the 1968 Transport Act, 75 per cent of the public finance being provided by the government and 25 per cent by the GLC with a contribution of £400 million from private sector developers in Docklands (though some of this was forfeited because the line was completed twenty months later than scheduled). It was the first line to use sound-absorbent panels instead of tiles, making it a somewhat quieter line than the others, and the first to place glass screens on the platform edges with sliding doors through which passengers board the trains. Most of its stations have been applauded as fine examples of modern architecture. It cost £3.5 billion.

MOORGATE: THE ACCIDENT THAT REMAINS A MYSTERY

On 28 February 1975, at 8.46 a.m., a Northern City Line train from Drayton Park, driven by a cautious, experienced man called Leslie Newson, entered the terminus at Moorgate faster than it should have been travelling. As it passed them, two railwaymen on platform 9 recognised Newson, apparently calm, alert, his hands on the controls. At nearly 40mph the train smashed into the 5ft-thick concrete tunnel wall beyond the end of the platform. It took police, ambulance staff and 1,324 men of the London Fire Brigade from all over the capital four days to remove the casualties from the wrecked train in the confined tunnel. Newson's body, buried deep within the wreckage, was the last to be removed. In all, 43 were dead, 74 injured. Lieutenant-Colonel McNaughton, Chief Inspecting Officer of Railways, carried out the first enquiry. He found nothing wrong with the train or track and concluded that the accident had been caused by the driver. Newson had a small amount of alcohol in his body, consistent with the level that could be produced by the natural decomposition of a body after four days. There was no reason to suspect suicide and much evidence to suggest that he had been a cautious, responsible, sober driver. A second, coroner's inquest heard Professor Keith Simpson, the country's leading pathologist, testify that he had found no evidence of incapacity due to illness, drink or drugs. The possibility of the sudden onset of various medical conditions was discussed, with no evidence of any having occurred. The jury returned a verdict of accidental death on all the victims, thereby accepting, in the coroner's words, that there was no evidence to support 'wicked, reckless behaviour or suicide'. In the words of Colonel McNaughton's report: 'No previous incident in the whole history of London Transport Railways can be regarded as in any way comparable with the Moorgate accident.' The true cause of the accident remains a mystery.

---

oil was raised by OPEC, with a direct effect upon the network's costs of generating electricity, and a series of highly inflationary pay deals in all sectors, unaccompanied by productivity increases, had disastrous effects on the network's costs without significantly easing its recruitment problems. The government imposed a freeze on fares and the GLC insisted on free travel for pensioners outside the peak hours. The result was a deficit of £24 million for London Transport in 1974 and a 60 per cent fares increase in 1975 when inflation reached an unprecedented 26 per cent. In the same year occurred the Moorgate disaster.

THE CUTLER YEARS

In 1977 the Conservatives returned to office at the GLC under the leadership of Horace Cutler, whose attitude to London Transport was very different from that of his Conservative predecessor Sir Desmond Plummer. In his memoirs he described the organisation as 'the world's largest public transportation organisation and an albatross round the neck of the capital's ratepayers'.[36] He added, 'The Board was weak . . . and couldn't make up its mind whether it was a commercial undertaking, a social service or a mixture of the two.' This charge could have been levelled at most nationalised undertakings at the time but it misses the point. Their directors were expected to run efficient, profitable operations while constrained by political factors that they couldn't control. Thus they were prevented from closing unprofitable operations for 'social' reasons, which usually meant the loss of votes. A conspicuous example was the loss-making rural line from Epping to Ongar, which London Transport wanted to close in 1970. They had to wait until 1994 before permission was finally granted, running at a loss in the meantime. Their fares were held down by governments who did not want to alarm passengers or risk inflation. Negotiations with the powerful trade unions were held under the watchful eye of governments anxious not to upset their supporters in the trade union movement by closing inefficient workshops or by insisting upon greater productivity. Nor did they wish to antagonise passengers through strikes in essential services. Profitable services were expected to subsidise loss-makers so that the profitable ones, instead of reinvesting in improved facilities, saw their profits drained away.

In the circumstances it is hardly surprising that the boards of directors were unclear about their roles but this did not stop Horace Cutler from attacking them, almost literally with an axe. In 1978 a former civil servant called Leslie Chapman published a book called *Your Disobedient Servant* which criticised the government machine for waste and inefficiency. Cutler sent Chapman a telegram summoning him to a meeting with the dramatic message 'Imperative I see you as soon as possible'. Chapman thought he could axe costs at London Transport by £60 million a year and his appointment was announced in the *Evening Standard* under the headline 'The Axeman Cometh', accompanied by a picture of Chapman brandishing an axe. He proceeded to antagonise the management of the network by publishing reports with titles like 'London Transport's Failure to Carry out its Functions Satisfactorily' and another book called *Waste Away*, with accounts of executive cars and restaurants which were normal practice in private companies of the period but which provided fine newspaper copy. Sir Horace Cutler, meanwhile, was amassing evidence in the form of letters from unidentified employees about 'Communist shop stewards who are allowed to sit in the canteen all day'.[37] A series of 'leaked' letters between Chapman, Cutler and the beleaguered London Transport chairman Ralph Bennett, who was the particular object of Cutler's wrath, added to the mayhem. At one point during the hostilities Horace Cutler arrived at 55 Broadway for lunch with Ralph Bennett. The security guard on duty failed to recognise Cutler who, offended, stormed out of the building.[38]

There were certainly weaknesses in the management of the network at the time. A report by PA consultants which was leaked to the press in 1980 identified lack of clear objectives, concern with short-term problems against long-term planning and greater strength in diagnosing problems than in tackling them. But, as observed above, many of the problems were beyond the power of management to solve: loss-making services kept open by government decree; controlled fares; labour shortages accompanied by trade union opposition to real productivity increases; and a nervous government anxious not to upset anyone. The same criticisms could have been levelled at most public and many private concerns at the time. The respected transport journalist Richard Hope, editor of the *Railway Gazette*, distributed the blame more equitably when he wrote of the consultants' report that: 'The impression is that London Transport is managed to some extent by bumbling idiots. It comes as a shock to recall that most of the idiots [including Ralph Bennett, author's note] were appointed by Sir Horace.'[39]

On 24 July Cutler dismissed Ralph Bennett, who was replaced as chairman for a short period by Sir Peter Masefield, who had been chairman of the British Airports Authority at the time of the construction of the Piccadilly extension. Cutler later wrote that he really wanted the cut-price airline magnate Freddie Laker to run the network. The following year Laker's airline went bankrupt. Perhaps this says more than anything else about the atmosphere in which London Transport's management was obliged to work at this time. One of Masefield's first acts was to get rid of the gadfly Leslie Chapman. In November 1980 a board meeting listened in silence to a particularly outrageous radio interview that Chapman had given and Chapman went, at Masefield's insistence. There was one sting left in the gadfly's tail. Three years later he published a book called *Waste in Public Expenditure*, in which he dredged up the fact that Dr Keith Bright, the recently appointed successor to Masefield, was running an Aston Martin car, acquired from his former employers, Huntley & Palmer's biscuits. The story ran for a while but lost momentum when the offending vehicle turned out to be third-hand. Such were the preoccupations of Underground management as the network entered its second decade under GLC control. In the words of London Transport's chief secretary of the time:

> Men who had worked hard all their lives, often in difficult conditions and with irregular working hours, under the impression that they were helping to provide a valuable service to the community, suddenly felt that they were being branded as wasters and parasites.[40]

More excitement was shortly to come.

THE LIVINGSTONE YEARS

In 1981 the Labour party gained control of the GLC with Ken Livingstone as Labour leader. Dave Wetzel, a former employee of London Transport, was elected chairman of the Transport Committee and the new councillors proceeded to implement one of the policies on which they had been elected – 'Fares Fair'. In October 1981 fares were cut by 32 per cent in a bold attempt to win passengers for public transport. The consequent huge drop in revenue was only marginally offset by a 9 per cent increase in the number of passengers using the service and an annual subsidy from the rates of £125 million was required to cover the gap, thus making the network more dependent than it had ever been upon its political masters. Councillors from the Conservative borough of Bromley, which had no Underground stations, challenged the 'Fares Fair' policies, arguing that its ratepayers were being unfairly penalised since they benefited less than inner-city residents from the policies and paid disproportionately towards subsidising them. The challenge made its way through the legal process and finally, on

17 December 1981, the Law Lords delivered their judgement in Bromley's favour. There followed another lurch in the opposite direction. On 21 March 1982 a 96 per cent fare increase was announced and this, to no one's surprise, produced a 17 per cent drop in passenger journeys: fewer people were using the system than before the 'Fair Fares' were introduced. There followed a process of consultation and debate as a result of which a 'Balanced Plan' was proposed, involving a 25 per cent cut in fares. London Transport, by now thoroughly nervous at the activities of the GLC, mounted what they described as a 'friendly action' in the courts to check that the 'Balanced Plan' would not be overturned and were reassured when Lord Justice Kerr approved it as a 'carefully researched strategy for transport in London as a whole'. The management, relieved, returned to their task of running the system.

'Fares Fair' left a valuable legacy. The principle of zoned fares, which had been introduced with the 'Fares Fair' policy and which simplified ticketing and fare structures, was kept and has remained a strong feature of the network's pricing strategy ever since. At the same time travel cards were introduced, simplifying journeys which used main line, Underground and bus travel, thereby reducing the need to issue several tickets for one journey: good news for travellers and staff.

THE END OF THE GLC

By this time, however, the GLC's days were numbered. Margaret Thatcher fought the 1983 general election promising to do away with the noisy neighbours at County Hall and she won with a large majority. A Bill was quickly introduced by the new government to do away with the GLC and hand over its responsibilities to a new body called London Regional Transport. Ken Livingstone and his colleagues fought a strong rearguard action against this fifth post-war management regime under the slogan 'Kill the Bill' but the government prevailed. The GLC was abolished and London Regional Transport took over its responsibilities for the Underground.

Since the GLC, in its latter years, sometimes received a bad press in its dealings with London Transport it is perhaps worth recording the views of the Director of Transportation Planning of the time, Eric Ellen, in a lecture at London's Transport Museum in 1994, after ten years of reflection on the events he described:

> Ken Livingstone and his henchmen, including particularly Dave Wetzel . . . had the interests of public transport at heart more than any other politicians of any colour since, probably, Herbert Morrison. . . . In public, also, where other politicians had often taken pleasure in deriding London Transport, Dave Wetzel, in particular, as chairman of the GLC Transport Committee . . . was always meticulous in giving London Transport a fair hearing and giving respect to our views, although not of course always agreeing with them.[41]

This is not how events were always portrayed at the time in the more excitable sections of the press.

LONDON REGIONAL TRANSPORT: NEW SYSTEMS, NEW FINANCE, NEW EQUIPMENT

In 1984, by Act of Parliament, London Regional Transport was established, responsible to the Minister of Transport, with London Underground Limited assuming responsibility for running the trains. The chairman, Dr Keith Bright, was charged with cutting costs and reducing the level of subsidy without significant fare increases.[42] These must have seemed to be tough targets but the record of the 1980s was very different from that of the previous decades. London Regional Transport's annual reports from 1985 onwards contain a steady stream of news about increases in passengers carried, automation and productivity rises.[43] In the ten years from 1983 staff numbers fell by 35 per cent and passenger kilometres travelled rose by 35 per cent.[44] From 1986 new rolling stock was introduced on the Central Line following the trial, in service, of three prototypes built by different manufacturers. This system had been tried with some success in the 1950s when a series of fires on Central Line trains had rendered more urgent the replacement of the ageing pre-war stock. After years of unproductive negotiations with trade unions in the shadow of the GLC the new industrial climate of the 1980s enabled the management to introduce one-person-operation on the Circle and Hammersmith and City Lines in 1984. This was followed on other lines in subsequent years, the Piccadilly being the first deep-level tube to convert to the system in August 1987. This was the first significant improvement in the productivity of train crews since the abolition of 'gatemen' in the 1920s. A further development was marked by the opening of the Docklands Light Railway with its driverless trains. A train captain checks tickets and is available in an emergency but the trains themselves are governed by computers from a central control at Poplar.

Further improvements were made with the introduction, from 1986, of the Underground Ticketing System, its wholesale use of ticket-issuing machines and automatic barriers being made easier by the zonal fare structure. It had the further benefit of cutting down on the numbers of staff required to check tickets and of reducing fraudulent travel by £21 million a year. A marketing initiative led to the issuing of Travelcards jointly with British Rail and Visitorcards were sold through a network of overseas agents to tourists. Since most of these were used outside the morning and evening peak periods the additional cost of carrying these extra passengers was marginal. The number of passengers grew rapidly, new records being set each year (*see* details in Appendix).

At the same time began the process of contracting out services which could be more effectively performed by others. The 1985/6 annual report identified 190 activities

The Docklands Light Railway

In the 1970s the Port of London's freight-handling facilities moved to the deep-water container port at Tilbury, leaving the London Docklands, east of Tower Bridge, derelict and bereft of jobs. In 1981 the London Docklands Development Corporation (LDDC) was formed with the task of regenerating the area, formerly the world's largest docks complex. In 1981 the unlikely combination of Sir Nigel Broackes, chairman of the LDDC and of the property developers Trafalgar House, and Ken Livingstone, left-wing leader of the Greater London Council, published *Public Transport Provision for Docklands*, recommending the construction of a light railway to improve access to the area and generate employment at a cost of £77 million: twice the cost of the alternative express bus service. Margaret Thatcher's government, not noted for its kindly attitude to such uses of public money, agreed to the scheme but specified that it be a 'design and build' contract in which the contractor, GEC-Mowlem, would have to bear the burden of any cost overruns. It was the first such contract of any size in the public sector. The line was built with three termini at Tower Gateway, Stratford and Island gardens (on the Isle of Dogs). It incorporated Automatic Train Operation, controlled by a computer from Poplar, thus dispensing with the need for lineside signals. It was officially opened by the queen on 30 July 1987, her inaugural train being briefly delayed because the computer wouldn't let it depart two minutes early. The public opening a month later, on 31 August, saw the system overwhelmed by 40,000 passengers. Six weeks earlier contracts had already been let to extend the line and upgrade its capacity since it was clear that it would not be able to handle the increased passenger traffic travelling to the new docklands. With a contribution from the developers of Canary Wharf, Olympia and York (who subsequently went bankrupt) the line was extended in 1991 from Tower Gateway to the Bank and in 1994 to Beckton. A further extension to Lewisham opened at the end of 1999. The Docklands Light Railway is under separate management from the Underground but has come under the authority of *Transport for London* from 1 July 2000.

which could be subjected to competitive tendering in which private companies could bid to take over activities ranging from station cleaning and staff catering to payroll processing and escalator maintenance. In 1991 the Underground adopted the management structure which would take it into the new century and which it would hand over to the new London mayor. The board consists of a chairman, managing director and directors of engineering, finance and passenger services. Each line has a manager who is responsible to the director of passenger services. In 1998 the new rolling stock for the Northern Line began to enter service under the government's 1993 Private Finance Initiative. The 106 trains are supplied, owned and serviced by ALSTOM,[45] London Underground paying about £450 million a year to lease them but thereby eliminating the need for the network to undertake elaborate and lengthy procedures to justify a capital outlay ten times that figure: a procedure that bedevilled the Victoria Line for so long. The introduction of London Transport's 'Big Yellow Duster' also enabled the network to improve its tunnel cleaning procedures and dispense with the services of most of the night-time army of 'fluffers'.

The King's Cross Fire

The new regime suffered a setback with the catastrophe of the King's Cross fire on 18 November 1987, when thirty-one people died as the result of a fire which began when a passenger dropped a lighted match on a Piccadilly Line escalator. It was not the first such accident but it was the final, disastrous consummation of the Underground's uneasy relationship with smoking passengers. In 1868, in one of his last acts as

THE 'BIG YELLOW DUSTER' AND THE UNIMOG

Unventilated tunnels like those on the deep tubes become clogged with dust and debris from passengers and from passing trains. Hair and skin cells are shed by the network's three million daily passengers and the process of braking casts off particles of brake lining every time a brake is applied. This dust, over time, becomes a health and fire hazard as it accumulates. Until the 1970s this debris was removed by a night-time army of 'fluffers' who descended into the tunnels after services had ended, armed with brushes, brooms and face masks, and removed the debris by hand. The job is now mainly done by the five-car Tunnel Cleaning Train (painted bright yellow and colloquially known as the big yellow duster) which was built at Acton Works in the 1970s. It is equipped with two sets of nozzles: one set to blow the debris into the air above the track and another set, following behind, to suck it into containers as the unit makes its way at a speed of up to 6mph along the tracks. In 1982 this unusual piece of track-cleaning equipment was joined by another: a 'Unimog' vehicle, powered by a Mercedes-Benz diesel engine which can run on road or rail and is used for clearing leaves from the tracks in autumn on the stretch of track between Rickmansworth and Amersham on the Metropolitan Line.

The 'big yellow duster' that cleans the tunnels instead of the army of 'Fluffers'. (London's Transport Museum)

Member of Parliament for Westminster, the philosopher John Stuart Mill[46] had argued, in accordance with his libertarian principles, that every Underground train should have at least one carriage that accommodated smoking passengers and this was incorporated in the Railway Regulation Bill of that year.[47] The enquiry into the King's Cross fire[48] established that, between 1956 and 1988, 46 escalator fires had occurred, 32 of them caused by smokers. In 1981 a fire caused by burning rubbish at Goodge Street had killed one person and in 1984 a fire at Oxford Circus led to an experimental ban on smoking on Underground stations. Paradoxically this may have helped to cause the King's Cross disaster. Passengers alighting from trains were wont to light up as they left the no-smoking platforms via the escalators. At King's Cross a discarded match or cigarette fell through a gap in the escalator floor and ignited the greasy debris beneath. In the words of the report this was 'a seed bed for a fire and it was into that bed that the match fell'. A forensic scientist found evidence of several previous fires beneath the escalator, none of which had been detected before they burned themselves out. The author of the report, Desmond Fennell QC, detected a fatalistic attitude among the management: 'the management remained of the view that fires were inevitable in the oldest and most extensive Underground system in the world. In my view they were fundamentally in error in their approach.' He made 157 recommendations which included the replacement of wooden escalators and installation of fire detectors, and in the years that followed the report the priority given to this programme led to a reduction in expenditure on other improvements in rolling stock and stations. It also had a slightly comical sequel. While the new safety equipment was being installed, hourly patrols were instituted on some stations, many of them by retired staff re-employed specifically for the purpose. Inevitably they became known as 'Dad's Army'.

Despite this setback the effects of the changes in policies, fare structures and patterns of travel can be seen in the chart that follows. In the years after the war passenger journeys increased steadily as the economy recovered, employment in central London grew and newly affluent consumers took advantage of opportunities for leisure travel and spending. In the 1960s and 1970s there was a downturn in passenger journeys as television and car ownership offered alternatives to the cinema, the zoo and the train. In the 1980s and 1990s the growth of London as a tourist centre[49] led to a substantial increase in leisure travel, a process assisted by the introduction of zonal fare structures which made Underground travel easier. These trends may clearly be seen in the tables and charts in the appendix. The spectacular inflation in receipts, of course, owes more to post-war inflation than it does to the fortunes of London Transport.

Other improvements have followed, some of them in the best traditions of Frank Pick. The station renewal programme which was approved by the GLC in the 1970s has continued and over thirty stations have been the subject of major refurbishment, of which many have won design awards. Prominent among these have been the new Charing Cross station which was formed by merging Strand and Trafalgar Square stations upon the opening of the Jubilee Line in 1979. David Gentleman, well known as a designer of postage stamps, decorated the Northern Line platforms with medieval scenes depicting the construction of the Eleanor Cross from which Charing Cross takes its name.[50] The Bakerloo platforms are decorated with reproductions of pictures from the National Gallery and National Portrait Gallery while the Jubilee Line platforms have a 'Nelson' theme. At the Oval a speeding cricket ball directs passengers to the exit. At Paddington the Bakerloo platforms show machinery including, appropriately, Marc

Long-term trends						
Year	1949	1959	1969	1979	1989	1999
Passenger kilometres (m.)	2861	5108	4653	4670	6256	6716

Loss of traffic to TV and the car in the 1960s and 1970s has been offset by traffic from other sources such as tourists in the later decades

Brunel's tunnelling shield; and at Baker Street the Hammersmith and City Line platforms have been restored to something like their original Victorian condition while profiles of Sherlock Holmes decorate the Bakerloo Line platforms. The tradition of using well-known artists to do the work has been continued with (later Sir) Eduardo Paolozzi's striking mosaics at Tottenham Court Road station reflecting the musical and entertainment traditions of the area with colourful representations of saxophones, cameras, electronics and music shops. Egyptian figures draw attention to the proximity

Sir Eduardo Paolozzi's striking mosaic designs for the new Tottenham Court Road station. (London's Transport Museum)

Canary Wharf station on the Jubilee Line Extension, designed in the very best traditions of Charles Holden and Frank Pick. (Author)

of the British Museum. In 1986 the Royal Academy mounted an exhibition to celebrate the completion of Paolozzi's design for the station. In the exhibition catalogue the President, Roger de Grey, wrote:

> Passengers on the London Tubes are not notable for the keen interest they take in their surroundings; now on arrival at Tottenham Court Road they are confronted by a tumult of colour in designs reflecting the particular nature of the locality.[51]

Frank Pick would surely have approved of this, as he would of some of the fine stations on the Jubilee Line extension. In April 2000, in an attempt to speed up the refurbishment programme, London Underground invited five major property companies to bid for the right to redevelop and manage its stations, thereby removing them from the short-term political and financial problems which have caused schemes to be postponed in the past.[52]

THE CURSE OF ANNUALITY

The problems of under-investment remain, however. In 1991 the Monopolies and Mergers Commission produced a report on the Underground.[53] While acknowledging that 'the public's perception of an erratic, overcrowded and poorly maintained service

More striking architecture on the Jubilee Line Extension is to be found at Canada Water. (Author)

in many areas is broadly correct', the report concluded that: 'For the most part the deficiencies in the levels of service are the result of chronic under-investment in both new capacity and the renewal and replacement of existing assets' – a diagnosis that echoes the conclusions of the Chambers Committee thirty-six years earlier. The report estimated that annual investment of £700–750 million was needed for ten years if the system was to reach a standard appropriate for one of the world's great cities, while the actual level was running at £290 million. It recommended that the Underground should 'seek firm political commitment' to its plans and establish 'a long-term contractual arrangement based on the review, discussion and approval of London Regional Transport's strategic plans', and that, in the event of politicians reneging on the arrangement, the network 'should receive a compensatory grant to make up for any shortfall in funds'. These well-intentioned recommendations were presumably written more in hope than faith since it is hard to imagine any politician agreeing to be so tied down, especially when governments change following elections. The Underground, like other public sector undertakings in the past, has continued to be constrained by the confusing policy represented by the hideous word Annuality. This expression, which is guaranteed to depress any public sector manager, refers to the practice by which the Treasury firmly commits investment funds one year at a time while announcing, usually to much publicity, longer-term plans. The plans, however, are not accompanied by any long-term commitment. It is well understood by Underground management that their investment plans for the following years could become casualties of other priorities such as a tax-cutting budget prior to an election. In fact, investment in the existing system averaged £463,000 annually in the decade following the report.[54] The only year in which the recommended figure was reached was 1992/3 when £730,000 was allocated and this resulted not from any change of heart on the part of government but from the King's Cross fire. The management of the Underground informed the government that much of the network would have to be shut down unless money was made immediately available for extensive fire detection and prevention measures: a prospect that concentrated ministerial minds wonderfully. It is possible that the solution to the problem of inadequate capital investment will be overcome by a radical proposal which has, falteringly, survived the transition from the Conservative to the Labour government: the much-discussed Public Private Partnership.

THE PUBLIC PRIVATE PARTNERSHIP (PPP)

The PPP is a logical development of previous initiatives by which the Underground operators have divested themselves of responsibilities which could be better undertaken by others. Reference has already been made to the process by which some jobs like station cleaning were outsourced in the 1990s and the further steps by which new rolling stock was leased rather than bought outright, thereby loosening the constraints on new capital investment which handicapped the network for so long. The PPP, though more radical, has the same aim: to inject private sector capital and expertise into improving the infrastructure of the network while leaving the running of the service in public hands. For this purpose the network has been divided into three infrastructure units (known as 'Infracos') as follows:

1. The sub-surface lines: Metropolitan, District, Circle, East London and the Hammersmith & City Line, known as the SSL
2. The Jubilee, Northern and Piccadilly tube lines: the JNP
3. The Bakerloo, Central and Victoria tube lines: the BCV

Suitably qualified consortia have been invited to bid to take over the management of the infrastructure of these lines, including the permanent way, the signalling, the stations and the rolling stock which they will be responsible for supplying and maintaining. The trains and stations will continue to be staffed and operated by the Underground Opsco as part of the public sector. Four consortia are involved in bidding for the concessions: Metronet, Tube Rail, Linc and Tube Lines Group/Surface Lines Group, each comprising companies with expertise in such areas as civil engineering, rolling stock construction and maintenance, and project management. The consortia include a number of well-known companies, such as Adtranz, ALSTOM, Balfour Beatty and the American project management company Bechtel. They also contain some more surprising names such as Thames Water and Anglian Water, whose experience of managing utilities and underground systems is no doubt considered to be of value to their partners. In May 2001 Tube Lines Group was nominated as preferred bidder for the Jubilee, Northern and Piccadilly contract, while Metronet was selected for the Bakerloo, Central and Victoria franchise. In return for injecting large amounts of capital and expertise into the systems and achieving specified standards of performance the consortia will be rewarded with a mix of passenger fares and public subsidies for the period of the concessions: thirty years.

For reasons that no economist has ever satisfactorily explained, capital investment by private consortia is regarded as more virtuous than investment from the public purse and less alarming both to chancellors and to City financiers. Nevertheless the PPP has not lacked its critics. Many, notably Ken Livingstone, have advocated the sale of 'London Transport Bonds' to public and private investors as a cheaper method of raising capital for the system. New York has raised $9 million in this way through the sale of 'Subway Bonds'. In Paris the mayor can divert parking fees into the Metro. These and other ideas became sidelined amid the drama that accompanied Ken Livingstone's election as mayor. They now seem to be lost causes. It is hoped that, through the Public Private Partnership, the shackles on investment which so frustrated the advocates of the Victoria Line[55] will be removed and the capital that the system needs will be made available, giving a more pleasant, efficient and profitable service. An injection of capital into the system would certainly bring some long-awaited improvements in the service and there are some encouraging precedents. Most now accept that the opening-up of telecommunications and other utilities like power and water to private capital have led to improved services in those sectors. The record in main line rail services is less impressive but it is to be hoped that lessons have been learned from that unhappy story.

There are also plans for new lines. A Chelsea–Hackney line is proposed, running from Wimbledon via Parsons Green to a new station in Chelsea and thence via Victoria, Piccadilly Circus and King's Cross to Hackney and possibly on to Epping. The Crossrail project, having been abandoned in the mid-1990s, has been reinstated in the government's ten-year Transport Plan, unveiled in July 2000. This would provide a route for main line trains from Paddington to Liverpool Street so that passengers can cross London from east to west, as they can from north to south, without having to change trains.

New Management, Old Faces

On 1 July 2000 Transport for London took over from London Regional Transport. The new body has a wider brief than its predecessor since it is responsible for taxis, river boats and the Docklands Light Railway as well as buses and, eventually, the Underground, which will be transferred to the new organisation once the Public Private Partnerships have been finalised. At almost the same time two old friends of the Underground returned to office: Ken Livingstone as mayor and Dave Wetzel as the member of the Greater London Assembly with responsibility for transport.[56] In the *Evening Standard* on 2 August 2000, Dave Wetzel outlined his plans for London's buses, writing that free travel was the 'ultimate aim'.[57] He did not mention the Underground but this arrangement would also presumably be extended to them, otherwise they would be deserted for free bus travel. It would certainly represent a radical departure. The precise relationship between the mayor, the GLA, Transport for London and the Underground management will become clear in time. There have been some early signs of tension. Ken Livingstone, speaking on the 'Today' programme on 18 August 2000, gave his verdict that the Underground management team were 'not the brightest' and threatened that, 'When I take over next April many of them will be heading for early retirement.' In September 2000 a report by the Industrial Society gave what its chief executive described as an 'amber light' to the PPP: a less-than-ringing endorsement which led Ken Livingstone to tell the BBC[58] that the report offered the government 'an honourable way out' of the PPP and that he reserved the right to seek a judicial review of the government's decision to proceed. On the other hand the appointment as London's Commissioner for Transport of Robert Kiley, former head of New York's Metropolitan Transportation Authority, demonstrated how seriously Ken Livingstone regarded this aspect of his responsibilities. Kiley is an experienced operator, not noted for undue deference to high-profile politicians, who raised $15 billion for New York's subway by the sale of bonds and turned it from a crime-and- graffitti-infested ruin to one of the best urban systems in the world. While recognising the importance of buses and other forms of transport Kiley saw the Underground as the key priority, telling the BBC South-East News on 16 October 2000: 'The Underground is where the real action is.'

However, some serious problems remain. Robert Kiley's verdict on the proposed Public Private Partnership was that, as a means of managing the system, it contained some vital flaws reminiscent of the Railtrack experience, with authority fatally diffused. Robert Kiley wanted to be able to direct the priorities of the private consortia so that they turned their attention first to improvements in signalling, permanent way and other facilities which will bring early improvements in safety and service. Station improvements, generating revenue from sources such as retailing, can come later. The consortia did not want to be bound by Kiley's directives. The government is anxious to involve the consortia because it does not believe that public servants, elected or otherwise, can manage major investment projects without getting into mischief. A long line of such embarrassments stretching from Concorde to the Millennium Dome explains why they feel that way. Discussions between Robert Kiley, the government and the consortia have so far produced only deadlock and Kiley's dismissal.

The Underground thus enters the twenty-first century amid a confusing blend of hope and uncertainty. The hope rests upon the prospect of the much-needed investment that the thirty-year concessions promise to bring with them. After the upheavals represented by frequent changes of regime in the second half of the twentieth century the prospect of a thirty-year time horizon over which to plan capital investment and marketing strategy is unprecedented in the history of the network as a whole.[59] Moreover the removal of capital investment from the dead hand of the Treasury should mean that such decisions will be made on their merits rather than when political priorities allow them. This could end the period of investment starvation with which the management has struggled since the time of Lord Ashfield and which has earned the sympathy of such well-informed bodies as the Chambers Committee and the Monopolies and Mergers Commission,[60] sympathy which was not, unfortunately, followed by money. The uncertainty surrounds the five-fold relationship between the new authority, Transport for London, the mayor himself, the private sector consortia managing the infrastructure, the Underground management operating the trains, and the national government watching nervously, tempted to intervene if the mayor does anything too radical or newsworthy. If the relationships between the higher-profile figures in this quartet can be managed sensitively then Ken Livingstone and his regime may well be remembered as the people who restored to London an urban transport system which is the envy of the world, as it was in the 1920s. If not, then much political mayhem, accompanied by further suffering for the travelling public, may confidently be predicted.

GHOSTLY PRESENCES

The Underground is not without its ghostly legends. On 29 November 1955 the London evening newspaper *The Star* carried on page 3 an alarming report of events at Covent Garden Underground station. It read as follows: 'Divisional heads of London Transport called to-day for reports on the "ghost" at Covent Garden Underground station. A West Indian porter at the station had asked for a transfer after claiming that he had seen an apparition of a six foot tall, slim, oval-faced man wearing a light grey suit and white glasses. Other staff at the station have told senior officials of London Transport that they had seen the same apparition.' In January 1956 the *Sunday Dispatch* offered as a likely candidate the Victorian actor William Terriss, who had been stabbed to death by a madman at the nearby Adelphi Theatre in 1897. As far as is known, no recent sightings have been recorded. The Elephant and Castle ghost is more persistent, running footsteps being reported there by night shift maintenance staff. In 1968 workmen building the new Victoria Line near Vauxhall station reported a ghost seven feet tall whom they nicknamed 'The Quare Feller'. As far as is known, no disturbances to services have arisen from these ghostly presences. Perhaps in the next century they will be joined by the ghosts of Ken Livingstone and Robert Kiley.

POSTSCRIPT
'SEE YOU IN COURT'

On Monday 23 July 2001 in the High Court, the scene of Whitaker Wright's downfall, Mr Justice Sullivan began to examine 2,600 pages of documents outlining Transport for London's case against the Public Private Partnership. On 24 July Ken Livingstone and Robert Kiley made a grand entrance at the High Court amidst the applause of their many supporters. Ken Livingstone's counsel argued that the Public Private Partnership would prevent the mayor from carrying out his statutory obligation to run the London Underground in a 'safe and financially efficient manner'. Negotiations having failed, lawyers were added to the cast list of those concerned with the future of the world's oldest underground railway system. They joined the politicians, the Treasury, the Department of Transport, public servants and private financiers whose interests in the future of the network were already well advertised. On 30 July Mr Justice Sullivan ruled that it was for the government 'to have the last word' on the matter, though he criticised ministers for inept handling of the legislation concerned, without which 'false hopes might not have been raised only to be dashed'.

Perhaps the shades of Sir Robert Perks, Sir Edward Watkin, Lord Ashfield and Frank Pick will inspire the contesting parties to bury their differences and work together to make the London Underground once again the finest urban transport system in the world, a status it last enjoyed in the 1930s. Certainly some intervention of that kind now seems necessary if Londoners are to be spared further suffering.

NOTES

INTRODUCTION

1. J. Hollis & A. Seddon, *The Changing Population of the London Boroughs* (Stat. Series No. 5, 1985), ONS Library.
2. Parliamentary Papers, 1854–5, vol. 10, *Report of the Select Committee on Metropolitan Communications*, is the source of these figures and those which follow.
3. Parliamentary Papers, 1846, vol. 17, *Report of the Commissioners Appointed to Investigate Projects for Railway Termini within the Metropolis*, contains an account of the evidence to the commission, and its findings.
4. Ibid., the quoted passage is on p. 21.
5. Ibid., questions 2283 *et seq.*
6. Pamphlet 10884, dated 1852, Guildhall Library.
7. Possibly the origin of the phrase 'bull in a china shop'.
8. *Herapath's Railway Journal*, 14 March 1857, pp. 284–5, has an account of the Great Northern meeting where the extent of Redpath's misdeeds was revealed.
9. Pamphlet 17557, dated 1859, Guildhall Library.
10. Parliamentary Papers, 1854–5, vol. 10, includes a full account of the committee's evidence, report and conclusions.
11. Ibid., pp. 78 *et seq.*, contains an account of Paxton's evidence.
12. Ibid., p. 89.
13. Ibid., p. 81.
14. Ibid., pp. 158 *et seq.*, contains Pearson's evidence.
15. Ibid., p. iv; Metropolitan Archives, 28.3, *Report from Select Committee on Metropolitan Communications*, 23 July 1855.

CHAPTER ONE

1. House of Lords Record Office, I.K. Brunel's evidence, 30 May 1854.
2. These are the modern station names. The original names are shown on p. 16: thus Euston Square was originally Gower Street.
3. *The Times*, 2 December 1858, p. 5.
4. Quoted in *Herapath's Railway Journal*, 14 March 1857, pp. 284–5.
5. An account of the dramas and veiled threats which preceded the meeting is given in A.A. Jackson, *London's Metropolitan Railway*, David & Charles, 1986.

6. Sir Samuel Morton Peto (1809–89) built railways, much of London's clubland and Nelson's column; Thomas Brassey (1805–70) built railways throughout the world and, under Bazalgette's direction, much of London's main drainage.

7. An eye-witness account by F.S. Williams, recorded in *Our Iron Roads*, 1884.

8. *The Times*, 30 November 1861, p. 5.

9. Institution of Civil Engineers, *Minutes of Proceedings*, vol. 81, 1884–5; Baker's reputation earned him much consultancy work overseas, including Australia, South Africa and Egypt, where he worked on the first Aswan dam.

10. *Illustrated London News*, 15 February 1862, p. 182.

11. Ibid., 28 June 1862, p. 648.

12. Ibid., 6 September 1862, p. 259.

13. Metropolitan Archives, Acc. 1297, Met 1/2, Board Minutes, 3 December 1862. *See* p. 34 for Fowler's conflict with Sir Edward Watkin over money.

14. *The Times*, 10 January 1863, p. 10.

15. Metropolitan Railway, *Minutes*; 25 February 1863; Metropolitan Archives, Acc. 1297, Met 1/2.

16. *Illustrated London News*, 17 January 1863, front page *et seq.*

17. Fares are given in old pennies; a new penny is equivalent to 2.4 old pennies. The level of the fares was strongly influenced by competition from omnibuses, which offered fares at less than a penny a mile for some routes. *See* for example the *Illustrated London News*, 21 November 1846, p. 327, reporting omnibus 'fares considerably less than one halfpenny per mile'.

18. Metropolitan Archives, Acc. 1297, Met 1/2, Metropolitan Railway Minute Books, July 1863, gives the details of the dispute.

19. Originator of *Willing's Press Guide*.

20. W.J. Passingham, *The Romance of London's Underground*, Sampson Low, 1932, p. 21; separately recorded in a 'lantern lecture' given by Underground management in the 1930s and held in the archives at Covent Garden.

21. This station no longer exists; it was close to the present site of the City Thameslink station opened in 1990.

22. *The Times*, 14 June 1879, p. 8.

23. Ibid., 7 October 1884, p. 9.

24. The proceedings of the committee are to be found in Parliamentary Papers, 1898, vol. 45; Bell's evidence was in response to questions 429–30.

25. F.M. Hueffer, *The Soul of London*, Alston Rivers, London, 1895, p. 28.

26. *R.D.B.'s Diary, 1887–1914*, Heinemann, 1930; the diary entry is for 23 June 1887.

27. To reach Hammersmith the joint venture had to purchase land which had been astutely bought shortly beforehand by its chairman, John Parson, who thereby turned a considerable profit and set a precedent for later developments: *see* Chapter Five.

28. Guildhall Library, Pamphlet 3592.

29. Parliamentary Papers, 1863, vol. 8, p. iv.

30. *See* panel on p. 4 for an account of Bazalgette's work.

31. Metropolitan Archives, 28.3: *Report of Select Committee on Metropolitan Railways*, February 1864; Fowler's evidence, 18 February 1864, pp. 33 *et seq.*; Bazalgette gave evidence the following day.

32. Parliamentary Papers, 1864, vol. 53, contains Bazalgette's evaluation.

33. Hansard, 26 April 1869, col. 1580, records this curious exchange.
34. *Illustrated London News*, 2 January 1869, p. 11.
35. *The Times*, 3 July 1871, p. 5.
36. Ibid., 4 July 1871, p. 8.
37. *See* for example Metropolitan Archives, Acc. 1297, MDR 1/2, accounts for half year ended 30 June 1872, pp. 429–31; net receipts of £51,044, of which £50,675 was taken by interest and preference shares.
38. Ibid., p. 241.
39. Frequently discussed at shareholders' meetings; e.g. Watkin, *Railway Times*, 26 July 1890, p. 94; Forbes, *Railway Times*, 9 August 1890, p. 194.
40. The Metropolitan Board of Works was London's first metropolitan government, taking office in 1856 and giving way to the London County Council in 1889. It showed much enthusiasm for the scheme; *see* the Board, *Minutes of Proceedings*, 22 May 1874, pp. 623–4; Metropolitan Archives.
41. *Herapath's Railway Journal*, 10 November 1877, the prospectus is on p. 1,184.
42. Ibid., 17 August 1872, pp. 884–5, contains a summary of the report.
43. Fowler's notorious avarice earned him enough money to buy a handsome Scottish estate.
44. Edwin was the brother of the distinguished Victorian architect, Alfred Waterhouse (1830–1905), who designed the Natural History Museum, Manchester Town Hall and many Cambridge buildings, notably the fine Victorian additions to Pembroke College's medieval courts.
45. *Herapath's Railway Journal*, 12 October 1872, p. 1,093, has Waterhouse's report.
46. Watkin's letter is in the Metropolitan Railway Minute Book; Metropolitan Archives, Acc. 1297, Met 1/4, pp. 134–6.
47. *See* p. 105 for an account of this escapade.
48. *Herapath's Railway Journal*, 15 February 1890, p. 178.
49. Metropolitan Archives, Acc. 1297, Met 1/17; Board Minutes, 14 January 1891.
50. *Herapath's Railway Journal*, 30 June 1888, p. 742.
51. *Railway Times*, 20 December 1890, p. 692.
52. *Herapath's Railway Journal*, 19 July 1890, p. 823, contains the account.
53. Ibid., 20 July 1889, pp. 789–90.
54. Ibid., 25 January 1890, p. 97; 26 July 1890, p. 842.
55. Ibid., 20 July 1889, pp. 789–90.
56. *See* for example the Metropolitan Board of Works, *Annual Reports*, 1879–1884.
57. Metropolitan Archives, Acc. 1297, Met 1/10, pp. 499–500, of *Metropolitan Railway Board Minutes*.
58. *See* p. 22, Steam, Smoke and 'Metropolitan Mixture'.
59. Author of *London's Metropolitan Railway*, David & Charles, 1986, the definitive history of the Metropolitan, from which this story is taken.
60. *Railway Times*, 18 October 1884, p. 1,332.
61. Metropolitan Archives, Acc. 1297, Met 1/13, Board Minutes, 23 October 1884, p. 378, contains a copy of the arbitration.
62. Ibid., p. 461, shareholders' meeting.
63. *Railway Times*, 9 August 1884, p. 1,000, gives an account of the District AGM.
64. Nine years later Watkin was still making reciprocal accusations; *see* Metropolitan Archives, Acc. 1297, 1/18, shareholders' meeting, 27 January 1893, p. 547.

CHAPTER TWO

1. Metropolitan Archives, Pamphlet 27.332 Moo: G.T. Moody, *London's Electrifications, 1890–1923*, Electric Railway Society, 1961, has an interesting short account of the electrification of the system.

2. *See* Chapter One for a description of the problems caused by steam and smoke on the Metropolitan and District Lines.

3. Much of the information on the Thames Tunnel is taken from *The Triumphant Bore*, sponsored by James Howden & Co., available from the Institution of Civil Engineers bookshop, Great George Street, London SW1.

4. *See* Chapter One for an account of these occasions.

5. *The Times*, 27 March 1843, p. 6, reported the event.

6. Replaced by the present structure in 1932.

7. An account of the Tower Subway is to be found in *Railway Magazine* 89 (1943), pp. 332 *et seq.*, written by Charles E. Lee.

8. Published by Spon, 1878, available in the Metropolitan Archives, ref. P.27.51.

9. *Herapath's Railway Journal*, 14 June 1888, describes the financing of the railway.

10. *The Engineer*, 7 June 1889, pp. 477–8, contains a detailed account of the engineering works.

11. Ibid., p. 478, contains this account of Greathead's precautionary work.

12. This experiment attracted huge crowds. *See* the account and illustration in the *Graphic*, 4 January 1879, p. 17.

13. An excellent account of the first underground electric railway and the later development of the tube system is to be found in R.I.M. Arthurton, 'The developing tube', *Railway Engineer*, 1990, vol. 3, pp. 3–29.

14. *The Times*, 5 November 1890, p. 12, described the event.

15. *Illustrated London News*, 8 November 1890, p. 579.

16. *Railway Times*, 8 November 1890, p. 545.

17. For this gem I am indebted to Passingham, *The Romance of London's Underground*, p. 54.

18. Metropolitan Archives, Greater London History Library, ref. 27.333 p. 12; booklet celebrating the reopening of the line after tunnel widening and linking to Hampstead Line, December 1924.

19. The medieval St Mary Woolnoth, on the corner of Lombard Street and King William Street, was repaired by Wren after the Great Fire of London, rebuilt by Nicholas Hawksmoor in 1716 and restored by William Butterfield in 1876. It holds the tomb of Edward Lloyd, owner of the coffee-house from which sprang Lloyds of London. Its most notable rector was John Newton (1725–1807), slave trader, later campaigner against slavery and noted hymn-writer. *See* Metropolitan Archives, Acc. 1297, CSL 1/5, especially 11 July 1899, p. 26, and 23 January 1900, p. 99.

20. As reported in *Railway Times*, 24 November 1894.

21. The *Illustrated London News* reported both the official and public openings on 16 July 1898, p. 76, and 13 August, p. 222.

22. Institution of Civil Engineers, *Minutes of Proceedings*, 14 November 1899, contains an account by H.H. Dalrymple-Hay and B.M. Jenkins of the technical processes involved in constructing and equipping the line.

23. T. Barker and M. Robbins, *A History of London Transport*, Allen & Unwin, 1974, vol. 2, pp. 47–8, gives an account of the gruesome conditions endured by commuters.

24. *Railway Times*, 23 April 1904, p. 434.

25. *Railway News, Finance and Joint Stock Companies Journal*, 30 June 1900, p. 960, attributed the raising of the capital to Cassel's persistence.

26. This situation continued to apply until the British Transport Commission Act 1955 conferred the power to make compulsory purchases of easements beneath property. The Victoria Line was the first to benefit from this opportunity to take a more direct line by cutting across streets, thereby avoiding sharp bends.

27. Metropolitan Archives, Acc. 1297, CLR 1/1, Central London Railway Minutes, 17 January 1900, pp. 288–92, contains Cuningham's recommendations on operations.

28. J.G. Bruce and D.F. Croome, *The Twopenny Tube*, Capital Transport, 1996, p. 7.

29. *Daily Mail*, 28 June 1900, p. 3.

30. *The Times*, 28 June 1900, p. 10.

31. *Daily Mail*, 30 July 1900, p. 3.

32. *Railway Times*, 25 August, p. 211, and 1 September 1900, p. 253, respectively.

33. This ritual is well described in Bruce and Croome, *The Twopenny Tube*, p. 18.

34. In 1903, 1904 and 1905.

35. The story was published in *Royal Magazine* in 1901, and is included in *Rivals to Sherlock Holmes*, ed. Sir Hugh Greene, Bodley Head, 1970. The extract quoted is on p. 220.

36. For much of the information in this panel I am indebted to Inspector Philip Trendall of the British Transport Police History Society.

37. Hansard, vol. 90, col. 188, 1 March 1901.

38. Metropolitan Archives, Acc. 1297, CLR 1/2, Board Minutes, 12 November 1901, pp. 118–21.

39. Ibid., pp. 114–17, contains the discussion from which the following quotations are taken.

40. Parliamentary Papers, 1905, vol. 30, questions 22063–5, contains Cuningham's evidence.

41. Details of the system are extracted from Howard Clayton, *The Atmospheric Railways*, London, 1966, and D.A. Bayliss, *The Post Office Railway*, Turntable Publications, 1978.

42. *The Times*, 10 February 1863, p. 5.

43. *See* Passingham, *The Romance of London's Underground*, p. 50, for an account of this alleged event.

44. *See* p. 4, for an account of Bazalgette's work in London.

45. *See* p. 8, for an account of Brunel's tribulations.

CHAPTER THREE

1. *See* pp. 22–3 above.

2. House of Lords Record Office, 23 June 1892: Baker's evidence to the Commons Committee on Baker Street and Waterloo Railway Bill; *see* p. 34–6 above for details of Watkin's Manchester to Paris ambitions.

3. Grandfather of Lord Hailsham, Lord Chancellor 1970–4 and 1979–87.

4. Hansard, 19 February 1903, vol. 118, cols 354–70.

5. Carson is better known for his earlier role in bringing about the downfall of Oscar Wilde and for his later role in the creation of Northern Ireland independent of the Republic.

6. Later Lord Chief Justice, Marquis of Reading, Ambassador to Washington and Viceroy of India.

7. *The Times*, 27 January 1904, p. 7, reported the judge's words and the drama which followed.

8. Ibid., 29 January 1904, p. 10, reported the inquest and this alarming discovery. Wright's son told the inquest that his father always kept a loaded revolver in his bedroom.

9. *Illustrated London News*, 30 January 1904, p. 144; the writer was confused – it should have read Ludwig of Bavaria or Rudolph of Bohemia.

10. *Dictionary of National Biography*, second supplement, vol. 3, p. 713.

11. The novels were called *The Financier* (1912), *The Titan* (1914) and *The Stoic* (1947).

12. Perks told the Royal Commission on London Traffic 1904 that he had approached Yerkes; the Commission's report is to be found in Parliamentary Papers, 1905, vol. 30.

13. The District only paid five dividends to ordinary shareholders between 1868 and 1900, the highest being 1.125 per cent in 1880; *see* records of the railway in the Metropolitan Archives, Acc. 1297, MDR 1/1 to 1/8.

14. *Tramway & Railway World*, 11 April 1901, p. 188.

15. *The Times*, 7 June 1901, p. 3, carried an account of the meeting.

16. T.G. Ashton, MP for Luton, 29 October 1902, Hansard, vol. 113, cols 1145–6.

17. The stratagems which Yerkes used in this manoeuvre are described in Alan A. Jackson and D.F. Croome, *Rails Through the Clay: A History of London's Tube Railways*, Allen & Unwin, 1962, pp. 83–4.

18. Parliamentary Papers, 1904, vol. 30, questions 6700 *et seq.*

19. *See* Chapter One for references to earlier disputes.

20. For example the shareholders' meeting reported in *The Times* on 27 July 1901, p. 5, earning a stinging rebuke from Yerkes on 31 July 1901, p. 10.

21. For example 27 July, p. 5; 31 July, p. 10; 28 September, p. 6; 30 September, p. 8.

22. The station remains in use but is due to be decommissioned shortly.

23. Whistler had created a celebrated painting of the Thames at this point. *See* for example the reference to the power station in Graham Greene's *The Ministry of Fear*, Heinemann Library edn, 1960, p. 104.

24. Metropolitan Archives, Acc. 1297, BKW 1/1, pp. 172–4; Board minutes, 26 February 1902, contains a copy of Yerkes' offer.

25. *See* Chapter Six for details of the work of Pick and Holden.

26. *The Times*, 12 March 1906, p. 14, carried an account of the event.

27. His pen name was Sekon, his real name spelt backwards.

28. *See* p. 68 above for details of this incident.

29. *The Times*, 16 December 1906, p. 12, carried an account of the opening.

30. *Railway Times*, 10 November 1906, p. 276.

31. Parliamentary Papers, 1901, vol. 6, questions 708–800; the witness was the eminent civil engineer Sir Douglas Fox.

32. Hansard, 18 July 1902, vol. 111, col. 663.

33. *The Times*, 25 December 1900, p. 9.

34. The underground railway reaches its greatest depth below the surface north of Hampstead station where it lies 221ft below the Heath.

35. Known at the time as *The Avenue* theatre. Alan A. Jackson, *London's Termini*, David & Charles, 2nd edn, 1985, pp. 250–1, contains a graphic account of the disaster.

36. *The Times* reported the ceremony and the speeches on 24 June 1907, p. 3, under the heading 'The Hampstead Tube'.

37. Ibid., 30 December 1905, p. 11.
38. Ibid., 9 February 1910, p. 9.
39. *See* p. 69 above.
40. The application form for the 'profit sharing notes' and the accompanying letter from Speyer are to be found in Metropolitan Archives, Acc. 1297, UER 1/1, pp. 95–9; Barker and Robbins give a full account of these manoeuvrings in their *History of London Transport*, vol. 2, pp. 113–15.
41. Jackson and Croome, *Rails Through the Clay*, Appendix 4a, contains a clear account of the tubes' failure to reach Sellon's forecasts.
42. Select Committee on Cabs and Omnibuses (Metropolis), 1906, [295] VII, p. x. In total, 521 petrol-driven buses were licensed by the Metropolitan Police by July 1906.
43. *Railway Times*, 16 February 1907, p. 174.
44. Beatrice Webb, *Our Partnership*, ed. Drake & Cole, Longmans Green, 1948, pp. 338–9.
45. Metropolitan Archives, Acc. 1297, UER 1/7, contains an account of these occasions.
46. Ibid., UERL 1/2, p. 151.
47. He was MP for Ashton-under-Lyne, Max Aitken (later Lord Beaverbrook) resigning the seat to make way for him.
48. Hansard, 26 June 1918, vol. 107, cols 1031–2.

CHAPTER FOUR

1. *See* p. 79 above for an account of this episode.
2. *See* p. 79 above.
3. Metropolitan Archives, Acc. 1297, UER 1/8 and 1/9, contains minutes of these meetings.
4. *See* pp. 29 *et seq.* above for an account of these hostilities.
5. Metropolitan Archives, Acc. 1297, UER 1/8, 26 February 1908.
6. Ibid., 24 March 1908.
7. The competition was won by W.J. Pawsey and announced in the *Evening News* on 18 May 1907.
8. Jackson and Croome, *Rails Through the Clay*, p. 104.
9. Eighteen pence worth of tickets were offered for sixteen pence.
10. *Evening Standard*, 14 May 1924, p. 4.
11. For this detail I am indebted to Alan A. Jackson, who saw the programme and reported the interview.
12. 1.25 per cent, 0.75 per cent and 1.25 per cent respectively; interest rates on gilt-edged stocks were about 4 per cent at this time.
13. Alan A. Jackson, *London's Metropolitan Railway*, David & Charles, 1986, pp. 212–15, gives an account of this Pullman service.
14. *Railway Times*, 9 December 1911, reported on the improvements.
15. H. Dalrymple-Hay, in a lecture to the London Society on 20 April 1928, stated that the idea of installing the escalator came from Stanley himself; Guildhall Pamphlet 17496.
16. Metropolitan Archives, Acc. 1297, MDR 1/11, Minutes 7896 and 8251; it cost £27,251.
17. *The Times*, 4 October 1911, p. 3.
18. A claim unhappily disproved by the King's Cross accident of 18 November 1987 when thirty-one people died following a fire on an escalator.

19. I am indebted to Sheila Taylor of London Transport for destroying this myth; the Museum received the information from a relative of Bumper Harris.

20. Jackson and Croome, *Rails Through the Clay*, p. 115.

21. Ibid., p. 154.

22. Lord Ashfield, *London's Traffic Problem Reconsidered*, Constable, 1924; Guildhall Pamphlet 2308.

23. For the information in this panel I am indebted to Paul Garbutt, Desmond Croome, *Underground News*, October 1987, and Alexander Edmonds, *History of the Metropolitan District Railway to 1908*, London Transport Publications, 1973.

24. For example the Select Committee on Transport (Metropolitan Area) Report, 1919, 147, vii.

25. *See* reference to Edgar Speyer's approach to the Progressive leader at the Webbs' house on p. 79 above.

26. Interest rates on gilt-edged stocks after 1918 were 4–7 per cent; dividends, as we have seen, were less than 2 per cent.

27. *The Times*, 27 October 1921, p. 7, reported the event; comments appeared the following day, p. 7.

28. Ibid., 28 November 1923, p. 12, carried a striking account of the incident.

29. One hastens to add that Anthony Bull, whose father was an MP and friend of Lord Ashfield, was accompanied by an experienced driver; the interview with the author occurred on 21 September 2000.

30. *Leave this and move to Edgware*, Underground Group poster, 1924.

31. *See* p. 74 for an account of their objections.

32. The letter appeared on p. 6 of the newspaper.

33. *The Times*, 23 February 1923.

34. As observed above (p. 88) the Great Eastern, another constituent of the LNER, had its own veto over the extension of the Central Line beyond Liverpool Street.

35. Hansard, 5 March 1924, contains the contributions quoted.

36. The paper's campaign extended intermittently over several months.

37. Witness evidence, 13 November 1925, questions 3805–916.

38. *See* p. 89 above for an account of this development.

39. Institution of Civil Engineers, *Minutes of Proceedings*, vol. 175, 1908–9, p. 214.

40. Reported in *Railway Times*, 12 December 1906, p. 637.

41. *See* above, p. 89.

42. *The Times*, 4 November 1935, p. 8.

43. Ibid., 14 November 1935, p. 10.

44. Ibid., 21 November 1935, p. 10.

45. Ibid., 22 November 1935, p. 15.

46. Ibid., 6 April 1937, p. 16.

47. *See* above, p. 92, for Ashfield's proposal.

48. *See* Chapter Three, pp. 68–9 and 77–80, for this reference.

49. In other words they belonged to whoever had them in his possession; they bore no name.

50. *See* Chapter Three, p. 64, for an account of Whitaker Wright's misadventures and suicide.

51. *Journal of the Institute of Transport*, vol. 20, May 1939.

52. Metropolitan Archives, Acc. 1297, LPT 1/13, 22 February 1935.

53. Some of the money was devoted to main line railway improvements, including some on the Great Western.

54. *See* p. 97 for an account of this anomaly.

55. *The Times* carried the letters on 9 April 1937, p. 10, and Pick's reply on 12 April, p. 15.

CHAPTER FIVE

1. Royal Commission on London Traffic, Perks's evidence, 17 March 1904, question 19552.

2. Alan A. Jackson, *London's Metropolitan Railway*, David & Charles, 1986, Chapter Nine, contains a full account of this fortunate turn of affairs for the company.

3. Royal Commission on London Traffic Report, 1905, vol. I, paragraph 216.

4. The Royal Commission on the Geographical Distribution of the Industrial Population, commonly called 'The Barlow Commission' after its chairman Sir Montague Barlow.

5. Metropolitan Archives, 28.02, 2 March 1938, questions 3462, 3485.

6. *Herapath's Railway Journal*, 26 July 1890, p. 841, reports Watkin's enthusiastic advocacy of the plan to his shareholders; *see also* Metropolitan Archives, Acc. 1297, Met 1/17, General Meeting 12/7/90 and 14/1/91, and *Herapath's Railway Journal*, 23/7/92, p. 787.

7. *Railway Times*, 26 July 1890, p. 94, has an account of this turbulent occasion.

8. *The Times*, 18 June 1890, p. 10.

9. *Wealdstone, Harrow & Wembley Observer*, 22 May and 29 May 1896.

10. *See* Chapter Three, p. 74, for an account of this project of Yerkes.

11. Royal Commission on London Transport, 1904. Perks's evidence, 17 March, question 19,556.

12. Dame Henrietta Barnett, *The Story of the Growth of the Hampstead Garden Suburb 1907–28*, pp. 5–6; Metropolitan Archives, 97.651.

13. Barnett, *The Growth of the Hampstead Garden Suburb*, p. 6.

14. The house now bears a blue plaque to commemorate Evelyn Waugh's residence there as a young man.

15. Figures are taken from F. Howkins, *The Story of Golders Green and its Remarkable Development*, London, 1924; Metropolitan Archives, 97.651.

16. *See* p. 88 for an account of these works, supported by the Trade Facilities Act.

17. Metropolitan Archives, Acc. 1297, Met 1/34, 21 November 1918.

18. An extract from *Metro-land*, broadcast by John Betjeman, BBC television, 1973.

19. Metropolitan Country Estates publicity brochure, December 1927.

20. *Hugh Casson's London*, Dent, 1983, p. 126.

21. Copies of *Metro-land* are held in the Metropolitan Archives, ref. 66.62 Met.

22. *Modern Transport*, 11 June 1921.

23. *Metro-land*, 1926 issue, p. 82.

24. *Evening News Homeseeker's Guide*, 19 February 1926.

25. Metropolitan Country Estates publicity brochure, December 1927.

26. The precise figures, as calculated by the Barlow Commission, were: 450,264 decline in the inner area, administered by the City Corporation and the LCC; 2,483,804 increase in the outer area, within the jurisdiction of the Metropolitan Police; Metropolitan Archives, 28.02.

27. *Census of Population*, 1901, vol. 2, and 1931, vol. 1; Library of the Office for National Statistics.

28. Metropolitan Archives, Acc. 1297, Met 1/29, p. 342 and appendix.
29. For much of the material that follows I am indebted to Alan Jackson, *Semi-detached London*, Wild Swan, 1991, which has a fuller account of the development of Edgware at this time.
30. George Cross, *Suffolk Punch*, 1939, Chapter 17, contains a full account of Cross's activities in Edgware.
31. *See* p. 104 for this reference.
32. *The Times*, 16 March 1937, p. 12.
33. Hansard, 26 April 1937, vol. 323, cols 128–30; Noel-Baker (1889–1982), MP for Derby, was a conscientious objector during the First World War but was decorated for bravery for his work in the Friends' Ambulance Unit; he competed in the Olympic Games in the 1,500 metres; and in 1959 was awarded the Nobel Peace Prize for his lifelong campaign for world peace.
34. LCC Minutes, 28 July 1891, p. 884.
35. *See* reference to Unwin on p. 106.
36. Greater London Regional Planning Committee, 2nd Report, 1933, Metropolitan Archives.
37. *See* Chapter One, pp. 34–6, for an account of Sir Edward Watkin's plans.
38. *The Times*, correspondence page, 5 December 1935 *et seq.*
39. *See* Chapter One, pp. 18–19, for a description of these engines.

CHAPTER SIX

1. E. Turner, *The Shocking History of Advertising*, Michael Joseph, 1952, p. 253.
2. Exhibition catalogue, 1978, p. 2.
3. Mornington Crescent station is another example of the style, which has survived almost unchanged into the twenty-first century.
4. *See* p. 89 for an account of this event.
5. This description was given in an interview with the author on 21 September 2000; the interview was also the source of the quotations from and personal memories of Frank Pick which are related in this chapter.
6. Letter dated 11 September 1939, in the possession of Anthony Bull.
7. *See* p. 106 for an account of the development of Hampstead Garden Suburb.
8. *See* for example Pick's article in *Commercial Art*, vol. 2, 1927, p. 137.
9. Adrian Forty, 'Lorenzo of the Underground', *London Journal*, vol. 5, no. I, May 1979, p. 114.
10. *See* Pevsner's *Studies in Art, Architecture & Design*, vol. 2, Thames & Hudson, 1968, p. 193.
11. Ibid.
12. H. Wanntig, *Wirtschaft und Kunst*, Jena, 1909, p. 292.
13. This quotation and the account of Pick's interest in the DIA are based on Pevsner, *Studies in Art, Architecture & Design*, Chapter 13.
14. *See* pp. 79–80 for an account of the drama surrounding this event.
15. The 'resignation' episode is described in C. Barman, *The Man Who Built London Transport*, David & Charles, 1979, p. 25, though I have not found supporting evidence and Anthony Bull expressed his doubts about its veracity.
16. Lord Ashfield, *London's Traffic Problem Reconsidered*, Constable, 1924, Guildhall Pamphlet 2308.

17. Barman, *The Man Who Built London Transport*, p. 36, is the source of this quotation and of much of the material that follows; a further source is Oliver Green, *Underground Art*, Laurence King Publishing, 1999.

18. The *Daily Mail* was launched in 1896 and the *Daily Mirror* in 1903.

19. Barman, *The Man Who Built London Transport*, p. 29.

20. *See* the colour section for examples of logo designs.

21. It was on this occasion that the marathon was lengthened by 385 yards so that the race finished in front of the royal box for the benefit of King Edward VII. The extra distance has remained a permanent feature of the race.

22. *See* p. 84 above for an account of this competition.

23. *See* for example J. Riddell and W. Stearn, *By Underground to Kew*, 1994, and J. Riddell and P. Denton, *By Underground to the Zoo*, 1995, both published by Studio Vista.

24. Published by Cecil Palmer in 1924.

25. Pevsner, *Studies in Art, Architecture & Design*, p. 199.

26. Ibid., p. 194; one of many other theories holds that it was based on Paris Metro signs observed by Albert Stanley during a visit to the French capital; *see* Oliver Green and Jeremy Rewse-Davies, *Designed for London*, Laurence King Publishing, 1995, p. 14.

27. Anthony Bull suggested to me that Pick, likewise, probably declined a knighthood on similar grounds.

28. Gavin Stamp, 'Tube Trauma', *Designers Journal*, November 1987, p. 47.

29. *Illustrated London News*, 15 December 1928, p. 1,145.

30. Metropolitan Archives, Acc. 1297, UER 4/78, contains the full report.

31. Ibid.

32. Metropolitan Archives, Acc. 1297, UER 4/83, contains Heaps's report.

33. Pevsner, *Studies in Art, Architecture & Design*, vol. 2, p. 197.

34. Interview with Anthony Bull, 21 September 2000.

35. The listed stations on this extension are Turnpike Lane, Arnos Grove, Southgate, Oakwood and Cockfosters.

36. B. Cherry and N. Pevsner, *Buildings of England*, Penguin, *London 2: South*, 1983, p. 123; *London 4: North*, 1998, p. 458. *See* illustration on p. 95.

37. David Leboff, *London Underground Stations*, Ian Allan, 1994, supports this view and contains an account of the history and architecture of all London's Underground stations; *see also* David Lawrence, *Underground Architecture*, Capital Transport, 1994.

38. *The Times*, 17 July 1929, p. 12.

39. Ibid., 26 July 1929, p. 12.

40. *See* Barman, *The Man Who Built London Transport*, pp. 128 *et seq.*, for an account of the drama which followed the unveiling of the statues.

41. Pick's offer to resign owed more to his loyalty to Holden than to his admiration for Epstein's sculptures, for which his enthusiasm appears to have been muted.

42. *The Times*, 1 December 1970, p. 9, printed this extract from *Khrushchev Remembers*.

43. Except the Waterloo and City Line, which was transferred to the Underground from British Rail in April 1994.

44. *See* p. 84 for an account of this common approach to publicity.

45. K. Garland, *Mr Beck's Underground Map*, Capital Publications, 1994, contains a full account of the origins of this icon of industrial design.

46. Published by Kegan Paul, London, 1941; the extracts are from pp. 13, 47 and 49.

47. For information about this episode I am indebted to Anthony Bull and for the subsequent detective work to Rowena House, archivist of the WRVS.

48. Anthony Bull's lecture to Friends of London Transport Museum, 20 April 1993, is the source of this information.

49. Letter dated 11 September 1939.

50. This incident is supported from many sources. Harold Nicolson, *Diaries and Letters, 1939–45*, Collins, 1967, p. 116, describes it and Anthony Bull heard it from Lord Swinton in 1942 and Sir John Colville in 1943, both of whom were present at the meeting. Anthony Bull suggests that Pick regarded himself as a railwayman rather than a busman.

51. For much of the material which follows I am indebted to *Poems on the Underground*, ed. G. Benson, J. Chernaik and C. Herbert, 8th edn, Cassell, 1998.

52. *The Guardian*, 30 December 1999, p. 17, leading article.

CHAPTER SEVEN

1. *See* Jackson and Croome, *Rails Through the Clay*, pp. 156 *et seq.*

2. *Railway Gazette*, 28 September 1917, p. 358.

3. Barker and Robbins, *History of London Transport*, vol. 2, pp. 198 *et seq.*, contains an account of these events.

4. *See* pp. 59–61 for details of this railway.

5. Published by Hutchinson, 1994; *see* pp. 100 *et seq.*

6. *See* pp. 30 and 66–8 for details of the District's financial misfortunes.

7. Hansard, vol. 270, 10 November 1932, col. 632.

8. *See* Nigel Pennick, *Bunkers Under London*, Valknot Productions, 1988, p. 4, Metropolitan Archives. In fact, total casualties in London throughout the six years of war were 80,000; according to the earlier calculations this figure should have been reached in the first three days of the Blitz.

9. For this information I am indebted to Mr Max Hageman, who was given the information under conditions of secrecy while training as a radar operator. His recollection was confirmed in correspondence with Professor R.V. Jones in 1994.

10. Barker and Robbins, *London Transport*, vol. 2, p. 308, gives the detailed figures.

11. Pennick, *Bunkers Under London*, p. 11.

12. *See* pp. 164 *et seq.* for details.

13. A Morrison shelter, named after the Home Secretary Herbert Morrison, was a metal plate placed protectively over beds or, in the case of the author, over his cot; an Anderson Shelter, named after Sir John Anderson, chairman of the Committee of Imperial Defence and later Chancellor of the Exchequer, consisted of two sheets of curved corrugated iron half buried in the garden.

14. *See* p. 98 for Morrison's role in the creation of the LPTB.

15. A substantial sum in 1940 – the cost of a night's lodging in a cheap hotel in normal times.

16. C. Graves, *London Transport Carried On*, 1947, Metropolitan Archives, 27.0615, gives a vivid account of life in the tubes, from which is taken much of the material which follows.

17. Philip Ziegler, *London at War*, Sinclair-Stevenson, 1995, pp. 155–8, describes these activities.

18. Constantine Fitzgibbon, *London's Burning*, Macmillan, 1970, pp. 94 and 89, is the source of this and the quotation which follows.

19. Recorded in T. Harrison, *Living in the Blitz*, Collins, 1976.

20. This and further extracts from *De Profundis* may be found in *Lines on the Underground, Bakerloo and Jubilee Line*, compiled by D. Meade and T. Wolff, Cassell, 1996.

21. This station no longer exists; it was incorporated in the new Charing Cross station when the latter opened in May 1979.

22. Graves, *London Transport Carried On*, pp. 47–50.

23. Nicolson, *Diaries and Letters, 1939–45*, p. 118.

24. George Orwell, *Collected Essays*, vol. II, pp. 377–8, diary entry, 25 October 1940.

25. Ibid., p. 399, diary entry, 6 May 1941.

26. Ibid., p. 384, diary entry, 1 March 1941.

27. L. Woolf, *The Journey, not the Arrival Matters*, Hogarth Press, 1970, p. 59.

28. Ziegler, *London at War*, p. 240, reports this phenomenon.

29. Graves, *London Transport Carried On*.

30. Brompton Road closed in 1934; the other stations used in this way were South Kensington, Hyde Park Corner, Green Park, Knightsbridge and Holborn.

31. For example Pennick, *Bunkers Under London*, p. 14.

32. *The Engineer*, 18 September 1942, p. 225.

33. *See* p. 30 for an account of these complaints.

34. P. Hennessy, *Never Again*, Jonathan Cape, 1992, p. 441, contains an amusing account of this episode.

35. *The Second World War*, vol. 2, *Their Finest Hour*, Reprint Society, 1951, p. 300.

36. P. Laurie, *Beneath the City Streets*, Penguin, 1972, pp. 182–4.

37. Graves, *London Transport Carried On*, p. 65.

38. London Passenger Transport Board report to Railway Executive Committee, 30 December 1940.

39. O. Green and J. Reed, *London Transport Golden Jubilee Book*, Daily Telegraph Publications, 1983, pp. 90 *et seq*.

40. *See* pp. 116 *et seq.* for an account of this aborted extension.

CHAPTER EIGHT

1. Though the branch closed permanently in September 1994.

2. Others were the Railway Executive; Docks and Inland Waterways Executive; Road Haulage Executive; Road Passenger Executive; and Hotels Executive.

3. Paul Garbutt gave me this account in an interview on 14 October 2000; Paul wrote the speech, expecting Latham to edit and cut it, but Latham delivered it in full.

4. Metropolitan Archives, ref. 27.03, holds this and the other reports from which quotations follow.

5. In 1954 the value was £121.7 million, in 1959 £127.7 million, as taken from the balance sheets.

6. Robertson's predecessor, the first chairman of the Commission, was Lord Hurcomb, (1883–1975), a civil servant.

7. *Report of the Committee of Inquiry into London Transport*, HMSO, 1955, Metropolitan Archives, 27.0616 TRA; the quoted extracts are from paragraphs 375–92 of the report.
8. The network would have incorporated the deep-tube shelters adjacent to the Northern Line described in Chapter Seven, pp. 166 *et seq.*
9. *Railway (London Plan) Committee Report*, HMSO, 1946.
10. David McKenna told me, in his letter of 20 July 2000, that the name arose in a discussion between himself and Sir John Elliot. John Elliot told Anthony Bull, later vice-chairman of London Transport, that the name was suggested by David McKenna.
11. British Transport Commission report, *London Transport in 1955*, pa.
12. *Report from the Select Committee on Nationalised Industries*, H., 1965, paragraph 447.
13. *London Transport in 1959*, p. 59, Metropolitan Archives, LTE 10/1.
14. For the account of this incident I am indebted to Paul Garbutt, who knew all three men at the time.
15. *Journal of the Royal Statistical Society* (A), 1963, pp. 46–92, 'Estimating the Social Benefit of Constructing an Underground Railway in London'.
16. *The Times*, 11 and 12 December 1962, p. 11 on each date.
17. The exception is Pimlico station, which was added to the Brixton extension in 1972 as an afterthought and had no interchange.
18. *See* pp. 135 *et seq.* for an account of this station reconstruction.
19. *See* p. 181.
20. This was three times the record set by the Price Rotary Excavator on the Hampstead Tube in 1905.
21. *See* pp. 40–2.
22. Northern, Piccadilly, Hammersmith & City, Metropolitan, Circle and Thameslink.
23. Though sites in Hampstead and Suffolk also claim to be her final resting-place.
24. Information obtained from a lecture given by Mr Anthony Bull, former vice-chairman of London Transport, on 20 April 1969.
25. *See* p. 97 for this statement, made on the opening of the Piccadilly Line in 1906.
26. The figures are: in 1955, 232,093 employed in food, clothing manufacture, etc.; in 1964, 180,777; in 1955, 217,082 employed in insurance, etc.; in 1964, 269,726; *London Statistics*, LCC, vols 2 and 7.
27. M. Collins and T. Pharoah, *Transport Organisation in a Great City*, Allen & Unwin, 1974, p. 224; figures extracted from the *Greater London Development Plan*.
28. *Report to the Minister of Transport by the Chairmen of the Central London Local Transport Groups*, 1949, Metropolitan Archives, P27.061 Tra.
29. *See* Appendix for the passenger figures for these years.
30. *Transport in London*, HMSO, 1968, Metropolitan Archives, MA 27.061 Tra.
31. Written by Dennis Brooks and published by Oxford University Press; the quoted passage is on p. 143.
32. *Falling Towards England*, Picador, 1986, pp. 137–8, describes the incident.
33. GLC *Minutes*, 22 October 1969, pp. 571–3, records the debate which preceded the transfer.
34. 'Passenger Movements' are passengers joining, leaving or changing trains. The system has at present 245 stations plus a further 32 on the Docklands Light Railway.
35. GLC *Minutes*, 6 July 1971, pp. 336–50, contains a statement of the GLC's policy.
36. Horace Cutler, *The Cutler Files*, Weidenfeld & Nicolson, 1982, p. 141.

37. Cutler, *The Cutler Files*, p. 145, quotes the letter; *see also* P.E. Garbutt, *London Transport and the Politicians*, Ian Allan, 1985, which gives a well-informed and entertaining account of these and other events at this difficult time.

38. Garbutt, *London Transport and the Politicians*, p. 149, describes the incident.

39. The source of this information is a conversation with Richard Hope in July 2000.

40. Garbutt, *London Transport and the Politicians*, p. 66.

41. Lecture at London's Transport Museum, 26 October 1994.

42. Letter from Nicholas Ridley MP, Secretary of State, dated 20 July 1984, in *LRT Statement of Strategy*, Metropolitan Archives, 27.061 Lon.

43. The reports from which the following facts are taken may be seen in the Metropolitan Archives and the Guildhall Library.

44. The figures, from LRT *Annual Reports* are: staff 23,900 to 17,900; passenger kilometres 4320m. to 5814m.

45. Formerly known as GEC-Alsthom.

46. In the general election that followed Mill was defeated by the stationer statesman W.H. Smith.

47. Hansard, 25 July 1868, vol. 193, col. 1789.

48. Prepared by Desmond Fennell QC, HMSO, 1988; the extracts quoted are on pp. 15 and 17.

49. Thus *Social Trends*, The Stationery Office, 1999, shows that between 1981 and 1998 visitors to the British Museum and the National Gallery, London's leading tourist attractions, increased from 5.3 million to 10.9 million per year.

50. So called in honour of Edward I's queen, Eleanor of Castile. The king erected a cross at each place at which her funeral cortege rested on its journey from Nottingham to London, Charing Cross being the last.

51. Exhibition catalogue, p. 6; Guildhall Library.

52. A clear exposition of the station refurbishment programme is given in *Changing Stations*, published by London Underground Ltd Architectural Services, 1993; a fine exposition of the network's architectural heritage is to be found in Lawrence, *Underground Architecture*.

53. *London Underground Limited: a report on passenger and other services provided by the company*, HMSO, 1991.

54. London Regional Transport *Annual Reports* 1990/1 to 1999/2000 are the source of these figures; in addition £3.3 billion was invested in the Jubilee Line extension.

55. *See* pp. 181–3 for an account of the tribulations of the Victoria Line.

56. *See* pp. 191–2 for an account of the period in the 1980s when these two gentlemen were grappling with the problems of London's transport.

57. *Evening Standard*, 2 August 2000, pp. 26–7.

58. 'World at One', 25 September 2000.

59. The Metropolitan Railway, of course, operated as a private company from 1863 to 1933 but it represented only a small component of the network as a whole.

60. *See* pp. 179 and 200 for references to the reports of these two bodies.

APPENDIX

year	1980	1981	1982	1983	1984/5*
Revenue £m.	254	252	279	287	298
Passenger kilometres m.	4224	4064	3632	4320	5344
Investment £m. (core)	72	83	77	106	117

year	1985/6	1986/7	1987/8	1988/9	1989/90
Revenue £m.	340	370	401	468	504
Passenger kilometres m.	5926	6179	6221	6256	5981
Investment £m. (core)	135	171	213	206	307

year	1990/1	1991/2	1992/3	1993/4	1994/5
Revenue £m.	577	610	642	688	718
Passenger kilometres m.	6128	5895	5758	5814	6051
Investment £m. (core)	459	370	730	485	528
Investment £m. (Jubilee)			96	301	401

year	1995/6	1996/7	1997/8	1998/9	1999/2000
Revenue £m.	765	797	961	1009	1101
Passenger kilometres m.	6337	6153	6479	6716	7171
Investment £m. (core)	561	374	367	415	342
Investment £m. (Jubilee)	511	600	476	282	655

* Until 1983 figures are for calendar year; from 1984 they are for year ending 31 March, extracted from London Transport's Annual Reports.

BIBLIOGRAPHY

In carrying out the research for this book I have been assisted by the work of previous writers who have sketched out the major themes in the history of the London Underground and have also identified many contemporary sources from which I have been able to extract original material. Where appropriate I have acknowledged these in the footnotes but no amount of such acknowledgement could do full justice to two seminal works. *A History of London Transport*, by T. Barker and M. Robbins (Allen & Unwin, 1974), was the definitive history of transport in the capital when it was published and remains a key source of information not only on the Underground but also on road and other forms of transport. *Rails Through the Clay*, by Alan A. Jackson and Desmond Croome (Allen & Unwin, 1962; 2nd edn, Capital Transport, 1996), is the definitive history of the deep-tube lines and I am further indebted to Alan Jackson for his many other works on London, especially *London's Metropolitan Railway* (David & Charles, 1986) and *Semi-detached London* (Wild Swan, 1991). These are included in the bibliography that follows.

PARLIAMENTARY PUBLICATIONS

Parliamentary Papers

1844, vol. 15	1863, vol. 8	1901, vol. 6
1846, vol. 17	1864, vol. 53	1904, vol. 30
1854–5, vol. 10	1898, vol. 45	1905 vol. 30

Hansard, 1868, 1869, 1902, 1903, 1918, 1924, 1932, 1937

RECORDS OF THE LONDON UNDERGROUND RAILWAYS HELD IN THE METROPOLITAN ARCHIVES

These are comprehensively catalogued, including shareholders' meetings, board minutes and reports to the boards. The records are prefixed Acc. 1297. This is followed by a three-letter abbreviation which specifies the railway company whose records are referred to, e.g.:

BKW: Baker Street–Waterloo Railway ('Bakerloo')
CLR: Central London Railway
CSL: City and South London Railway

LPT: London Passenger Transport Board
LTE: London Transport Executive
MDR: Metropolitan District Railway
MET: Metropolitan Railway
UER: Underground Electric Railways

OTHER RECORDS OF THE METROPOLITAN ARCHIVES, WITH CATALOGUE NUMBERS WHERE APPROPRIATE

LRT Statement of Strategy, Metropolitan Archives, 27.061 Lon

London Regional Transport *Annual Reports* 1990/1 to 1999/2000

G.T. Moody, *London's Electrification, 1890–1923*, Pamphlet 27.332 Moo

C. Graves, *London Transport Carried On*, 1947, 27.0615

Metropolitan Board of Works, *Annual Reports*, 1879–1884

Report of the Committee of Inquiry into London Transport, HMSO, 1955, 27.0616 Tra

Royal Commission on the Geographical Distribution of the Industrial Population, commonly called 'The Barlow *Commission*' after its chairman Sir Montague Barlow, 28.02

F. Howkins, *The Story of Golders Green and its Remarkable Development*, London, 1924, 7.651

Dame Henrietta Barnett, *The Story of the Growth of the Hampstead Garden Suburb 1907–28*, 97.651

Transport in London, HMSO, 1968, 27.061 Tra

INSTITUTION OF CIVIL ENGINEERS

Minutes of Proceedings, 1884–5; 1899; 1908–9.

GOVERNMENT AND LOCAL GOVERNMENT PUBLICATIONS

Census of Population, 1901, vol. 2, and 1931, vol. 1, Library of the Office for National Statistics

GLC *Minutes*, 22 October 1969; 6 July 1971

Greater London Regional Planning Committee, 2nd Report, 1933

LCC *Minutes*, 28 July 1891

London Underground Limited: a Report on Passenger and Other Services Provided by the Company, HMSO, 1991

London Statistics, LCC, vols 2 and 7, Library of the Office for National Statistics

Railway (London Plan) Committee Report, HMSO, 1946

Report from the Select Committee on Nationalised Industries, HMSO, 1965

Report into the King's Cross Fire, prepared by Desmond Fennell QC, HMSO, 1988

Royal Commission on London Traffic Report, 1905

Social Trends, The Stationery Office, 1999

BOOKS AND PAMPHLETS

Published in London unless otherwise stated

Ashfield, Lord, *London's Traffic Problem Reconsidered*, Constable, 1924

Bancroft, P., *London Transport Records at the Public Record Office*, Nebulous Books, Alton, 1996

Barker, T., *Moving Millions*, London Transport Museum and Book Production Consultants, 1990

Barker, T. and Robbins, M., *A History of London Transport*, Allen & Unwin, 1974

Barman, C., *The Man Who Built London Transport*, David & Charles, 1979

Bayliss, D.A., *The Post Office Railway*, Turntable Publications, 1978

Blumenfeld, R.D., *R.D.B.'s Diary, 1887–1914*, Heinemann, 1930

Brooks, D., *Race and Labour in London Transport*, Oxford University Press, 1975

Bruce, J.G. and Croome, D.F., *The Twopenny Tube*, Capital Transport, 1996

Casson, H., *Hugh Casson's London*, Dent, 1983

Changing Stations, London Underground Ltd Architectural Services, 1993

Cherry, B. and Pevsner, N., *Buildings of England*, Penguin, London 2: South, 1983

Churchill, Winston, *The Second World War*, vol. 2, *Their Finest Hour*, Reprint Society, 1951

Clayton, H., *The Atmospheric Railways*, London, 1966

Collins, M. and Pharoah, T., *Transport Organisation in a Great City*, Allen & Unwin, 1974

Connor, P., *Going Green, The Story of the District Line*, Capital Transport, 2nd edn, 1994

Croome, D.F., *The Piccadilly Line*, Capital Transport, 1998

Cross, George, *Suffolk Punch*, London, 1939

Cutler, H., *The Cutler Files*, Weidenfeld & Nicolson, 1982

Droste, M., *Bauhaus*, Bauhaus-Archiv Museum, Berlin

Edmonds, A., *History of the Metropolitan District Railway to 1908*, London Transport, 1973

Faulks, S., *Birdsong*, Hutchinson, 1994

Fitzgibbon, C., *London's Burning*, Macmillan, 1970

Garbutt, P.E., *London Transport and the Politicians*, Ian Allan, 1985

Garbutt, P.E., *World Metro Systems*, Capital Transport, 2nd edn, 1997

Garland, K., *Mr Beck's Underground Map*, Capital Publications, 1994

Green, O., *Underground Art*, Laurence King, 1999

Green, O. and Reed, J., *London Transport Golden Jubilee Book*, Daily Telegraph Publications, 1983

Guildhall Pamphlets nos 2308; 3592; 10884; 17557 (all Guildhall library)

Hardy, B., *London Underground Rolling Stock*, Capital Transport, 12th edn, 1990

Harrison, T., *Living in the Blitz*, Collins, 1976

Hennessy, P., *Never Again*, Jonathan Cape, 1992,

Hollis, J. and Seddon, A., *The Changing Population of the London Boroughs*, OPCS, 1985

Horne, M.A.C., *The Bakerloo Line*, Douglas Rose, 1990

Horne, M.A.C., *The Victoria Line*, Douglas Rose, 1998

Horne, M. and Bayman, R., *The Northern Line*, Capital Transport, 2nd edn, 1999

Hueffer, F.M., *The Soul of London*, Alston Rivers, London, 1895

Jackson, A., *London's Metropolitan Railway*, David & Charles, 1986

Jackson, A., *London's Termini*, David & Charles, 2nd edn, 1985

Jackson, A., *Semi-detached London*, Wild Swan, 1991

Jackson, A. and Croome, D., *Rails Through the Clay*, Allen & Unwin, 1962, 2nd edn, Capital, 1993

James, Clive, *Falling Towards England*, Picador, 1986

Kauffer, E.M., *The Art of the Poster*, Cecil Palmer, 1924

Laurie, P., *Beneath the City Streets*, Penguin, 1972

Lawrence, D., *Underground Architecture*, Capital Transport Publications, 1994

Lines on the Underground, Bakerloo and Jubilee Line, ed. D. Meade and T. Wolff, Cassell, 1996

Nicolson, H., *Diaries and Letters, 1939–45*, Collins, 1967

Orwell, George, *Collected Essays*, vol. II

Passingham, W.J., *The Romance of London's Underground*, Sampson Low, 1932

Pennick, N., *Bunkers Under London*, Valknot Productions, 1988

Pevsner, N., *Studies in Art, Architecture & Design*, vol. 2, Thames & Hudson, 1968

Pick, Frank, *Britain Must Rebuild, a Policy for Regional Planning*, Kegan Paul, London, 1941

Poems on the Underground, ed. G. Benson, J. Chernaik and C. Herbert, 8th edn, Cassell, 1998

Riddell, J. and Denton, P., *By Underground to the Zoo*, 1995, Studio Vista

Riddell, J. and Stearn, W., *By Underground to Kew*, 1994, Studio Vista

Rose, D., *The London Underground, a Diagrammatic History*, Douglas Rose, 7th edn, 1999

Teaspoons to Trains, Victoria & Albert Museum Exhibition Catalogue, 1978

The Triumphant Bore, sponsored by James Howden & Co., Institution of Civil Engineers bookshop

Trench, R. and Hillman, E., *London Under London*, John Murray, 1984

Turner, E., *The Shocking History of Advertising*, Michael Joseph, 1952

Wanntig, H., *Wirtschaft und Kunst*, Jena, 1909

Webb, Beatrice, *Our Partnership*, ed. Drake & Cole, Longmans Green, 1948

Woolf, L., *The Journey, not the Arrival Matters*, Hogarth Press, 1970

Ziegler, P., *London at War*, Sinclair-Stevenson, 1995

JOURNALS, MAGAZINES, NEWSPAPERS AND MISCELLANEOUS PUBLICATIONS

Commercial Art, vol. 2, 1927

Daily Mail, 28 June, 30 July 1900

Designers Journal, November 1987

The Engineer, 7 June 1889; 18 September 1942

Evening News, 18 May 1907

Evening News Homeseeker's Guide, 19 February 1926

Evening Standard, 14 May 1924; 2 August 2000

The Guardian, 30 December 1999

Herapath's Railway Journal, 14 March 1857; 17 August, 12 October 1872; 10 November 1877; 14 June, 30 June 1888; 20 July 1889; 25 January, 15 February, 19 July, 26 July 1890

Illustrated London News, 15 February, 28 June, 6 September 1862; 17 January 1863; 2 January 1869; 8 November 1890; 16 July 1898; 30 January 1904; 15 December 1928

Journal of the Royal Statistical Society (A), 1963

London Journal, vol. 5, no. I, May 1979

Metropolitan Country Estates publicity brochure, December 1927

Modern Transport, 11 June 1921

Journal of the Institute of Transport, vol. 20, May 1939

Railway Engineer, 1990, vol. 3

Railway Gazette, 28 September 1918

Railway News, Finance and Joint Stock Companies Journal, 30 June 1900

Railway Times, 9 August, 18 October 1884; 26 July, 9 August, 8 November, 20 December 1890; 25 August, 1 September 1900; 24 November 1894; 23 April 1904; 10 November, 12 December 1906; 16 February, 22 June 1907; 9 December 1911

The Times, 27 March 1843; 2 December 1858; 30 November 1861; 10 January 1863; 3 and 4 July 1871; 14 June 1879; 18 June, 5 November 1890; 28 June, 25 December 1900; 7 June, 27 and 31 July 1901; 27 and 29 January 1904; 30 December 1905; 12 March, 16 December 1906; 24 June 1907; 9 February 1910; 4 October 1911; 27 October 1921; 23 February, 28 November 1923; 17 and 26 July 1929; 4, 14, 21 and 22 November, 5 December 1935; 16 March, 6, 9 and 12 April 1937; 11 and 12 December 1962; 1 December 1970

Tramway & Railway World, 11 April 1901

Wealdstone, Harrow & Wembley Observer, 22 and 29 May 1896

INDEX